Egypt's Liberal Experiment: 1922–1936

PUBLISHED UNDER THE AUSPICES OF THE
GUSTAVE E. VON GRUNEBAUM CENTER FOR NEAR EASTERN STUDIES
UNIVERSITY OF CALIFORNIA, LOS ANGELES

Egypt's Liberal Experiment: 1922-1936

Afaf Lutfi al-Sayyid-Marsot

University of California Press

Berkeley   Los Angeles   London

University of California Press
Berkeley and Los Angeles, California
University of California Press, Ltd.
London, England
Copyright © 1977, by
The Regents of the University of California
ISBN 0-520-03109-1
Library of Congress Catalog Card Number: 75-22659
Printed in the United States of America

Contents

Preface   vii

Note on Transliteration   xi

Abbreviations   xii

Introduction   1

   I. Sons of the Nile   10

  II. Prologue: The Man of the Hour   43

 III. The King of Hearts   73

 IV. The Iron Grip   111

   V. "Allah Created the English Mad"   138

 VI. Détente and Return to Constitutional Government   171

VII. The Second Dimension: Socioeconomic Factors   196

VIII. The Third Dimension: Intellectual Eddies and Currents   217

Conclusion   244

Appendix: Treaty of Alliance   253

Sources and Select Bibliography   269

Index   273

To the memory of
Ahmad Lutfi al-Sayyid
and
Bahi Eddine Barakat

Preface

To some readers what follows may sound like an old-fashioned book about old-fashioned people, the kind today we patronizingly refer to as the ancien regime. It may seem so because it talks about people and events and does not pretend to express theories or even consciously to apply them, although like most of my generation I am influenced by the ideas of Marx, Mannheim, Eliade, Erikson, et alii. I started this work partly as a tribute to my parents and to their friends whom I love and respect, but who may never speak to me again, for much that I write about them is not laudatory, and many of their heroes are stripped bare. And while Egyptians, like all other people, love to gossip about their friends, they do not relish washing their dirty linen in public. One hopes that they may see behind my criticism of their generation and their actions my respect and admiration for their efforts, such as they were, right or wrong, successful or otherwise, and I appeal to them to realize that our generation is only a continuation of theirs and that our failures and successes are only an extension of theirs. This book is written partly in an effort to explain to this and succeeding generations that each era has its glorious moments as well as its abysmal failures, and that posterity should judge a generation in the light of its times as well as in the light of history. No man is absolutely hero or knave, and no man is entirely master of a situation, above all a political one. Lastly, it is written because I wanted to understand what happened and why. Curiosity may have caused the cat's demise, but where would all historians be without it? If I have not understood the situation entirely, my hope is that those who know better will speak up, so that subsequent works about this period may throw more light on it.

By natural inclination this book would have concentrated on the social history of the period. But, alas, some of the political information concerning 1922-1936 is unknown to Western readers, and it is lop-sided to write a social history where the political aspects are shrouded.

For that reason I ask the reader's indulgence for recounting the rise and fall of cabinets as though that were the sum of a country's history, but the cause and effect of such changes in themselves mirror the ruling elite with its alliances and alignment and reveal its attitude toward society, and vice versa. Nonetheless some of the chapters of the book are concerned with giving a picture of Egyptian society economically, socially, and intellectually, with showing how the political activities of the time impinged on the facets of the society, and with how society reacted to the politics of the age. Thus Chapter I is an introduction to the society, mores, and psychology of the Egyptian, while Chapter VII is a brief synopsis of the economy intended neither to be detailed nor complete and supplied simply to accentuate certain economic facets of that society. Chapter VIII is an equally brief introduction to the major intellectual ideas of that time, showing the different paths that the intellectuals, or the society that shaped them, had mapped out for the country.

I want to point out that any general reference in this book to Egyptians includes both Copts and Muslims who share the same characteristics and traits that make up the Sons of the Nile.

Much of the material for this book was obtained orally from the men who were involved in the period or from their wives and children. A great deal of the background has, of course, been absorbed through conversations with my uncle Ahmad Lutfi al-Sayyid (Pasha) and with my father Muhammad Said Lutfi al-Sayyid (Pasha). I spent many happy hours talking to Dr. Bahi Eddine Barakat (Pasha), the former Regent of Egypt, and laying my problems and questions at his feet. In 1971 he allowed me access to the memoirs of his father Fathallah Pasha Barakat. It is my regret that he died before he was able to see this work.

The Barakat memoirs are gathered in forty-seven notebooks, most of them written in the author's hand; when he was stricken with trachoma his secretary wrote them at his direction. The occasional gaps in the notebooks occurred when he was too busy as a cabinet minister to make entries. Frequently the memoirs are out of chronological order; for example, in 1935 he recounts an event that occurred in 1931, or if a subject comes up during a conversation with a friend he comments on something relevant that occurred the month before. Adding to the confusion is the fact that he did not number the notebooks except for recording the year and month of the entries. The volumes were numbered after his death, and some volumes have duplicate numbering, for example, two volumes are numbered volume 6, one pertaining to one year and the other to a period two years later, there are two volumes 16, and volumes 15-17 are followed by volumes 5-9. In spite of these minor difficulties, the memoirs, which cover the years 1922 to 1934—from the year of Fathallah's exile to the Seychelles with Zaghlul to the year of his death—are most informative. Only two volumes of this collection have ever been consulted by a scholar, and I am exceedingly grateful to have had the privilege of examining them in their entirety.

Other people have been most generous in giving me information concerning the period and the personalities involved: among them are H. E. Mahmud Muhammad Mahmud (Pasha), H. E. Sharif Sabri (Pasha), H. E. I. Tharwat, and Mmes. Husain Haikal (Pasha) and Makram Ubaid (Pasha). To all I am deeply grateful. I am also indebted to the late Hidiya Hanim Barakat for her vivid accounts, especially of when she smuggled revolutionary literature in shopping bags in 1919 and organized the women of Cairo in protest demonstrations. I owe a great deal to my mother Atiya Hanim Rashwan for her eyewitness accounts of the 1919 uprising and her tales of the times.

In England I had long talks about the Percy Loraine period with Gordon Waterfield, who gave of his time and vast knowledge as generously as he has always done. Sir Laurence Grafftey-Smith, whose anecdotes are a sheer delight and whose comments on the personalities concerned are invaluable, also gave generously of his time, and I am grateful to him and to Lady Grafftey-Smith for a lovely day at their house.

I am deeply grateful to Albert Hourani for his unfailing kindness in reading the manuscript and for his comments, to Rifaat Abul-Haj for his pertinent observations, and to Malcolm Kerr. I am also grateful to my husband who, with his customary patience, put up with the birth pangs of the book and sustained me not only with affection but with valid criticism. My warm thanks go to my research assistant Doha Sleiman for his help with some of the research. I am particularly indebted to my many colleagues at the Gustave E. von Grunebaum Center for Near Eastern Studies at UCLA, especially Speros Vryonis Jr., the then director, for his encouragement; Teresa Joseph, their editor, who has done a masterly job of editing the manuscript; and Evelyn Oder and Elahei Badkoubei who typed the manuscript.

I am indebted to the American Research Center in Egypt for the grant to conduct research there in 1971, and to the Social Science Research Council whose generosity helped me to carry out research in England in 1972. I am grateful to St. Antony's College at Oxford for

permission to consult their collection of private papers, and to the
Public Records Office in London for permission to consult theirs. I
would like to have consulted the Egyptian archives in Cairo for the
years 1922 and 1923 (the rest of the period under discussion comes
under the fifty-year rule), but I was unable to do so since in 1971 the
archives were still closed. On a trip to Egypt in 1975 for research on
another subject, after the manuscript was in the editor's hands, I was
allowed to consult the Saad Zaghlul papers and I have incorporated
that material into the book. I am most grateful to His Excellency the
Under-Secretary of State for Cultural Affairs, Dr. Sheniti, for his
permission to use these materials, to Jubran Jubran, the Director of
the National Archives in Egypt, and to the employees of the archives,
especially Sawsan Abd al-Ghani, Hashim Abd al-Azim, and Ibrahim
Fathallah Ahmad for their kindness.

Note on Transliteration

I HAVE simplified the transliteration of Arabic words and names as much as possible. Where a quotation from a text has used a certain form for a proper name, or where I know the person's preference in spelling his name, I have retained it. Ains and hamzas have been included in titles of books and in quotations, but all other diacritics have been omitted.

Abbreviations

al-Aqqad, *Saad Zaghlul*

Abbas Mahmud al-Aqqad, *Zaᶜim al-thawra: Saad Zaghlul.* Cairo, 1952.

Ayrout, *Egyptian Peasant*

Henri Habib Ayrout, *The Egyptian Peasant.* Trans. J. A. Williams. Boston, 1968.

Barakat Memoirs

Fathallah Barakat Memoirs. 1922-1934. Egypt.

Berque, *L'Egypte*

L'Egypte: Impérialisme et Révolution. Paris, 1967.

Cromer, *Modern Egypt*

Earl of Cromer. *Modern Egypt.* 2 vols. New York: Macmillan, 1916.

Grafftey-Smith, *Bright Levant*

Laurence Grafftey Smith. *Bright Levant.* London, 1970.

Haikal, *Mudhakkirat*

Ahmad Hussain Haikal. *Mudhakkirat fi-l siyasa al-Misriyya.* 2 vols. Cairo, 1951.

Issawi, *Mid-Century*

Charles Issawi. *Egypt at Mid-Century.* London, 1954.

al-Rafii, *Fi aᶜqab*

Abd al-Rahman al-Rafii. *Fi aᶜqab al-thawra al-Misriyya.* 2 vols. Cairo, 1958-1966.

al-Sayyid, *Qissat Hayati*

Ahmad Lutfi al-Sayyid. *Qissat Hayati.* Cairo, 1962.

al-Sayyid (Marsot), *Egypt and Cromer*

Afaf Lutfi al-Sayyid (Marsot). *Egypt and Cromer.* London, 1968.

Waterfield, *Professional Diplomat*

Gordon Waterfield. *Professional Diplomat: Sir Percy Loraine.* London, 1973.

Zaghlul Memoirs

Egypt. State Archives. Saad Zaghlul Memoirs.

Zayid, *Struggle for Independence*

Mahmud Zayid. *Egypt's Struggle for Independence.* Beirut, 1965.

Introduction

GENETICISTS inform us that an individual inherits traits that go far back in time to many generations of ancestors belonging to either parent. Psychologists, notably Jung, inform us of the presence of a collective atavistic memory. When we as historians put these two pieces of information together we may come to infer that peoples, like individuals, also have inherited traits and a collective political memory. It is the cement that binds a people together as a nation and causes them to develop characteristics which differentiate them from other nations and which we hint at when we talk of historical continuity.

History like memory is continuous and rarely shows abrupt breaks, although there are lapses in both. Above all, we must remember that social change in the past was a slow process, that new political and social impacts are at best plastered over an older traditional foundation, which may or may not become eroded in time, which under violent impulses may merge with the new, or may shed the new and show patches of the old traditional society. It is only in this our twentieth century that change has become so rapid that countries have whizzed from the camel age to the jet age and where homogeneity is slowly and inexorably spreading into a global norm.

The history of modern Egypt has frequently been written with a disregard for the past, and the modern age has been treated as though it had sprung fully grown like Minerva from Bonaparte's occupation of Egypt in 1798 and Muhammad Ali's subsequent rise to power in 1805. It is true that 1798 is a convenient date with which to begin the modern history of Egypt because one must obviously begin somewhere in time, and the French occupation was a novel experience. A new and different Egypt did slowly emerge in the nineteenth century but it carried with it the traits and scars of the past which can be traced further back to one constant that has had the deepest influence on Egypt, namely its agricultural configuration.

As far back as the dawn of civilization, Egypt has been—and in some ways still is—predominantly an agricultural country. That factor leads one not only to assume certain economic conclusions but also to understand certain psychological factors. The cyclical recurrence of the seasons, predictable yet varied; the inevitable repairs that Nature undertakes after periodic ravages; the helplessness of man in the face of the elements; the bounty yielded by a land that is well tended—all these factors have helped create the mentality of the Egyptian peasant. A succession of autocratic governments, frequent oppression and misery, like the presence of alien and alienated rulers, have added their share in creating other traits to which only a psychiatrist can give full justice in description. Translated into political-historical terms these traits can be summarized as a highly developed sense of individuality—a feeling of self-reliance—and a basic distrust of one's fellow-man; an even greater feeling of enmity toward and distrust of the *hukuma,* government, whose only purpose in the past had been to oppress and exploit the population, hence the need to placate it, or better still, to outwit it if that can be done safely and with impunity; a deep religious belief that man is guided by destiny, and that what is *maktub,* written, on the brow must come to pass, allied to which is a dualistic belief in which Iago's "Dio crudel" is balanced by equal faith in the Merciful, the Compassionate, *al-Rahman al-Rahim;* and lastly, and above all, an instinct for survival, a tenacity and an endurance which explains much in terms of political and human reactions. As L'Abbé Sieyès said after the French Revolution, the Egyptian can say that in spite of the elements, and in spite of his governments, his fate has allowed him to survive, "Il a vécu." More than that, in the twentieth century he has finally seized power in his own hands and fashioned his own government from among his own people. And while the 1919 revolution gave the country a limited autonomy, the revolution of 1952, for all its defects and shortcomings, was the first instance in their recorded history from the time of the pharoahs of an indigenous Egyptian government ruling over Egypt. For that reason, if for no other, that revolution is enshrined in the Egyptian collective memory.

The fact that no native Egyptian had ruled Egypt for more than a millennium was to give Egyptian political life a characteristic trait, that of the nonidentity of the population with the government. The historical fact of a majority that was oppressed by an alien minority came to be viewed by both rulers and ruled as the norm and created the so-called unpolitical outlook of the average Egyptian. When

Muhammad Ali and his family of Turco-Albanians overthrew the mamluks they were still alien rulers; and when in turn the authority of that family had degenerated into a British protectorate, veiled or otherwise, the average Egyptian, or the composite Egyptian, when he thought of the matter at all, probably shrugged to himself and muttered *kulluhum awlad kalb,* which translated in politer language implies that it is all much of a muchness.

It was indeed a different matter when Egyptians attempted to wrest independence from the British in 1919. Then the population shed its apathy and joined in the struggle of Egyptians against non-Egyptian authority. Many Western historians have argued over the uprising of March 9, 1919, whether it was spontaneous or manufactured, whether it was organized by the Wafd or took the Wafd by surprise, whether it was a genuine nationalist manifestation or simply an occasion for the rabble to express their many frustrations. The theme that runs through these inquiries (as though it were in the slightest bit relevant) is one of surprise at an uprising on the part of the Egyptians. Yet one need but go back to Jabarti's chronicles to trace the continuity of such uprisings in Egyptian political life. It is true that in the eighteenth and nineteenth centuries similar uprisings were limited in locale—save for the Urabi revolution—for obvious reasons such as lack of communications, but there are traces of protonationalist uprisings in almost every decade of Egyptian life, and though they may have been triggered by economic reasons—what revolution is not?—they were definitely couched in terms of protest against the alien government of the day, which justifies characterizing them as protonationalist movements. It is no accident that Umar Makram, who organized popular resistance movements on three separate occasions during his lifetime (twice against the French occupiers in 1798 and 1800 and once against the Ottoman governor when he helped put Muhammad Ali in the seat of government in 1805), has become a popular hero today. After the uprising of March 9, 1919, the members of the Wafd did create an organized movement in the capital and a few other urban centers. The students who went to their homes in the countryside after the schools were closed did take the message of an uprising to the rural areas. But the grass-roots organization of the Wafd succeeded the uprising and therefore does not explain it. What does explain it is that uprisings were a form of protest that Egyptians understood, and one of the few effective forms available at the time. Given sufficient stimulus or provocation they would break through their shell of apathy and flower into response and violence as they had many times in the past.

The reasons for the 1919 uprisings may have differed with each person (but that applies to every revolutionary or protest movement and only a psychiatrist can tell us the hidden motives that impel an individual to rise in protest) but the magnitude and promptness of the response can only be construed in terms of a spontaneous protest on the part of all individuals who joined in the uprising.

Egypt had no Eisenstein to record on film the impact on the population of the Wafd's message and to show the exuberance of the masses—men, women, and children—as they faced the rifles of the enemy and fell under the bullets. British official reports underplayed the events and attributed them to that catchall word they used whenever they failed to understand the currents prevailing in colonized countries, "fanaticism." Like all colonizers they could not comprehend nationalist movements in their colonies—for had they not governed them fairly and well and saved them from native tyranny?—and therefore chose to deny their existence or to minimize their magnitude. Since the British could not grasp the essential irrationality that goes with a revolution, or an ideology that differed from theirs, they assumed that it was based on "untruths" and for a long time Egyptian and British officials talked past one another, in a pattern typical of all colonial situations.

Today in the light of hindsight, and contrary to some prevalent attitudes, we must admit that the 1919 uprisings were without doubt an expression of nationalism, with all that the word implies: a desire to be rid of the British occupation, frustration suffered by an oppressed people and attributed to the hukuma and to the British occupation which had brought the government to power and kept it there. Many Egyptians, including some members of the Wafd, were not sure that their attempt would succeed, but that has never prevented man from trying and is an added reason to respect these men who were not daunted by such seemingly insuperable odds. The success of their movement surprised both the Wafd and the British. Saad Zaghlul, who became the epitome of popular resistance to the British authorities, especially after his first exile to Malta in 1919, was enthroned among a pantheon of awliya, saints, and for a long time could not be displaced, not even by Nasir.

It is one of the weaknesses inherent in hero worship that the hero is viewed in almost holy or mystical terms as infallible and without defect. All his faults are glossed over as though were one to admit that he had a failing it would redound unfavorably on his movement and discredit or weaken it. So simplistic an approach may succeed during the hero's lifetime, or for a short period after his death when myth-making is paramount; it is a natural process of spell-weaving in any movement. It is equally inevitable that succeeding generations should try to measure and weigh the facts in more objective fashion, not out of a need to destroy the myth but out of a spirit of curiosity, of objectivity, out of a need to know, which presumably motivates all historians. Above all, it is necessary because each generation sees history with different eyes and from a different perspective. Thus modern Egyptian scholarship, while fully realizing the debt Egypt owed Saad Zaghlul, tries to depict him as he really was. Unlike our forebears we know that the value of a movement is not always predicated on the personalities of its supporters or leaders, and, because we are more cynical than our forebears, we know that everyone has flaws and that in historical terms the flaws of heroes are more tragic than those of the average man. After Erikson's study of Luther it is difficult to look upon heroes with the same eye as before. The first modern attempt at reexamining Saad Zaghlul was A. Lajin's *Saad Zaghlul: Dawruh fi-l siyasa al-Misriyya hatta 1914* (Cairo, 1971) and the second his volume *Saad Zaghlul: Wa dawruh fi-l siyasa al-Misriyya* (Beirut, 1975). The present work is an attempt to depict Egyptian political life from 1922 to 1936, to present the forces at work and the limitations placed on the main characters both through personality and circumstance, and thus to draw the general lines without too many minutiae. It is also an attempt to sketch the role of political personalities on the Egyptian scene other than Zaghlul and to give credit where credit is long overdue, as in the case of Adli Yakan.

That period of Egyptian political life has generally been regarded as an experiment in constitutional life which failed. When the Nasir era in midcentury ushered in a more extreme period of repression than Sidqi's, it accentuated the belief that constitutional institutions were incapable of taking hold in so hostile a political soil as Egypt seemed to be. The Egyptians have therefore been described as servile, unaccustomed to self-government, and incapable of appreciating it. From there only a small step led to the conclusions that Egyptians understood only force and tyranny and had not the slightest need for any other form of government, that Egypt was "une terre d'oppresseurs et d'opprimés" and would continue to be so either because of a tragic flaw in the Egyptian national character or because of Islam, which was believed to encourage authoritarian predilections.

It is my contention in this book that most of that criticism was not only unjust but also one-sided, based on only part of the story. The

liberal experiment was a partial success, and in fact saw the burgeon-
ing of several elements that were vital to the future development of
Egypt, such as the beginning of industrialization, the emancipation of
women, the spread of education and of better hygiene, and the
Anglo-Egyptian Treaty of Alliance of 1936 — which for all its defects
was a step in the right direction.

To the extent that the liberal experiment failed, the failure was
attributable not to Islam or to the Egyptian national character but to
specific reasons, political and social. The political reasons were the
presence of the British and of the King. Liberal growth is a tender
plant that needs the proper political atmosphere in order to flourish,
and that plant was smothered before it could grow. It would be more
correct to qualify the period 1922-1936 as an abortive attempt to give
birth to liberal institutions, for while the framework for the institutions
was there it was hemmed in by so many restrictions as to render it
unworkable. There cannot have been a monarch, a foreign occupant,
and a local government all pulling in different directions and then
claim that the institutions have failed. As long as the Egyptian government was forced to defer to the monarch, and the monarch was
subservient to the occupiers, no stable government could develop.

Added to the political situation were social and economic factors
which acted as supplementary barriers to the development of a
constitutional government, notably the low level of literacy, the existence of a tiny indigenous bourgeoisie who could not balance the power
of the landowners, let alone challenge it, and an economy that was
dominated and manipulated by foreign interests.

Yet throughout that period Egyptian society was continuing to
undergo a process of change which had begun in the nineteenth
century but which accelerated in the twentieth. The outcome was the
extension of a bourgeoisie, the growth of a working class, the spread
of education which produced the unemployment of intellectuals,
because of limited possibilities, the start of an articulate professional
class, and changes in thought and in economic realities. And while
the process of change developed political instability, which culminated
in a military revolution, it also produced a modern society, and one
more capable of working a constitutional government than the society
of the previous decades. Thus the political events of the twenties and
thirties and the socioeconomic and thought processes they bred have
pushed Egypt squarely into the modern age.

A phenomenal change in thought which occurred in Egyptian
society was that it is possible for Muslims to become part of the modern

world and still remain Muslims. And yet in carrying out my research for this book I was struck by the difficulty some Western historians had in understanding that a person can be westernized and still remain a Muslim. The roots for that mental block lie in the fact that these authors could not separate the essence of Islam from its forms. One can sympathize with that difficulty since many Muslims face it too, but it seems usually to arise from an outmoded, if not static, notion of what a religion is. It is as though religion were gelled in a mold fashioned in the distant past and hence unchangeable, a notion many clerics of many religions firmly believe, or have induced their adherents to believe. Today we can accept the reality that a religion is a changing and developing thought process, that some practices which in the past were regarded as essential to salvation, like not eating meat on Friday to Catholics, can be discarded without trauma. We know that Muslim beliefs and practices at the time of the Rashidun changed under the Abbasids and continue to change in the modern age, just as early Christian beliefs and practices differed from those of the Middle Ages and from those of the modern age. The difficulty I am referring to is one that authors had as the result of a conscious or unconscious belief in the inferiority of Islam as a religion and a culture; the assumption seems to be that once a Muslim is exposed to Western thought he must reject Islam in favor of a superior religion and culture.

A second phenomenon, closely allied to the first, is the inability of some writers to grasp the fact that a person may be westernized intellectually and remain nonetheless an Egyptian and a nationalist. The assumption underlying that notion goes back to a statement made around the turn of the century by Cromer, the British consul general and uncrowned ruler of Egypt, which implied that once an Egyptian was westernized he must perforce lose his roots or reject them, because he would become overwhelmed by the superiority of Western civilization and ashamed of his own.[1] It was the obvious basis for France's *mission civilizatrice* and the excuse given by all colonizing powers. When Egyptians have tried to expose the fallacies underlying such reasoning they have been accused of indulging in apologetics.

To a more modern generation the alienation of an intellectual is taken for granted without the implication that it is stripping him of his culture and his national identity, not that it cannot happen as we have seen in Algeria. But it is possible for alienation to be viewed as

1. Cromer, *Modern Egypt*, II, 228.

a psychological and social crisis without it being a national one. My generation of Egyptians is therefore very conscious of its roots and its traditions because we frequently had to learn them in a distorted fashion through a Western reflection, or at least, the Western model was held up in comparison before our eyes. We therefore tried to learn where the truth lay. As a person who sees himself in a distorting mirror is more conscious of his defects than a person who looks into an ordinary mirror, so an Egyptian intellectual learned more about himself and his people through exposure to intellectual sources other than his own. A heightened awareness of self and of nation is the result of foreign exposure, not a rejection of either. Hence the phenomenon familiar among many nationalists of the Third World, of humanists steeped in an alien culture, who in consequence have become more acutely aware of their own with its values and defects than the person who was familiar only with the narrow milieu of his own culture. Rather than produce a de-Muslimized Muslim and a de-Egyptianized Egyptian, as Cromer firmly believed education would do in Egypt,[2] we find that modern education has produced a generation of people of culture who, because they were familiar with the humanist tradition of two cultures, were more perceptive of Islam and of Egypt and consequently rejected neither. They sought on the contrary to accentuate the values of both.

To the Western mind those people were of necessity a fraud, because Western man could not accept both cultures simultaneously. He could not say, "My culture is fine for me and theirs for them"; he needs always to say, "My culture is the best." Thus the statement made by Cromer that Abduh was an agnostic[3] was picked up by some modern scholars and passed on as fact, without verifying the statement for validity, because it concided with the basic beliefs and prejudices of Western authors regarding Islam and Egypt. They disregarded the fact that the statement came from a man who despised both Islam and the Egyptians and who certainly never carried out a theological discussion with the Imam. Had they bothered to dig deeper they might have learned how devout a Muslim Abduh was. At one time when Abduh and Lutfi al-Sayyid were spending a summer in Geneva, Abduh confided to Lutfi that he hoped to live long enough to rid Islam of its superstitions. Lutfi flippantly inquired whether anything of Islam would then be left. Abduh was so offended by the remark, even though

2. Ibid., p. 228.
3. Ibid., p. 180.

it was made in jest, that he refused to talk to Lufti for two days when he made proper amends for slighting Islam.

The same attitude is to be found in authors who claim, for instance, that Haikal and Taha Husain were going through a "reactionary" phase when they chose to write on Islamic subjects. There are many other examples but it is not my intention to justify and argue. It is my intention to point out that prejudices and "fanaticism" were and are practiced as much by Western authors as by Eastern and that today we are striving to free ourselves of these traits, although we may develop others equally reprehensible. But that is inevitable and a later generation of historians will no doubt point out our defects in turn. For while every generation must rewrite its past history in the light of its present principles and world view and state of knowledge, it must also write with its readers in mind. A historian today has a wider audience and therefore must adopt a more rigorous standard since he knows, nay urges, that any slip may be challenged, and hopes that some of what he writes may raise interest and controversy. For as in *Areopagitica* the historians' prayer should be: "Give me the liberty to know, to utter and to argue freely according to conscience, above all liberties" (Milton).

I

Sons of the Nile

To this day the backbone of Egypt is agriculture; in 1936 it supplied more than half the national output and it still mobilizes half the work force of the nation.[1] Although by 1930 industry was beginning to develop rapidly, the predominant physical characteristics of Egypt were that of an agricultural land pitted by urban-industrial pockets which were few and wide apart in Upper Egypt but which formed a closer linkage in the Delta region. In order to grasp the essence and logic of Egyptians one has to understand the fallah and his society, to trace his values and beliefs in the political pattern of the land; for Egypt's political configuration is the outcome of the interaction among the fallahin, the native Egyptians, and the rulers, whoever they might be.

The Egyptian fallah is a microcosm of Egypt. His society and culture are homogeneous and characterized by centuries of exploitation and abuse by alien rulers and native superiors alike. He has been at the mercy of the elements, which were capable of devastating him equally with drought and flood, trailing in their wake epidemics and starvation. He has been comforted and gulled by his religious mentors. Everything and everyone seemed to conspire against him to render his life miserable and his condition pitiful, yet not one of his rulers had pity on him. It would seem that he epitomized all the travails that the fall from Paradise entailed, and yet he was also granted a divine gift, that of survival. Ground as he was into the mud, he derived from that mud a strength that sustained him and on occasion rewarded him

1. Patrick O'Brien, "The Long-Term Growth of Agricultural Production in Egypt: 1820-1962" in *Political and Social Change in Modern Egypt*, ed. P. M. Holt (London, 1968), p. 162.

bountifully, and for that rich mud he developed a love that surpassed all others and to which he devoted his life. To a fallah, a plot of land was the ultimate boon, and to acquire it he would do anything. And yet the supreme irony of fate was that the fallah who loved and tilled the land was denied its possession, and the legal owners of the land were frequently those who lived away from it and who regarded it simply as a source of income. Even more ironic was the fact that although landed property was owned by absentee landlords, Egypt had never had a landed aristocracy so that the owners could not even justify their ownership by an appeal to tradition. Egypt has never had a *noblesse terrienne*. Not even the mamluks could claim that right for landed property was not hereditary.

Land ownership in Egypt was based on a complex system which I shall attempt to simplify and summarize. From the time of the Ottoman conquest in 1516, land was regarded as the property of the crown, but for administrative and economic purposes it was parceled into tracts called *iqta* and *iltizam*, which were tax-farmed either by public auction to a *multazim*, or given to a mamluk bey or to the head of the Ottoman regiments as reward for services rendered. The function of the multazim was to act as tax collector on his parcel of land, to remit the sum agreed upon with the authorities to the treasury, the *ruznama*, and to keep a portion for his pains. The iltizam included *ard al-usya*, a piece of land, which the multazim was allowed to farm free of encumbrance; it was exempted from taxation and tilled by means of corvee labor by the fallahin of the iltizam. In time some of the usya land became private property, and much of it was transformed into waqf land. Waqf endowments became the principal means of preventing land confiscations by the authorities, and also of making sure that extravagant heirs did not become destitute too rapidly.

The only right the fallah, the tiller of the soil, had under that system was the right to till the soil, the *athariyya*, for as long as he and his heirs continued to remit the taxes to the multazim. The fallah could not be dispossessed except in cases of continued nonpayment of taxes. Land taxation devolved on the village as a whole, and the appropriate amounts were divided amongst the fallahin by the village elder, the shaikh, according to the amount of acreage each man tilled and the degree of fertility of the land. Any default in tax payment by one person was perforce made up by the majority of the villagers, so that tax payment was a communal project, and punishment fell on the village as a whole.

Muhammad Ali (1805–1848) had annulled the iltizam system as a wasteful means of collecting taxes and had cut out the middleman, the multazim, substituting the state as the direct tax-collector. Later on when his need for money outran the contents of the treasury he resorted to various systems known as *uhda, ibadiyya, chiflik,* all methods of parceling the land among the rich and collecting from them taxes which were in arrears, or of bringing new land under cultivation.

He also tried to distribute land to the fallahin in lots of five acres, which could have spelled the beginning of a class of small landowners. Unfortunately he did not give the fallah any capital with which to work his land, and taxed him unmercifully, which caused many peasants to desert the land. At the same time Muhammad Ali distributed large tracts of land to his friends and relations and the large latifundia tended to gobble up the smaller plots of land which were insolvent.

In 1858 the Ottoman land law became applicable in Egypt, and from that period onward land could become privately owned in return for proof that taxes had consistently been paid over five years, and title deeds were accordingly issued. But just as had been so over the past centuries, the tiller of the soil seldom owned the land he cultivated. Half the land came to be owned by 2 percent of the population. Although the large majority of landowners had come from fallah origins, many new landowners did not. The largest landowners in the country from the time of Muhammad Ali onward were members of the royal family who replaced the mamluks as the largest landed group. The new element in the landowning picture was the advent of foreign landowners, land companies, and members of local minority groups, especially the Copts. The rise of these groups as landowners occurred with the British occupation. Foreign landlords, however, never formed more than 0.5 percent of the total, although their holdings covered large tracts of land and in 1932 reached a total of 700,000 faddans.

The landless condition of the fallah had preoccupied the British authorities in Egypt, but little was done to remedy the situation, and when government land was sold, it was parceled into large tracts which were too expensive for the average fallah to buy. For example the sale of the Daira Saniyya lands from 1900 to 1906 increased the number of large proprietors, as Cromer pointed out in his report of 1906, rather than create a new group of small landholders. Much of the land that was bought in that era was financed by mortgage credit offered by foreign banks, and credit was given only to those who already owned property. Mortgage credit continued to be a major reason for the increase of landed property among those who already owned land or collateral.[2]

Successive Egyptian governments had paid lip service to their intention of selling state lands to the small fallah — Zaghlul in 1924, Muhammad Mahmud in 1928, Nahhas in 1942 — but they always ended by selling large tracts beyond the range of the fallahin. Land reclaimed by individuals or land companies rarely went to the fallahin since it was retained by the individual or the company and never subdivided into small plots.

The improvements in the irrigation system initiated by Muhammad Ali and Ismail Pasha (1867-1879) enabled the country to turn from basin to perennial irrigation. The new system increased the number of crops per year and increased the area of cultivated land by nearly 1.5 million faddans. But it also brought related evils like parasites, which thrived in the stagnant canal waters, and problems of drainage, salination, and soil depletion. Ismail had also given the first big boost to cotton production and for a brief span, during the American Civil War, the fallah had money in his pocket. The boom did not last long, and the fall in cotton prices at the end of the war caused hardship to many, landowners and fallahin alike. With British occupation in 1882 Egypt was turned into a one-crop country. The insatiable cotton mills of Lancashire and Egypt's foreign debt were two good reasons for Lord Cromer to direct the country's economy toward cotton, and the large landowners who thereby made great profits were only too happy to comply, until ultimately the former "granary of Rome" was forced to import grain for its local consumption.

The realization that so lopsided a development of the economy was detrimental in the long run arose with the nationalist movement under the inspiration of Mustafa Kamil, for it was he who underlined the evil effects of British economic policy in Egypt. Nothing much was done to remedy these defects, however, until after the 1919 revolution.

In the words of Charles Issawi, Egyptian agriculture was characterized by a highly developed system of irrigation, a labor-intensive technique, lavish use of fertilizers, dependence on cotton, and markedly unequal distribution of property accompanied by very small-scale tenure and farming.[3]

2. Abd al-Rahim Abd al-Rahim, *al-Rif al-Misri fi al-qarn al-thamin ashr* (Cairo, 1974). See as yet unpublished but important dissertation by Ali M. M. Barakat, "tatawwur al-milkiyya al-ziraʿiyya fi-Misr wa atharuh ʿala-l haraka al-siyasiyya" (Cairo University, 1972).

3. Charles Issawi, *Egypt in Revolution* (London, 1963), p. 126.

Landed property in Egypt derived its basic income from cotton; even the leading industries dealt with cotton: spinning, weaving, ginning and pressing. Cotton was the most expensive crop to plant in terms of labor and capital outlay, but it brought in the highest financial returns. For example Issawi estimated in 1948 the relative cost of cultivating the four main crops (see table 1).

Fruits and vegetables brought in much higher profits but they also required that the owner possess a more specialized degree of agricultural knowledge especially of the newer fruits like mangoes; they represented a larger capital outlay since the owner had to wait a number of years for the trees to grow before he could see any profit; and lastly they represented problems of spoilage and storage. Cotton therefore continued to form the basis of the Egyptian economy; it was easily marketed, the banks accepted it as collateral on loans, it was not consumed by the peasantry, and could be stored without spoiling. As a general rule small landowners with holdings of less than 3 faddans grew cereals for their own consumption and barsim for animal fodder. The larger landowners grew cotton, when they could afford to pay for the seeds and fertilizers, and they made the highest profits. Twenty-one percent of the land was planted in cotton (1,716,000 faddans), 19 percent in maize (1,562,000 faddans), 17 percent in wheat (1,410,000 faddans, which was not even enough for local consumption and was supplemented by imports of wheat), and 18 percent in barsim (1,510,000 faddans); the rest of the crop area, some 25 percent of the total 8,101,000 faddans, grew a variety of crops like flax, sugar cane, onions, and rice, which were also export crops.[4] The agricultural land had not increased much in the twentieth century, growing from 5,280,000 faddans in 1912 to 5,845,000 faddans in 1952, but extensive and expensive irrigation projects had been carried out and they allowed the land to turn to perennial irrigation and plant three crops in a two-year cycle, so that the crop area rose from 7.7 million faddans in 1912 to 9.3 million faddans in 1952. Thus from November to May wheat and barsim were sown, in June and July the land lay fallow, August to November was the maize season, December and January were fallow, and February to November was cotton time. Many of the landlords have turned to a triennial cycle in order to allow the land to rest longer than with a biennial cycle and thus they have appreciably increased the yield of the crop.

4. A. E. Crouchley, *The Economic Development of Modern Egypt* (London, 1938), p. 223.

TABLE 1

COSTS OF CULTURE

OF FOUR MAIN CROPS, 1948 (*in percentage*)

Crop	Rent	Cost of Cultivation	Total	Value of Crop	Profit
Cotton	16.6	16.7	33.3	44.1	12.6
Maize	7.0	12.4	19.4	16.9	-1.8
Wheat	11.4	11.2	22.6	16.2	-3.8
Barsim	11.7	6.6	18.3	28.8	11.8

SOURCE: Charles Issawi, *Egypt in Revolution* (London, 1963), p. 140.

That picture was to continue without major modification until the revolution of 1952 when the passage of the land reform law limited landholding to 200 faddans per person. The law was subsequently amended to 100 faddans and then to 50 faddans per person, thereby breaking up the large latifundia and weakening the hold of the landlord on the peasant. Recently it has become customary to castigate large landlords as "feudalists," *iqta῾iyyun,* but one must not overlook the important economic role these same landowners and their predecessors played in effecting national integration. As Iliya Harik pertinently pointed out, it was through their efforts that urban and rural economies became interdependent. "Their concern for the protection of their recently acquired private property rights and the security of trade routes drove them to advocate the presence of a constitutional and centralized system of government,"[5] and made them the advocates of a national movement against royal autocracy and foreign occupation.

The relationship between the landlord and the fallah was an exploitative one, hence the accusation of "feudalism." The fallah could be a tenant, a sharecropper, or a day laborer. In all three roles he was at the mercy of the landlord who set the terms of payment, could raise the rent at will, and evict the fallah for nonpayment. As a tenant the fallah usually paid the rent in crops, and by 1939 it was estimated that only 17 percent of the land was under money rent—by 1952 the figure had gone up to 75 percent. As a sharecropper the fallah

5. Iliya Harik, *The Political Mobilization of Peasants: A Study of an Egyptian Community* (Bloomington, 1974), p. 19.

delivered the valuable crop, cotton, to the landowner, shared the wheat and the rice, and kept maize and barsim for his own use. Thus while the landlord was oriented toward a market economy, the fallah remained on a subsistence economy. With the growth of absentee landlords, a group of middlemen developed, who leased the land from the landowner for cash—*min al-batin*—and rented it to the fallah, a process that inevitably raised the rent and cut down on the fallah's profit.

A great number of large landowners resided in the urban centers and returned to the land in times of sowing and harvesting. Others were totally absentee and appointed overseers to do the work. The reasons for absentee landlords were many, but let us keep in mind that mamluks had also been absentee landlords, so the system was not new. The first and major new reason was the development of representative bodies which siphoned off bona fide landlords to the capital. It was the landlords who pushed for representative, constitutional government, where they would have a majority voice, and protect their property from arbitrary governments, especially in a hydraulic economy where irrigation was controlled by the government and could be manipulated in a way that could make or break a large landowner. Landowners therefore had to forge links between the town and the country which were not only economic but also political. Thus whatever assemblies existed, whether under British aegis or after the constitution of 1923, were stacked with landowners who were forced to spend their time between their estates and the parliamentary sessions in town. Government officials, by virtue of their employment, were also forced to follow the same pattern.

The second reason was that some landowners knew little about agriculture. Either they did not stem from a fallah milieu and had invested in land as a means of making profit, or, if they did, had been trained as bureaucrats. For men with social pretensions, possession of land was a sine qua non. In a country that was predominantly rural in mentality, those who were rich but landless were made in some subtle way to feel their lack of solid worth. The rich but landless therefore hastened to remedy that defect, even when they could more profitably invest their money elsewhere. That was one of the reasons many of the post-1919 revolutionary elite, a large number of whom came from fallah families, but some of whom came from the professional bourgeoisie, rapidly joined the ranks of the large landowning group. A landowner belonged to the ranks of the *ayan*, the rural gentry, where he could not aspire to penetrate the ranks of the *dhawat*, the elite.

Otherwise he remained in some sort of social limbo where his wealth was recognized but did not confer on him any standing.

The third reason was that the towns, and especially the political capital, Cairo, and the commercial capital, Alexandria, were centers of power that held the lure of modernity and comfort. Inevitably those with political ambitions and economic acumen moved to the cities and commuted to the country only when it was strictly necessary. Families with children of school age moved to the towns, since boarding schools were extremely rare. In time they came to prefer the comforts of town to the hardship of rural life.

The normal links that a landowner might have had with the land at one time weakened with every urbanized generation and frequently died out. He then came to regard the land and the fallah who worked it in the same light as a cash register. Cynics could point out that landowners had always had that attitude toward the fallah, but where in the past it may have been taken for granted, in the twentieth century it simply weakened the fabric of society, weakened the rise of a real representative government, and brought about the social instability that ended in another revolution in 1952.

The fallahin of an estate lived in hamlets called *izba,* of which there were some 1,500 in Egypt. The houses of an izba were provided by the landlord to the peasant free of rent, but if the fallah was evicted from the land he also lost his house. The inhabitants of an izba form a tightly knit unit and are frequently related to one another by blood ties or through marriage links. An outsider is seldom admitted into the group. If for some reason a plot of land in the area was sold to someone outside the community the fallahin of the izba would unite against the newcomer and attempt to drive him away either by burning his crops, stealing his cattle, or even attacking him to force him to sell the land to someone within the community. Buying up land was therefore no guarantee of ownership, unless the landlord showed he was more ruthless than the local opposition.

Each izba had a certain land area allotted to it, which formed the *zimam* and which could only be cultivated by the inhabitants of the izba. Should new land be reclaimed and new izba put up, however, fallahin were imported from overpopulated areas and set up in the new territories. In the twentieth century Egypt became a land-hungry country and there was never enough land for all the fallahin, especially when holdings were inevitably cut down through inheritance. Even today when the large latifundia have been limited in size, there is still not enough land to meet the demands of an ever growing rural population, especially when every fallah dreams all his life of saving enough money to be able to buy an acre or two.

The life of the fallah has remained outwardly unchanged since the time of the pharaohs. Dressed in a tattered *galabiyya,* with a cap, *libda,* on his head, he works barefoot in the mud from sunrise to sunset, as did his ancestors depicted on the bas reliefs of the tomb of Ti, 4000 B.C. In the past basin irrigation dried out the mud for part of the year, during the dry season, and killed off all the parasites dwelling in it. When the Nile rose and flooded the fields, the rich silt fertilized the land and revived and strengthened it. Perennial irrigation put an end to that system. Fields could now be irrigated the year round through canals which stored the water, so that the mud never dried out and instead turned into the perfect breeding ground for parasites like bilharzia and ankylostoma, which enter the human body when, for example, the bare feet come into contact with the mud, and lodge in the intestines, causing an extremely debilitating disease characterized by hemorrhaging and consequent diminution of resistance to all germs. Three years after the introduction of perennial irrigation in the districts of Qina and Aswan the incidence of bilharzia and ankylostoma rose from 0-2 percent to 43-75 percent, while 75 percent of the total rural population developed bilharzia.[6] Thus the strong Egyptian peasant who could work tirelessly under the merciless sun for 12-14 hours a day found his energy sapped and his body a prey to a parasite that weakened his resistance and led to his early demise. To counteract the lethargy induced by the parasites in his body the fallah turned to hashish, which gave him the illusion of continued strength and sexual potency, and to drinking a strong sweet tea in enormous quantities.

The sand of Egypt has also brought disease in its wake, in the shape of trachoma. The ancient Egyptians had deified the sand as the god Seth, the enemy and brother of the god of verdure, Osiris. The enmity between the two brothers symbolized the eternal conflict between the desert and the sown. The dry, choking dust that trails every footstep in rural pathways and a low rate of hygiene have earned Egypt the unenviable reputation of having the highest rate of blindness in the world.[7] Widespread belief in the evil eye has encouraged parents to keep their children as filthy as possible, to allow flies to gather undisturbed on small faces, in order to hide a child's good looks and ward off the envious glances which might harm him through the evil they emit.

6. Issawi, *Egypt in Revolution,* p. 92.
7. Ibid., p. 93.

The fallah's ignorance of primary notions of hygiene has been the cause of the high incidence of infant mortality, and hence of the urge to procreate as much as possible since many children were sure to die. Childbirth for a young wife is an imperative, and her constant pregnancies turn her into an old woman prematurely if she is not carried off at an early age by puerperal fever or any of the other mishaps related to childbirth. Ignorance of hygiene in the cities was the cause of the constant epidemics that raged over the country unabated until the advent of modern medicine and the imposition of stricter methods of hygiene, and especially of clean drinking water.

Both male and female peasants share a high degree of illiteracy and its ally superstition. The 1937 census revealed that 82 percent of the population over five years old was illiterate: 74 percent of the men and 91 percent of the women.[8] In spite of this handicap, or maybe because of it, the fallah is capable of performing incredible feats of mental arithmetic, since calculations are an integral part of his working life, and he is also gifted with a good, retentive memory, much in the fashion of the bedouin of the Jahiliyya who was able to recite long qasidas after one hearing.

The artistic sense of the fallah has long amazed his urban neighbors, who wrongly assumed that because the life of a fallah is hard and he is untutored he must also be totally ungifted. An artistic sense is instinctive in the fallah. Children are capable of weaving the most elaborate rugs with complicated color combinations and designs after the simplest training in weaving techniques, as Wisa Wasif has so admirably proved in his work with the children of the village of Harraniyya, near the pyramids. The straw mats which every village weaves for its own use, the textiles, the water pots, all are witness to the sense of beauty that has been a natural part of their heritage from time immemorial and is nurtured by the variety of color and species that abound in the countryside.

Another artistic gift possessed by the fallah is that of poetry, of rhyme and rhythm. Perhaps those who live close to nature are rewarded by such gifts. Continued repression over centuries had caused the fallah to develop the faculty of extemporaneous folk poetry, which was frequently set to music and sung as a *mawwal* or recited as *zajal*. Folk poetry was invariably a commentary on a fallah's life and was the safety valve that allowed him to express his fears, doubts, miseries, and hopes. It is one of the most ancient art forms and a very flexible one. Any major incident in a fallah's life, the visit of the tax collector, the

8. Ibid., p. 91.

hangings of Dinshwai, the accession or deposition of a ruler, is cele-
brated extemporaneously. Snatches of folk poetry have lasted through
the ages thanks to the retentive memory of some elders and to the
efforts of modern scholars like Ahmad Rushdi Salih, who have strived
to collect these poems and the related folk arts as an important part of
the Egyptian cultural heritage, a link that is traceable back to
pharaonic days. Most of the poetry, alas, is lost, since it was entirely
oral, but as every generation produces its own poets the art form lives
on. One of the most perceptive documents that we possess on rural life
in the eighteenth century is in the form of a long folk poem written by
one or several unknowns, who have chosen the nom de plume of Abu
Shaduf.[9] The poem describes in poignant terms the poverty of the
countryside, the abject fear of the visit of the tax collector which
turned men into cowering creatures, the aspirations of a rural dweller.
The language of the poem is coarse and vulgar to delicate ears, but
the images conveyed are unforgettable, more vivid than the sophisticated account of a traveler, government bureaucrat, or even a more
polished poet.

The fallah sings almost as soon as he can talk. He sings as he works,
and during harvest days the best singers of a village are hired just to
sing and supply the rhythm by which the harvest is picked. On any
building site today one can still hear a leader sing the verse while the
laborers work to the refrain. Singing seems to lighten a burden and to
while away the monotony of labor, and so to have become part of the
labor itself. The songs tell of life and death; they also satirize, eulogize,
and criticize. Many are songs of praise to God, *madh,* or to the
Prophet, as a form of prayer in song, which may have its roots as much
in sufi as in orthodox Islam. The famous "Nightingale of the East,"
Um Kalthum, started her career as a rural child who chanted the
Quran, and then turned to secular song. Quran chanting to a Muslim
Arab is tantamount to song in other cultures, and, to a people
enthralled by the magic of the Word, to listen to a good chanter is a
universal treat, for while it pleases the auditory senses, it also rouses
religious fervor and induces in the hearers a mystical sense of com-
munion. Some of the famous Quran chanters, like Shaikh al-Shishai,
Shaikh Muhammad Rifaat, and more recently Shaikh al-Naqshabandi,
had exquisite voices which they refused to desecrate by singing secular
songs. Music sacred or profane therefore plays a basic role in rural life,
and is one of the few means at the fallah's disposal which was not
censored, punished, taxed, or confiscated, unlike everything else he

9. Yusif al-Shirbini, *Hazz al-quhuf fi sharh qasidat Abi Shaduf* (Bulaq, 1857).

owned. The music that one hears on approaching a field is the same music that was heard thousands of years ago, for the reed flute, or *nay*, which any child can gather from the banks of the canals and blow into, is the oldest musical instrument. The plaintive sound of the nay echoing through the fields, punctuated by the monotonous squeak of a water wheel as it turns, and the occasional chirp of a bird is an integral part of the Egyptian countryside. Now and then the busy staccato of a donkey's hooves, followed by that incredible braying, disturbs the peace, as it has done almost forever. Today the noise of an exhaust pipe badly in need of repair and the loud toot of a horn signal the advent of a motor car, usually obscured by a cloud of dust in the midst of which it travels at a dangerous speed loaded with humans, baggage, or poultry, and followed by every self-respecting dog in the village and every urchin who is not out in the fields. But that sign of the industrial age rapidly disappears and gives way to the immutable and eternal sounds of the countryside, which lull and soothe the senses, which have led city dwellers to write ecstatic prose about the country-side, until the monotony of life drove them back to their familiar hubbub. Underneath the serenity of rural life is a harshness and a cruelty that is awesome in its intensity, but out of which the character and personality of the fallah has been fashioned, a personality that can cope with extremes of joy and misery with equanimity, even indifference, because of having been bred in the belief that sooner or later the tide will turn. Abd al-Rahman al-Sharqawi, who came from the fallah milieu, has given us an acute and disturbing picture of those who have been called *al-muᶜadhabun fi-l ard*, "The Tortured on Earth." The condition of the fallah has inspired Egyptian writers from Haikal in his romantic novel *Zainab* and Taha Husain in his equally romantic but more perceptive *Duᶜa al-Karawan*, "The Call of the Curlew," to the more realistic treatment of contemporary authors. While these novels all describe the miserable existence of the fallah, they also portray his long-suffering patience and his stoic qualities which have earned him both admiration and opprobrium. The term "fallah" is thus used as a term of praise, to denote strength of character and solid worth, and as a term of blame, to denote crudeness and apathy—an ambivalence that is intrinsic to the fallah.

In his book on the fallahin of Egypt, Father Ayrout, who spent much of his life in the rural areas, talks about the "traditional feminism" of the country.[10] That statement may surprise many who are familiar with the stereotype of the subservient female who defers

10. Ayrout, *Egyptian Peasant*, p. 139.

to her husband on all matters. And while that description may indeed fit a small section of the urban middle and lower bourgeoisie, in no way does it fit the rural society that comprises a large part of the Egyptian population. Perhaps one can trace the origins of so positive a female role back to the ancient Egyptians where the mother was the "focus of the house" during the family religious ceremonies, rather than the more common father focus in other cults.[11] Or it may simply be that rural life has no room for a pampered, subservient person; everyone must pull his weight or fall by the wayside.

The fallaha is much more liberated than her urban sister. She has never known the veil, although she may coyly draw a head cover over her grinning mouth when strangers pass by; and she has never known the harem. As an active participant in the economic life of the household she is not restricted in her movements; she is free to circulate among the men, but woe betide her if she is found alone with a man, or if she infringes upon the men's circle in the evening. She works in the fields during the harvest; she raises chickens to sell or barter; she milks the cow, makes butter or cheese, and is the one who sells and haggles during the weekly market days. She in fact supplies the brains of the outfit while her husband supplies the brawn. The fallah defers to his wife's judgment in most economic dealings, where an urban husband would not even mention finances to his wife. In most cases the fallaha is the family banker and investor. She decides when it is time to buy a young heifer, or baby chicks, or when they have saved enough money to make a down payment on the plot of land they have always coveted. The fallaha chooses her son's wife with an eye to her family's affluence, and her ability to work in the house and assist her mother-in-law, and then supply her with strong grandchildren. Every young bride who has had to live under the iron rod of a mother-in-law (who may be her aunt) has perpetuated the same system when her turn to rule the roost came. The sons defer to their mother to the extent of handing her their earnings until they set up houses of their own.

Like the fallah, the fallaha wants as many children as possible. They are her guarantee, her social security, against the day when she can no longer work. They are the links that bind her husband to her and, she hopes, militate against his taking another wife. She knows that many of her children will die before they reach five years of age, but every one of those who survive will bring money into the family. Any child under the age of five, male or female, can take the cow to pasture, fill the family pots from the well or the river, carry food to the men in the

11. Joachim Wach, *The Sociology of Religion* (Chicago, 1944), p. 62.

fields. A child over five works during the harvest gathering cotton, which needs a child's nimble fingers to extract the fibers; at other times the child picks the cotton larva before it turns adult and wreaks havoc on the crop. Thus every child is regarded as a contributor to the family budget rather than as an extra mouth to feed. And while an economist can prove that a child costs more than it contributes to the family, such sophisticated reckoning never convinces the peasant (consequently the recent birth control program has not proved successful to date). A fallah wants his children to acquire an education—which he interprets as the ability to read, write, calculate, and recite the Quran—but only for as long as it does not interfere with their earning power. At harvest time all schools are emptied of children, as in rural areas the world over; they are to be found out in the fields earning their keep. Usually peasant children never go beyond the most rudimentary education unless they are blind, when those who have a pleasant voice become Quran reciters and those who have brains become faqihs. Only the more affluent fallah, the small landowner, can afford to do without his children's wages and send them to elementary and secondary school, both of which are free. By so doing the child is likely either to become an effendi if he can find a job in town, or become a member of the rural administrative group, wich means that he becomes eligible to seek a post as an overseer, a *khawli*, or an accountant, a *sarraf*, or, if he proves highly intelligent, even better posts.

In an agricultural society every member has to have a niche, and if there is none available then that "surplus" person must go elsewhere. He can go into the next village and hire himself out as a laborer, or he can go into the urban society and become absorbed within its system as a day laborer, a domestic servant, gardener, or porter, or swell the ranks of the unemployed and the semi-employed. Agricultural surplus was not an issue in Egypt until the twentieth century. When industrialization expanded, the rural surplus became a necessary part of the system. The "push" of overpopulation in rural areas and the "pull" of industrialization caused a rapid rise in the urban population. Where the population of Cairo in 1917 was 791,000, 25 percent of whom were Egyptian-born migrants, in 1937 it rose to 1,312,000, 34 percent of whom were migrants.[12] These figures acquire more meaning when we note that the population of Egypt in 1917 was 12,751,000, in 1927 it became 14,218,000, and in 1937 it became 15,933,000.[13] Given

12. Janet Abu Lughod, *Cairo: 1001 Years of the City Victorious* (Princeton, 1971), p. 174; also, Issawi, *Egypt in Revolution*, p. 84.
13. Ibid., p. 77.

the relatively small population increase in the country the swell in
urban population was noticeably large. Today Egypt has reached the
danger level of overpopulation, since its crop surface has increased but
slightly and its population has topped the 38 million mark. But the
problem was becoming acute even in 1937, hence the need for rapid
industrialization to employ the surplus. But even by 1960 only 10
percent of the population was employed in industrial activities, so that
more and more people were working the same plot of land as in the
previous four or five decades—a greater degree of impoverishment for
an already impoverished country.

For millennia Egypt's hydraulic society has imposed a strong central
government, so the world view of the fallah is limited to his contacts
with the government, the dreaded hukuma. In the past this contact
was identified as the tax collector and his notorious rapacity, the
abusive corvée, and the kurbaj, the lash. Later on under Muhammad
Ali the bane of conscription was added to the list of government
blights. For these reasons he bore toward the government a resentment
which is the hallmark of an oppressed group that had not yet developed an aspiration to rule, so that his outlook was unpolitical, and it
further developed the "ethic of fatalism . . . of submission to higher and
inscrutable pwoers."[14] From time to time he broke out in uprisings,
but they were rarer in the rural areas than in the urban society,
where contiguity and the presence of more enlightened and more vocal
elements developed a pattern of at least one uprising every ten or
fifteen years throughout the late eighteenth century.[15]

With the advent of the British occupation the fallah came to know
a greater measure of fairness in tax collecting, while the kurbaj,
conscription, and the corvée on the lands of the rich were abrogated.
(In times of crisis such as a flood the corvée is willingly offered by the
peasantry to safeguard their fields and homes.) And since irrigation
depends on a centrally planned organism, he grew to appreciate the
fairness of the British irrigation engineers, who saw to it that the fallah
had a steady and free supply of irrigation water for his crops and that
the rich landlord did not monopolize all the water. For that reason
the irrigation engineer remained the only foreigner who did not earn
the opprobrium of the fallah. Of all the improvements and the new

14. Karl Mannheim, *Ideology and Utopia* (New York, 1936), p. 191.
15. André Raymond, "Quartiers et mouvements populaires au Caire au XVIIIème
siècle," in Holt, *Political and Social Change in Modern Egypt*, pp. 109 ff., and Afaf
Loutfi el Sayed, "The Role of the Ulama in Egypt during the Early 19th Century" in
ibid., pp. 264 ff.

systems introduced during the British occupation, the most incomprehensible to the fallah were the new laws passed, which no one bothered to explain to him. Fines were imposed on him for the infringement of rules which he never even knew existed, for law was made by the effendis in town and imposed on the population in a callous manner that left the fallah no recourse but to follow village custom and unwittingly or deliberately break the law. A case in point is criminal law. Any government arrogates to itself the right to punish a wrongdoer, but peasant society denied it that right and regarded it as due the injured party. Thus it is a village custom dating back to tribal days that a homicide could only be wiped out by a vendetta, *al-thar*. Likewise a dishonor to one's family such as the real or suspected loss of virginity in a sister or a daughter was punishable by the death of the girl and of the offender at the hands of her nearest male relatives. Hence a murder could be committed in broad daylight in the middle of a busy marketplace, and no witnesses would be found. The investigating police officer would be met by denials when he tried to carry out an investigation, and no lips would become unsealed. Frequently when a father was questioned by the authorities he would freely admit having killed his daughter for being unchaste, and neither he nor his society could understand why he had to stand trial and go to prison for righting a wrong done to his honor, *sharaf*. On his release from prison a felon would be greeted with great rejoicing by his village. As Ayrout pertinently quotes, "Egypt is a land of much crime without being essentially a criminal country."[16]

The gap between legislation and social realities was due to a number of causes, but it was basically the result of an attempt at westernization. Legal systems were imported wholesale from Western legal codes and imposed on the society without making any attempt to justify or explain the value of these codes. Custom and some elements of sharia law were set aside in the process of modernization which began with Muhammad Ali and was accelerated under Ismail and under the British occupation. Thus the law of the land and the law of the people were at loggerheads. The gap between the two has been closing over the years, but it still exists though to a lesser degree. The obvious manifestation of the gap in legal understanding was patent in the breakdown of public security which was a problem during the days of Cromer, and continued to be a problem for a long time. It remains a problem in some remote areas today although brigandage can be more severely repressed by the authorities who have many more means at

16. Ayrout, *Egyptian Peasant*, p. 145.

their disposal than they had in the past. Brigandage is one manifestation of the defiance of authority, others less obvious continue to abound;
they are generally expressions of an unwillingness to cooperate with the
government unless coerced, and disinclination to believe anything the
government says.

The "otherness" of government in the fallah mind was an outgrowth
of centuries of foreign domination, but it continued into the present as
a carry-over even with a wholly Egyptian administration. At no time in
the period under examination here, save when Saad Zaghlul was in
power, did the fallah feel that those men ruling in the capital were
fallahin like himself. Zaghlul was different; he talked like a fallah; he
understood the fallah; he made the fallah understand him and identify
with him. No one else had that ability, for while Nahhas did have the
popular touch, it perhaps was more urban in nature and more popular
there. Hence voting procedures did frequently become farcical, unless
the electoral process was left free of government interference, which
was seldom the case. The Wafd was the only party in Egypt which had
a grass-roots organization based on a thorough understanding of the
village pecking order. But even when the fallah would have voted
Wafd on his own, the Wafd could not trust his judgment and paid the
fallah to vote for the party.

Aside from the large landlords, absentee or otherwise, the village has
a very definite hierarchical system. At the top level of the power
structure is the umda, or village shaikh, *shaikh al-balad,* who controls
a variety of posts, such as that of ghafir, or local constable. The umda
is able to disburse patronage, punish the opposition or harass it by
arresting them or imposing fines. Often he was the richest man in the
village, and some umdas were sufficiently affluent to climb the social
ladder and buy their way into the title of a pasha by donating sums
to the government or to a certain party. The umda acts as a buffer
between the members of the village and the outside world, notably the
landlord, government official, or irrigation inspector. He was also the
main channel of communication, if only by virtue of the telephone, the
symbol of office, in his house. The traditional functions of the umda
were to offer hospitality to travelers and succor to the needy, both of
which enhanced his image in society, for generosity is a much-prized
virtue. He also mediated in quarrels of every variety from personal to
economic, and settled the disputes that might otherwise involve the
disputants in a long and costly process of litigation. Within his milieu
the umda has practically unlimited authority for good or for harm,
because his society recognized and acquiesced in his special standing as

the local leader and the prime politician. The umda who was a government appointee was effective only if he also happened to be recognized as a leader by his community; otherwise his election was of no consequence, and the government would find itself in the position of having to replace him, so that in fact the appointment of an umda was the official recognition of his already important status in the community. But since one community usually numbered several important and rival people, the choice of one member over the others determined the pecking order.

The umda was supported by a council of elders who represented different village factions and families. An ad hoc member of village councils was frequently the local faqih, or the alim or the priest, both of whom were enshrined in a special position by virtue of their religious lore. On occasion he too developed into a settler of disputes and a purveyor of wisdom, depending on his personal talent. He also functioned as teacher, judge, and mentor to the community. His powers rivaled and, if he was especially able, even eclipsed those of the umda. The rest of society was arranged in descending order of importance according to the degree of wealth, judged in terms of size of landholdings of the members of the family, their connections with the government through other members of the family, and the function of the individual members. The *nazir,* supervisor, of a large estate, the khawli, the sarraf, the manager of a flour mill, the guardian of the pasha's house, while they were all private functionaries, nonetheless belonged to the rural elite because of their control over the hiring and the firing of laborers and because of their proximity to a greater authority, the large landlord, absentee or present. Within the elite group age played an important role, and youth usually had to await its turn to assume power, unless the youthful person occupied some position of power. At the bottom of the scale were the day laborers and the dispossessed in the community.

The landlord of a large latifundia managed his estates, or *daira,* through his overseer, who was as often as not a poor relation who lived in the village, or the son of one of his men who had been educated by the landlord in order to fill that position. For while in the past the large landowners had been Turco-Circassians, Egyptians had been joining the ranks of the large landowning group throughout the nineteenth century. Since many of the newly affluent urban groups had at one time been fallahin, it was rare to find a rich landowner who did not have many poor relatives in his village. Because of his city connections the landlord was expected to help out his poor relations, and indeed to help out the whole village when it came to a problem involving the government.

As in the old days of the iltizam the nazir frequently enriched himself at the expense of the landowner, especially the absentee owner or one who had lost his links with the rural area through a generation of residence in the urban milieu. The nazir was more feared than the distant pasha in town for having recently risen from fallah status he was harder on the fallah than his master would be. It was not at all unusual to find the overseer of a large estate come to own it. The landlord who sent to the nazir for money whenever he needed it indebted himself to the nazir who became a money lender to his employer, when he was not also a usurer. Rich or poor, the absentee landlord had a limited contact with the peasantry and relied on the overseer to carry out his orders, economic and political.

At election time all the elements of the rural society were marshaled by the umda to summon, cajole, threaten, or bribe voters into voting as he wished. The umda was responsible for the whole voting procedure and therefore for delivering the votes according to the dictates of the party to which he belonged. The pattern could only be upset when the government gave the umda orders contradictory to those of his party and upheld them by the presence of a provincial official flanked by a troop of police, or when the territory contained more than one landlord with different political affiliations.

Election time then became a bloodbath with the toughs of each group bidding for the votes of the fallahin, or cracking skulls to show they meant business. The outcome of such continuous politicking on the part of government and parties was that the fallah seldom voted out of political conviction. He was constantly manipulated, and lied to, and so voted out of self-interest when he was offered a bribe, or out of fear when faced with a threat. The fact that even so important an official as the mudir, or governor of the province, interfered in the electoral process simply confirmed in the fallah his cynical opinion of the political process and rightly or wrongly encouraged him to attempt to skirt the law when he could safely do so.

Government authority was therefore never regarded as a source of assistance or succor, but was solely identified with repression and the manipulation of the law in favor of the powerful. The fallah sought redress for injustice through private channels. He rarely resorted to the law but appealed either to the umda or to his landlord, if he could reach the ear of either. Every village had its local equivalent of the mafia, with the landlord or the umda playing godfather.

The only source of comfort the fallah had was his religion. Unlike Christianity which stresses the concept of original sin and imbues people with a sense of guilt, the unsophisticated Muslim is devoid of guilt and assumes that he will be saved by virtue of his submission to God, his Islam. Whatever sins he commits he assumes will be wiped off the slate by the performance of a good deed. In any case, pre-destination plays an important part in his philosophy of life. When an evil day falls upon him, he will mutter "It is God's will," and if fortune smiles upon him he will say "That is from God's bounty." Every sigh he emits is automatically followed by ꜣafwak, wi satrak, wi ridak, Your Pardon, Your Protection, Your Approval; just as a sneeze in Western society is countered by a *Gesundheit*, in Egypt it is greeted with *al-hamdu-lillah*, Praise be to God, one of the most frequent ex-clamations heard. Although the fallah's knowledge of the details of his religion is limited and his faith is simplistic and dominated by saint cults and superstition, it nonetheless contains a greater degree of the "sacred" in it than that of the more learned, for as Eliade pertinently said, "it is the scale that makes the phenomenon."[17] Obviously the experience of the masses is different from that of the elite, but that does not mean that their interpretations are any less "sacred." The evil eye and Shaitan's blandishments are very real to the fallah and believed to be the source of all misfortune. If he is caught stealing the fallah will deny personal responsibility and claim *wazz al-shaitan*, the incite-ment of the devil. If the boll weevil attacks his crops he will call on the faqih to recite al-Bukhari, the Prophet's sayings, at the four corners of the field, and when his crop is devastated he will deny any negligence, for had he not had the Holy Words recited? and blame the evil eye.[18] Today the fallah is not likely to place so much faith in Shaitan, or al-Bukhari for that matter, and will first spray his fields with insecticide, and then recite the Holy Writ.

In the past, therefore, the most influential member of the village community aside from the umda, and on occasion before the umda, was the alim, although in recent history he has been displaced by the schoolteacher, and after the 1952 revolution by other functionaries such as the members of the Socialist Union. The shaikh or alim was respected because of his religious knowledge. He therefore served as moral tutor, arbiter, confidant, and example to the whole community. His society was sought because his "possession of the word of God"

17. Mircea Eliade, *Patterns in Comparative Religion* (New York, 1958), pp. 1-33.

18. Husain Haikal recounts a similar story in his memoirs and I have heard the story from both my father and uncle.

made him a special being whose blessing was frequently besought. If the shaikh also happened to be a sufi, or if he was a sufi without being an alim, which was much more common, then he was believed to have a direct line of communication with the saints, the *awliya*. For while saint worship is frowned upon by the more rigidly orthodox, it is encouraged by the sufis, who claim sanctity and miraculous powers for many of the famous mystics. Appeals to a holy man are a basic feature of rural (as well as urban) life. A shaikh is frequently enjoined to cast a spell on an enemy, or break a spell woven by an enemy. If he is an honest man who refuses credit for nonexistent miraculous powers people still believe that recitations of Quranic passages will work miracles, and beg his indulgence.

The most blessed events of a fallah's life are visits to a saint's tomb to invoke his blessings, *baraka,* upon himself and his family. The mawlid of al-Sayyid al-Badawi in Tanta is attended by over one million pilgrims every year. Only the truly affluent can afford to dream of a pilgrimage to Mecca as the culmination of all the labors of a lifetime.

The hold of religion, or the nearest equivalent as interpreted by the local authority, was thus very strong on the fallah, and had been so recognized by those in power at all times. It was the ulama who told the people to accept the rule of tyranny for that was preferable to anarchy. Before the age of the mass media the government had used religious figures to encourage the adoption of certain reforms. When a water pump was installed in a village, the alim was encouraged to expound on the blessings of clean water and to incite the villagers to use it instead of drinking polluted canal water, which was credited with powers of fertility, but which was also a major source of epidemics. Today the ulama of al-Azhar are incited to preach on the virtues of contraceptives and they participate in television debates to point out that their value was not inconsistent with religious beliefs. When an epidemic struck, the umda and the alim were summoned to help the authorities vaccinate the population by becoming the first in line to set a good example. By the same token the men of religion were used by the opposition to rouse the people against the government as King Fuad used al-Azhar University in 1924 against Zaghlul and the Wafd, or later, in 1936, when King Faruq used the Azhar against the Wafd.

The fallah's mind was thus filled with a mixture of a little Islam, much popular religion, and a little animism as an atavistic throwback to his pharaonic heritage. Many of his ceremonies concerned with birth, death, and the land were in fact purely pharaonic in origin, overlaid with a thin veneer of Islam or of Christianity.

The influence of the religious factor on the rural population was one of the reasons for the success of the Muslim Brethren movement as we shall see later. The Ikhwan al-Muslimun talked in terms the fallah understood. They preached a return to Islamic rules of government, to social justice and equity. No one could quarrel with these sentiments. But the Brethren went a step beyond when they showed, by personal example, how to lead a pure life, and more important, how to become financially successful through leading a pure life. In almost puritan terms they sought to link material success with a Godly life, by means of self-help or by "operation bootstrap" which used available resources rationally, and successfully, thereby demonstrating the truth of their preaching. Although no figures are available it is my belief that the large majority of the rural population were, if not themselves active Ikhwan, at least, close sympathizers. At present the movement is politically proscribed after its leaders were executed for treason, but I have no doubt that were the ban to be lifted they would regroup in great numbers.

Many local and foreign authors writing about Egypt have made the mistake of assuming that because the fallah was ignorant he was also stupid. Jokes abound in all the chronicles, ancient and modern, about the credulity of the fallah, and how easily he was gulled by the townsman when he came to sell his wares. The reality is quite different. There are obviously clever fallahin and stupid ones, as in any society, but the major characteristic of the Egyptian peasant is one shared by many other peasants, distrust of the stranger. The fallah may be gulled by his shaikh, but rarely by anyone else except by the foreigner. In the past, however, his major handicap was his illiteracy, so that he often signed documents that he could not read and was cheated out of his land by the foreign moneylender. His mistrust of the outsider was born of oppression and exploitation and honed during his struggle for survival and his hunger for land. His confidence is gained with difficulty, and city people rage at what they call the "ill will" of the fallah. He is described as "childlike" even by Father Ayrout, because he does not behave in the same fashion as the urban dweller. The logic of the fallah is different from the logic of the urbanized individual. His environment is different, his life-style is different, his needs and hopes are different, so his responses are different. When asked how far it is to the next village, the fallah will answer, "a 2 P.T. fare," for everyone in his society is familiar with the distance covered

by a 2 P.T. fare, and to them the fare is of more importance than
the distance in terms of mileage. The urban dweller castigates such a
response as "stupid." In brief, behavioral responses within the same
culture vary with the environment, but since the fallah on emigrating
to the city took with him his cultural standards, it is with justification
that Egypt was regarded as a nation of fallahin.

Most of twentieth-century Egypt's political and intellectual figures
were of fallah origin: Saad Zaghlul, Ahmad Lutfi al-Sayyid, Abd
al-Aziz Fahmi, Taha Husain, Mustafa al-Nahhas, Makram Ubaid. All
grew up in a rural environment, or in a small rural town, and they
possessed many of the fallah traits, modified in some degree or other
by their urban training and their westernized education. But the
formative years of their lives were strongly influenced by peasant
society. In their later years they either continued to accept wholly or
partly the values of that society or to reject them entirely. Zaghlul
continued to think like a fallah, Ahmad Lufti al-Sayyid, while retaining sympathy and emotional links with that milieu, rejected it in
intellectual terms. The fallah therefore identified with Zaghlul, but
rarely responded to anything Lutfi al-Sayyid said or wrote, for that
was couched in urban terms and had an urbane logic, and the gap
between his frame of reference and that of the fallah was enormous.
For example in 1913 during the elections for the Legislative Assembly
Lutfi had run for office on a "democratic" platform. The opposition,
who knew that the fallahin had no idea what democracy was, spread
the rumor that democracy meant atheism, whereupon the fallahin
voted for his opponent who did not use any newfangled terms.[19]

The problems of the fallah therefore continued under any regime to
be those of poverty, exacerbated by increasing overpopulation which
turned half the rural population into "surplus" with no adequate
employment in the countryside waiting to be siphoned off into industry
whenever industrialization on a sufficiently large scale began. Allied
to the fallah's poverty was disease which exacted a heavy toll in terms
of life, labor capacity, and degree of alertness. Lastly there was
ignorance which inhibited the fallah from exercising his rights as a
citizen, since he was not even cognizant of those rights and obligations,
which turned him into a "silent majority" to be manipulated and
dominated by all who reached power, and which left him at the mercy

19. al-Sayyid, *Qissat Hayati*, p. 140. This work is erroneously cited as Lutfi's autobiography when actually it was written by Tahir Tanahi after a series of interviews
with Lutfi.

of the politicians. Thus if the history of Egyptian political life seemed to be written in terms of the rise and fall of cabinets, and in terms of backstairs haggling between the members of the elite, that was justified in Egypt to some extent, for the population had reached a nadir of apathy, and of noninvolvement in the political process.

In 1897 less than 15 percent of the Egyptian population lived in the 17 cities and towns listed as having at least 20,000 inhabitants, of which 6-8 percent lived in Cairo. In 1937 almost 30 percent of the population was living in the 57 communities of urban size of which 12-15 percent lived in Cairo.[20] It is to this urban population that we turn next.

In the period 1920-1936 industrialization was still limited in scope and, save for the Misr Bank founded by Talaat Harb in 1920 and its affilitates,[21] was dominated by non-Egyptians. Urban workers were seldom grouped in work units that were larger than a workshop and labor legislation was slow to develop, as were labor movements. Early nationalist leaders had little interest in the urban workers and concentrated on organizing only the student communities. The sole exception was Muhammad Farid of Hizb al-Watani who did push for labor legislation, and the child labor laws of 1909 were attributed to his party's efforts.[22] That law prohibited the employment of children under nine in cotton ginning, tobacco, and textile factories, and regulated employment for children under the age of thirteen. Labor conditions in general were horrifying, but social consciences were as yet not sufficiently awakened to the plight of the urban worker, who did not have enough power to push his problems to the attention of the rulers.

The fact that urbanization was proceeding rapidly did not mean that rural ethics when transported to town were changing equally rapidly. As Janet Abu Lughod has shown in her brilliant study of Cairo,[23] migrants brought their cultural values with them and created

20. Abu Lughod, Cairo: 1001 Years of the City Victorious, p. 121.

21. The shareholders and administrators of the Bank Misr were required to be Egyptian nationals. Misr Ginning, 1924; Misr River Traffic and Transport, 1925; Misr Cinematographic Production, 1925; Misr Spinning and Weaving in Mahalla al-Kubra, 1927; Misr Fisheries, 1927; Misr Linen, 1927; Misr Cotton Export, 1930; Misr Dyeing and Tanning, Misr Steamship, and Misr Insurance, 1934; Misr Oil Company, Misr Mining, 1937; Misr Kafr al-Dawar for Spinning and Weaving, Misr Cement Works, Misr Pharmaceuticals, 1938.

22. Abd al-Rahman al-Rafii, Muhammad Farid (Cairo, 1962), p. 110.

23. See n. 12.

rural pockets within the urban milieu. Nonetheless there was a small urban society which had its own characteristics, some of which resembled those of the rural society and some of which differed radically.

Urban society was also divided into hierarchies and groupings which were more sharply delineated than those of rural groups. The gap between one group and the other was wider in the cities, and contacts between them more limited because of various factors like distance, mobility, and living quarters. At the bottom of the social scale were the working classes who like the fallahin were illiterate, superstitious, and disease ridden. They shared the same mistrust of the hukuma. Throughout the eighteenth century the urban groups had been wont to demonstrate their opposition and defiance of the hukuma through uprisings. The different regime imposed by Muhammad Ali had changed many things, including urban uprisings, and city people then were manipulated as often as the fallahin. Both urban and rural groups shared a basic economic insecurity, which was however worse in urban terms. For while the fallah could live off the land, the urban worker needed a cash economy in order to survive. Both groups shared a philosophy of *ma⁽lish*, "never mind," which does not have its roots in Islam since Copts as well as Muslims share it, but which rather is the outcome of capricious government and governors. The city workers, however, who had to cope with insecurity of work, with hazardous labor conditions, without the benefit of that close bond with nature which breeds hope, developed character traits that differed from those of the fallah. The city dweller refers to himself as *ibn al-balad,* or *bint al-balad,* son or daughter of the country, in opposition to the foreigner, the *khawaja,* the white-collar worker, the *muwadhaf,* and the elite, the *dhawat.* Today the term has come to acquire the added connotation of one who continues along traditional cultural lines, and is not westernized, or *mutafarnij.* In a recent sociological study carried out on ibn al-balad, his salient characteristics were believed to be the following:[24] He was gay, jovial of spirit, possessed a keen sense of humor that could make him turn any situation, painful or pleasant, into a subject for mirth—levity being the saving grace of an otherwise dreary life. Humor is a safety valve that keeps people going in the face of overwhelming odds, a means of exorcising calamity by holding it up to mockery. The basic ingredient

24. Quoted in a lecture given by Dr. Laila al-Hamamsi, Director of the Social Science Research Centre in Cairo at the University of California, Los Angeles in December 1973.

of conversation was therefore the *nukta,* or anecdote, the joke which summarizes the public reaction to any situation, tersely and wittily.[25]

Ibn al-balad lives for the moment and is often accused by the more affluent of lacking foresight. His philosophy of life seems to be: why save for a rainy day when every day seems rainy, and the Good Lord will provide, or else a friend or neighbor will always lend a helping hand. The two qualities which distinguish ibn al-balad from the fallah are summed up in two Arabic words, *fahlawa* and *shahama.* Shahama implies gallantry, chivalry, audacity, machismo, decency, and sagacity. Fahlawa is more difficult to describe. It means sharp, shrewd, adaptable, quick-witted, it can imply something of the con man, or can imply that its possessor is a manipulator, but with panache. The term suggests suppleness and politeness which leads to a surface acquiescence. Instead of proffering a blunt "no" to a request, ibn al-balad will say instead *"insha² Allah,"* "if God wills." An Egyptian at once recognizes the negative implications of the term by the tone of voice, but the British refused to see beyond the surface expression, and characterized that trait as double-dealing or hypocrisy, as proof of lack of moral courage. On the other hand the Egyptians regarded British plainspokenness as rude and lacking in breeding and certainly in social acumen.

The contrast then between the quick-witted, slightly unscrupulous ibn al-balad and the slow thinking, deliberate fallah was one that has inspired the talents of numerous comedians. The urban crowd admired those political figures who possessed shahama and fahlawa, those who were flamboyant, and identified with them, hence their love for Zaghlul and to a lesser extent of Nahhas.

Like the fallah, ibn al-balad is an individualist, and, like the fallah who had to learn to cooperate with his co-villagers in order to survive the tax collector and nature and who lived a more communal life, the city dweller, too, learned to live communally, not perhaps in order to survive but for historical and psychological reasons.

In past centuries artisans had all been grouped into guilds as a convenient tax-collecting device. The guilds, which converged along topographical lines, offered a certain measure of cooperation and security to their members, and the guild head acted as a buffer between the individual and the government agencies in much the same way as the umda or shaikh al-balad had done for the village.

25. See Afaf Lutfi al-Sayyid (Marsot), "The Cartoon in Egypt," *Comparative Studies in Society and History,* 13, 1 (Jan. 1971), 2-15.

Taxes were distributed to each guild and the head of the guild was enjoined to collect them from the individual members according to the extent of their trade and profit. The first blows to the guilds came with Muhammad Ali's policy of state monopolies and his encouragement of European merchants and cheap imports which overwhelmed the local mercantile community. Throughout the century the influx of cheap Western goods killed off some artisanal guilds, while the change in tax-collecting finished off the rest. In 1890 a law was passed which taxed workers and employers individually, and established the principle of freedom to practice any trade or profession. A hiatus therefore occurred before the industrial workers became numerous enough to realize the advantages to be found in a modern system of cooperation and in the strengthened bargaining power a trade union could offer.

The total industrial population of Egypt in 1927 was estimated at 507,148 men and 48,821 women (see table 2) out of a total population of 14,177,864. There were a reported 70,314 industrial establishments in 1927 of which 4 percent employed more than 10 persons, so that the large majority of industrial establishments were of the craftsman or workshop variety. By and large those workers who were grouped in large working communities such as the cigarette-manufacturing establishments were of foreign nationality and foreign owned. That explains why the first trade union movements in Egypt were begun by the foreign communities, who also organized the first strike. Since workers were not yet grouped in large working communities and did not have the comfort of the guild system, they underwent a long period of insecurity and frustration as we shall see later.

But if workers were not grouped professionally they were certainly grouped socially. Social groupings centered in the local cafe, or *qahwa baladi*, in their quarter, or *hayy*, and in the precincts of the sufi *zawiya*, meeting place. In the 1930s the sufi zawiya was displaced by the more active Muslim Brethren circles, who supplied the same social and religious needs in a more dynamic mold. Nonetheless we must not fall into the common error of assuming that mysticism was on the road to disappearance. While sufi orders may have lost much of their wealth and influence as the result of rival secular organizations, they are still active and gaining new adherents.[26] In the zawiya or the Ikhwan circle the urban person found a warmth and a social response which in other societies is found in the social "club."

26. Told to me by Shaikh Mashayikh al-Turuq al-Sufiyya in Egypt in 1963.

TABLE 2 REPARTITION OF POPULATION
ACCORDING TO OCCUPATION

Occupation	Men	Women
Agriculture	3,001,274	523,932
Industry	507,148	48,821
Transport	198,358	1,631
Commerce	414,990	44,373
Public services	184,920	4,929
Professions	98,389	12,262
Domestic service	131,931	80,906
Unproductive and unknown	473,577	122,224
Unemployed (including children under 5 and housewives)	2,051,486	6,280,713

SOURCE: Egypt, Annuaire Statistique: 1932-33 (Cairo, 1932), Table
XII, p. 36.

The hayy or quarter is a coherent social unit dating back centuries
when members of the same guild tended to live in the same quarters,
when each *hara,* or alley, had its own gates which were closed at
nightfall, and when it had its own toughs and dogs to protect it.
While the gates of the haras have long disappeared, the sociological
implications of the hara are still alive. *Awlad haritna,* the children
of our alley, is a common expression, and not only the title of Najib
Mahfuz's fascinating work which depicts urban Cairo more vividly
than anyone can hope to do. The term implies primary contacts,
intermarriage, mutual assistance, and a propinquity that verges on
the claustrophobic in intensity. In brief, every hayy or hara supplies
the human warmth that is necessary to mankind and diminishes the
need to further human contacts outside the periphery, hence turning
urban society into discrete entities, much like the rural izba. These
baladi quarters were to be found in the old parts of town, for example
in Fatimid and Mamluk Cairo, as well as in Bulaq, where the more
affluent had moved out into the Khedive Ismail's new quarters to the
west, planned by Mahmud al-Falaki, his urban designer. The European quarters were in the new area of Garden City surrounding the
British Residency, and were to grow on the Island of Jazira around the
Sporting Club; in Maadi, a rural suburb some 10 miles to the south

of Cairo on the Nile; or Heliopolis, an oasis in the desert some 15 miles to the north.

Each hara had a traditional institution in the *futuwwat*.[27] In the past the term was applied to a chivalrous grouping of artisans, but in the twentieth century it had degenerated to mean the city "toughs." The futuwwat gathered in the local cafe around a leader, and, oddly enough, there have been cases of futuwwat bossed by a woman, a *mu'alima*. The gang was for hire: to beat up an opponent, to smash the neighboring cafes, to join in political demonstrations, to rough up political opponents. Some were known to be gangs of thieves and cutthroats who would do anything for a price. Some were, of course, only the rough elements of the street and not necessarily outlaws in the strict sense. The futuwwat of al-Husainiyya quarter near al-Azhar enjoyed a redoubtable reputation, as did those of the abattoirs, *al-madbah*, for obvious reasons. The madbah crowd were not averse to using their meat cleavers and hooks in a fight, but the Husainiyya crowd could wreak as much havoc with the use of a deadly weapon, the *nabut*, or stave, assisted by the human skull, the *rusiyya*, which was devastatingly effective. The sickening thud of one skull bashing the other inevitably left one of the two an ambulance case. Violence was usually coordinated and the signal, a rallying cry of *Yalla ya gid'an* (Let's go, guys), was also a warning for the uninvolved to get out of the way, as quickly as possible. Violence was therefore no stranger to the harat of the city, and was successfully harnessed by the political parties who used it in demonstrations and other organized forms of opposition.

Aside from the working groups in the urban milieu the other gradations of society were those grouping the students, the bureaucrats, and the elite.

The student population in the urban society formed the most politically committed and involved members of the community and cut across all sections of society in Egypt. Once again in the eighteenth century the ulama and students of al-Azhar had been among the first to demonstrate against mamluk inequity and to organize resistance to Bonaparte's occupation and Ottoman misrule. In 1895 Mustafa Kamil revived student activism in the service of the nationalist movement. Mustafa al-Nahhas, a former member of Kamil's party, organized the students round the Wafd when the movement swept the country.

The reasons for student activism were not that they had time on their hands, as the disgruntled claimed, or had nothing better to do,

27. Lutfi al-Sayyid, *Qissat Hayati*, p. 24.

but were deeper. Psychologists tell us that young people in their late teens and early twenties go through an identity crisis when "those vague inner states and those urgent questions arise in consequence." They feel a need to repudiate part of their culture as well as a need for discipline. They are "ready to provide the physical power and the vociferous noise of rebellions, riots and lynchings, often knowing little and caring less for the real issues involved. On the other hand, [they are] most eager to adopt rules of physical restriction and of utter intellectual concentration." It is this identity crisis which "even when there is no ideological commitment or even interest, [makes] young people offer devotion to individual leaders and to teams, to strenuous activities and to difficult techniques."[28]

Since many of the students were poor and most of them were ready to become politically committed, political parties were successful in gaining the allegiance of students and in using them in public demonstrations. In time parties were to carry a large number of student leaders on their payrolls and to call upon them to organize agitation of one sort or another.

In Cairo there were two main centers where the students could mass: the Azhar and the University of Cairo campus in Giza. The campus grounds were inviolate to the city police and the only steps the police could take in the event of a student outbreak was to surround the campus with a cordon sanitaire. If the police were not on time or unable to control them, the students would break through the cordon and hitch a ride on one of the trams going into town, crossing over two bridges until they reached the Dawawin area where the ministries were situated, which was adjacent to the house of Saad Zaghlul. The first clashes between students and police were to occur in the 1919 uprising and it set a pattern that is followed to the present day whenever students break out in protest. In time the police devised a rapid method for containing the students, and that was to open the swing bridges across the Nile thus marooning the students on the west bank of the Nile. Student demonstrations were to become one of the constants of Egyptian political life in time of crisis, and not a few cabinets have fallen when they reacted in too harsh a fashion against the students. For in a country of illiterates the students had a definite standing as the intellectuals of the future and the leaders of the coming generation, and since the student body cut across class groupings the whole population found itself involved when the students demonstrated. Those who did not have children of university age had children

28. Eric Ericson, *Young Man Luther* (New York, 1958), p. 42.

in secondary or even primary schools who rapidly followed suit when a major move was in the air. When the schools and the universities were closed down during drastic eras the students went to their homes all over the country, and they carried with them their ideas which they spread rapidly to the remote corners of the land. Thus as an instrument of propaganda, the diffusion of ideas, of agitation and activism, the students were the most effective in the land.

The rest of the urban population rose in an ascending hierarchy of occupations, from blue-collar workers, who were then exiguous, to the bureaucrats, the *mawadhafun*. Government service was highly valued for it promised a regular salary, security of tenure, and an adequate pension on retirement. The war years had destroyed that premise since people with fixed salaries were the ones to suffer most from rampant inflation. Nonetheless the government employee could hope to rise in the ranks, and that was a good vehicle for vertical social mobility. A position in the hukuma could open many doors, political and social, but not financial unless the official was given to accepting "gifts." The top echelons in urban bureaucratic groups obviously acquired political clout since they were in communication with various sources of power in the other ministries and with the members of parliament and of the parties. In rural areas government employees had even more importance as the voice of authority or as representatives of the government. Most officials disliked transfer to the rural areas since they had none of the amenities of life and had the added disadvantage of being removed from the center of power. Unless he had "influence" of some kind through a relation, an official could be forgotten in the periphery for long periods of time. The use and abuse of influence, known as *wasta,* was to become the subject of the brilliant satires on Egyptian life and officialdom, written and acted by Badi Khairi and Najib al-Rihani who together founded the modern theater in Egypt.

The top echelons of urban society comprised the people referred to as the dhawat, the elite. I hesitate to call them the notables for that term seems to have been appended to the ayan, which in Egyptian Arabic refers to the rural notables, whereas the term "dhawat" has a distinctly urban connotation. They are also called the *bashawat,* the pashas, and I hesitate, again, to call them a class because hereditary standing was only one factor for membership in that group; it was applied solely to those of Turco-Circassian origin. These last had been in a steady decline since the Urabi revolution of 1882 and were inexorably being displaced by native fallah Egyptians. Membership in the pasha group was defined by government service; theoretically, to

become a pasha the person had to have rendered the state some
service even if only monetary, for the title could be bought. In brief,
the pasha group was composed of men who wielded influence and
who represented the Establishment. One must also keep in mind that
the real rulers of Egypt were still the British Resident and the British
advisors in government service. The pasha, who was the nearest
equivalent to a life peer, was followed by the bey, something like a
baronet, and then by an effendi, which in modern Egypt, unlike in
Turkey, was an honorific title. The religious hierarchy had a different
set of titles, the top ones being imam, which applied to the grand
mufti, and shaikh al-Islam, which applied to the rector of al-Azhar
University. Lesser luminaries were called *sayyidna* or *mawlana* depending on whether they belonged to the regular orthodox hierarchy or
were members of sufi orders.

In the past century the hierarchies had been well defined and clearly
demarcated, and no one could mistake an Egyptian for a pasha even
when he was one, like Ali Mubarak. Pashas generally were Turks.
But the lines of delineation were becoming blurred by the end of the
century. Education and westernization were rapidly creating new
groups, while others who in the past were subservient groups found
new wealth and aspired to a higher standing in society. In brief, the
social changes that Muhammad Ali and his successors had inaugurated
were coming to fruition, aided by the British occupation of Egypt.
The Urabi revolution and the British occupation, which had exacerbated the rise of the nationalist movement, confused former social
distinctions and produced a new society of native Egyptians who were
affluent and well educated, and who sought to rule their own country
themselves and thus escape from the dual dominance of the British
overlordship and the Turkish elite as represented by the Palace and
the men who served it. This they thought to effect by establishing
a popularly elected constitutional form of government.

It is commonplace knowledge that a sound parliamentary form of
government can only thrive in a society with the following characteristics:[29] First, a certain level of education which would allow a literate
electorate to balance a highly educated ruling elite, make possible a
two-way exchange of ideas, and, of more importance, create a basic
common ideology among the nationals. Second, a degree of industrialization and even distribution of wealth among the population. A society

29. Charles Issawi, "Economic and Social Foundations of Democracy in the Middle
East," *International Affairs*, 32, 1 (Jan. 1956), 27-42.

composed largely of peasants and landowners is one in which the former are dominated by the latter and where government is limited to the landowning class. A society in which the wealth of the nation is concentrated in the hands of a small elite leaving the greater mass preoccupied with scrambling for a living will be more subject to demagoguery and manipulation than a society where the wealth is more evenly distributed and where the population has the means and the leisure to busy themselves with public matters. Lastly, a certain level of communications is necessary. This means a need for roads, railways, mass media in order to create channels of communication branching all over the nation and linked to the centers of power.

All these elements were lacking in Egypt in 1919. There was a small literate elite that led the nationalist movement, and this was followed by a large illiterate mass. There was a minimal degree of industrialization and what there was was concentrated mostly in the hands of foreigners. There was a certain amount of infrastructure and of mass-media diffusion, but 80 percent of the country's population was illiterate.

Egyptian society was a perfect but vicious circle. So long as the land was occupied by a foreign element it could not become independent and could not establish constitutional government. But if it did not become independent it could not progress and reform its society. So long as the economic lifeline of the country was controlled by foreigners and capitulations economic measures could not hope to succeed, and without industrialization and the rise of a bourgeoisie and a working class to balance the landowners a real democracy could not be created. Everything needed to be done simultaneously and yet it could not, because each element was delicately balanced by another. In the abstract one could say that the Egyptian nationalists could have fought on all fronts, political, social, and economic, but in the concrete we know that no society has ever progressed in such a fashion, and that reforms come piecemeal. The nationalists therefore concentrated their efforts on the political situation and shelved the rest of Egypt's problems for later. In doing so they could only hope for partial success, but that partial success laid the framework for a modern Egyptian society and was therefore a distinct advance.

The decades of Egyptian history that followed the 1919 revolution could well have been called "The Struggle for Mastery in Egypt," to paraphrase a famous title, a struggle that involved the British, the Palace, and the rest of the Egyptians in giving Egypt the shape of its future society.

II

Prologue:
The Man of the Hour

EGYPT'S political condition for four cen-
turies up to 1919 was determined by her legal position as a vassal of
the Ottoman Empire, even though from the eighteenth century onward
she had achieved quasi autonomy under the rule of the mamluks and
the presence of a nominal Ottoman governor, or *wali*. Muhammad
Ali (1805-1848) had almost won independence for Egypt when he was
balked by the Powers, especially the English, in 1840, but he had at
least installed his family as the hereditary rulers of Egypt. The British
occupation of 1882 instigated by the Egyptian ruler, the Khedive
Tawfiq, to help quell the Urabi revolution changed the picture. From
then on Egypt came to be dominated by the British consul general,
Lord Cromer, who set up a system known as the Veiled Protectorate,
by means of which Egyptian executive authority was abrogated and
replaced by that of the British Resident and the British advisors in
Egyptian service. As a consequence political life in Egypt became a
mirror of the conflict between the Ottoman Empire and the Powers,
or among the Powers themselves. The system of capitulations, grants
of extraterritoriality that removed foreign residents in Egypt (as in
other parts of the Ottoman empire) from the jurisdiction of the
Egyptian legal system and hamstrung legal and financial authority,
also allowed the Powers to inflict their international antagonisms on
Egyptian affairs. In sum, Egyptians had no control over their country;
they had no protection from abuse of authority by their rulers or by
the men who governed them save the moral conscience of the British
administrators and the House of Commons and the moral conscience

of the Khedive. Neither alternative was satisfactory for the British were motivated by the interests of the British Empire, and the Khedive by an ingrained sense of autocracy and self-interest.

The British presence in Egypt allowed the country a period of calm and reflection after the throes of revolution, which brought a sense of stability but at the same time induced a nationalist movement to rise in 1895 under the aegis of Mustafa Kamil. The young nationalists chafed under alien domination. Not having known the rigors of the rule of Ismail, they felt secure in their assumption that they could contain the monarchy and harness it in the service of the state. Under Ismail and his son khedivial tyranny had provoked a movement for constitutional government which culminated in the Urabi movement. Subsequently constitutional government was also adopted by the nationalists, for that was a safeguard against British interference in affairs of government as well as a safeguard against khedivial pretensions. Thus the nationalist movement under Mustafa Kamil sought to bring to an end the British occupation of Egypt, to remove the onus of the capitulations which fettered the administration legally and financially, and to institute constitutional rule.[1] Other nationalist groupings, like Hizb al-Umma, agreed with all of Kamil's aspirations but laid greater stress on the need for constitutional government to limit their monarch's autocracy and added another factor, the desire to sever links with the Ottoman Empire and render Egypt legally autonomous.

In 1912 Ahmad Lufti al-Sayyid, the spokesman of the Hizb al-Umma, had developed a plan for autonomy from Turkey which was then enmeshed in a war with Italy over Tripolitania. Kitchener, the British consul general, did not think the moment opportune, and Prime Minister Muhammad Said considered it treasonable, but the Khedive Abbas was pleased with it and suggested that a delegation, or *wafd*, composed of Adli Yakan, Saad Zaghlul, and Ahmad Lutfi al-Sayyid go to London to sound out the British government.[2] Adli Yakan had been Minister for Foreign Affairs in the prior cabinet, Zaghlul was the elected vice-president of the Legislative Assembly and

1. For a more expanded study of the period see Berque, *L'Egypte;* Robert Tignor, *Modernization and British Colonial Rule in Egypt: 1882-1914* (Princeton, 1966); Anouar Abdel Malek, Idéologie et Renaissance Nationale (Paris, 1969); P. J. Vatikiotis, *A Modern History of Egypt* (New York: Praeger, 1969); al-Sayyid (Marsot), *Egypt and Cromer;* Abd al-Rahman al-Rafii, *Mustafa Kamil* (Cairo, 1945); and Ahmad Abd al-Rahim Mustafa, *Misr wa-l masʾala al-Misriyya* (Cairo, 1964).

2. al-Sayyid, *Qissat Hayati,* p. 132.

the leader of the opposition, and Lutfi al-Sayyid was editor of *al-Jarida*. But they could not take any steps because public opinion in Egypt was firmly in favor of support for Turkey in her need. The three friends realized that any move toward autonomy at the present juncture would not meet with public approval, so the move was temporarily shelved.

During World War I the legal link between Egypt and the Ottoman Empire was broken. In 1916, with the assent of the Egyptian government, Egypt was declared a British Protectorate on the understanding that conditions would change for the better once the war was over. The Egyptians did not then anticipate that they were to have a more difficult time ridding themselves of the Protectorate than of Turkish suzerainty. The war brought martial law in its wake and a ban on public gatherings among other vexations, not the least of which was a military occupation of Egypt by vast numbers of Allied troops. Compared with the handful of British troops that had been stationed in Egypt since 1882 the influx of troops bent on rest and relaxation before and after battle was demoralizing to the population, caused inflation and profiteering, and exacerbated many of the wounds that had been inflicted by colonial presence.

The war years and martial law prohibited public discussion of nationalist desires and issues, but private discussion was current among the politicians and the intelligentsia. No firm plans could be made until the tide of war had subsided and revealed the victors. In 1918, after President Woodrow Wilson issued his Fourteen Points and the Allies their declaration which promised self-determination to previous Ottoman possessions, five friends — Saad Zaghlul Pasha, Ahmad Lutfi al-Sayyid Bey, Abd al-Aziz Fahmi Bey, Muhammad Mahmud Pasha, and Ali Pasha Shaarawi — met to discuss Egypt's future. From that meeting and the discussions that followed the Wafd party was born.

The five men were native Egyptians of fallah background. Zaghlul, Lutfi, and Fahmi were the sons of fairly affluent village umdas, and had grown up in a rural milieu where they had attended the village kuttab. Mahmud and Shaarawi were among the richest landowners in the country, yet the latter still retained his local dialect from Upper Egypt. All belonged to the same generation — Zaghlul and Shaarawi were the senior members by about ten years — and all had a local and a Western education. All except for Zaghlul had been members of the Umma party or at least, like Zaghlul, strong sympathizers. All had married into the Turco-Circassian elite, but they could still vividly remember the days when an Egyptian was called a *pis-fellah,*

"dirty fallah," by his Turkish superiors, and when Egyptian umdas
and ayan were whipped when they failed to deliver the village taxes
on time.[3] Distaste for and resentment of the Turkish elite were more
deeply ingrained than dislike for the British occupation. Their need to
humble the Turks and the desire to replace them as the elite in the
land were therefore important motivating forces, and formed the basic
difference between them and the members of Hizb al-Watani who were
not averse to espousing a pan-Islamic policy in befriending the Sultan.
The other basic difference between these two parties was that while
the members of the Umma party were mostly landed gentry, *ayan*,
with vested interest they sought to protect, the members of the Watani
party were mostly from the urban petty bourgeoisie who never had
grass roots support or even rural backing.

Zaghlul was born in the village of Ibyana either in 1860 or 1857,
where his father was umda. His father died when the boy was six
years old and his eldest half-brother undertook his upbringing.[4] Like
other children of his age he attended the village kuttab and at the
age of twelve entered al-Azhar. Then he became a disciple of Shaikh
Muhammad Abduh and of Jamal al-Din al-Afghani, and became
Abduh's assistant editor in *al-Waqa'* al-Misriyya, the *Journal Officiel.*
He joined Abduh in the Urabi revolution and played a small part for
which he was briefly imprisoned, and it seems to have left him with
a distaste for political action for a long time. Eventually he started
to practice law and in time received a law degree from France. He
was befriended by the Princess Nazli Fazil, the Khedive's cousin and
antagonist, met the British officials of the day at her salon, became
friendly with Harry Boyle, the Oriental Secretary, and then Lord
Cromer. His star rose and in his late forties he married the daughter
of Mustafa Pasha Fahmi, the most pro-British premier Egypt had
known. He made a name for himself as a judge in the Court of
Appeals, where his lucidity earned him the respect of the lawyers
pleading before him.[5] In 1905 Cromer appointed him Minister of
Education, a particularly sensitive appointment since Mustafa Kamil
had by then galvanized the students into action and they were continually demonstrating and organizing strikes in the name of nationalism. At that time Zaghlul thought that independence was a chimera

3. Ibid., p. 20.

4. al-Aqqad, *Saad Zaghlul,* p. 9.

5. Abd al-Aziz Fahmi, *Hadhihi hayati* (Cairo, 1952), p. 25. This book was written
by Tahir Tanahi after interviewing Fahmi and is not an autobiography.

and Mustafa Kamil's agitation that of a lunatic baying at the moon.[6] Thus the man who was later to become the focus of student and mass adulation was for most of his life a sympathizer with British rule in Egypt, which he deemed better by far than khedivial misrule.

Zaghlul's rapprochement with the nationalist movement came around 1913 when, as the elected vice-president of the Legislative Assembly, he headed the opposition in parliament. The cause for his change of attitude was attributed by some to the fact that former Consul General Eldon Gorst's policy of rapprochement with the Khedive Abbas had made it plain to the moderate political elements in Egypt that their hope for an eventual Egyptianization of power was not to be realized and that their attempts to found a constitutional government to end royal autocracy were not to meet with encouragement from British officials.[7] Others attributed Zaghlul's change to his antagonism toward Lord Kitchener, Gorst's successor, who in turn disliked him and refused to allow Zaghlul to become appointed cabinet minister. From that period on we detect the beginnings of joint opposition to British rule in Egypt by pro-British moderates, members of Hizb al-Umma, and members of Hizb al-Watani, Kamil's party.

Throughout his public career Zaghlul had not believed that the British could be made to evacuate Egypt through agitation or any other element of Kamil's program of action. The war years, however, and the subsequent declarations made by the Allies promising independence to their "friends" under Ottoman dominion had reinforced the belief that self-rule, if not independence, was in the offing. Like other Egyptians and Arabs, Zaghlul believed the promises made by the Allies.

Abd al-Aziz Fahmi was the most brilliant legal brain in the country. He and Lufti had been friends since their student days in the School

6. Rashid Rida, *Tarikh al-Ustadh al-Imam al-Shaikh Muhammad ʿAbduh* (Cairo, 1931), I, 593.

7. al-Sayyid (Marsot), *Egypt and Cromer.* p. 8. It is notable that Barakat gives a different account (Fathallah Barakat Memoirs [1930], 16b:40). Barakat said that after Ghali was assassinated Zaghlul should have been chosen premier by right of seniority, *al-aqdamiyya;* Muhammad Said was appointed instead and the Khedive told Said that Gorst had refused to accept Zaghlul as premier. Fathallah claimed that from that time on "Zaghlul became filled with rancor, *al-daghina,* against the Khedive." May one add against the "British" as well? Zaghlul gives another version. In 1915 there was a further attempt to bring Zaghlul into the ministry. Kitchener, who was then in London, refused in spite of the fact that MacMahon, the high commissioner, was in favor of the appointment (Saad Zaghlul Memoirs, vol. 29, p. 1591). See also A. Lajin, *Saad Zaghlul: Wa dawruh fi-l siyasa al-Misriyya* (Beirut, 1975), p. 65.

of Law along with Ismail Sidqi and Abd al-Khaliq Tharwat. He and
Lutfi had been cofounders of a secret society aimed at ridding Egypt
of the British presence, a society that had briefly merged with Hizb
al-Watani, which was at the time a small secret society with the same
aim. Fahmi was a lawyer, had become one of the most eminent in
the land, and in 1913 was elected to the Legislative Assembly where
he joined Zaghlul in the ranks of the opposition.

Lutfi was the intellectual of the group. He too was a follower of
Shaikh Muhammad Abdul. He had been the ideologue and cofounder
of the Umma Party in 1907 and had served for eight years as editor
of the party organ, *al-Jarida*. In time he was to help found the Liberal
Constitutionalist Party, al-Ahrar al-Dusturiyyun, as he had the Wafd
and the Umma parties, and he became its unofficial theorist. His most
enduring achievement, however, was not in creating political parties
but as an educator. He perhaps did more for Egypt as rector of Fuad
al-Awal—now Cairo—University than as a politician and earned the
title of Teacher of the Generation, *ustadh al-jil*.

Muhammad Mahmud was the son of a rich landowner, Mahmud
Pasha Sulaiman, and himself owned vast latifundia in Upper Egypt,
so he was born with the proverbial silver spoon.

Shaarawi, who was equally wealthy, had married Huda Hanim
Sultan, whose father was believed then to be one of the richest
Egyptians. She later founded the feminist movement.

The five men had been politically active in the prewar years, and
the end of the war revived the need for a concerted plan of action on
the part of the Egyptian leaders. Ironically, Zaghlul, the "Father of
the Revolution," at first did not see the need for taking any initiative
with the British authorities but believed the initiative should come
from them; although later he came round to the need for further
planning when he met the encouragement of Husain Pasha Rushdi,
the Premier, and Adli Yakan, the Minister of Foreign Affairs.[8]

Three of the group—Zaghlul, Fahmi, and Shaarawi—who were all
members of the Legislative Assembly, were chosen by the other two
to form a delegation, a wafd, to meet with Sir Reginald Wingate,
the high commissioner, on November 13, 1918, to discuss the future
of Egypt. Although at first the comrades were not quite sure what

8. Rushdi and Adli both informed Zaghlul of their intent to travel to London and
discuss Egypt's case and agreed that the project of a Wafd party would greatly
strengthen their hand in negotiating with the British authorities. Many others had
similar plans for the future of Egypt, see Lajin, *Saad Zaghlul*, pp. 120 ff.

they wanted beyond some form of self-rule, they got carried away during their talk with Wingate. Fahmi, who was a very touchy individual, felt that Wingate had made a snide remark at Egypt's ability for self-rule and bluntly announced that they had come to ask for complete independence, *al-istiqlal al-tam*.[9] Wingate was fairly sympathetic to the Egyptians' request, but unfortunately the British government was too busy with postwar questions to pay attention to the Egyptians, and a few months later this neglect precipitated a crisis.

Ten days after the meeting with Wingate, the five friends, plus two more recruits, Abd al-Latif al-Mukabati and Muhammad Ali Alluba, formed an organization known as al-Wafd al-Misri, the Egyptian Delegation, and drew up a body of rules expressing its aims: "The purpose of the Wafd was to strive for the complete independence of Egypt by peaceful means (article 2); . . . the Wafd derived its strength from the will of the Egyptian people and their desire (article 3); . . . the Wafd opened its membership to all who sought to achieve the same goals (article 8).[10] In an effort to obtain maximum public backing the Wafd went to the people and requested they be given a mandate to speak for Egypt. In an unprecedented show of unity, the government backed the Wafd, and thousands of signatures were obtained from the people, authorizing the members of the Wafd to act as delegates of the Egyptians in their struggle for independence. The membership of the Wafd grew to include representatives from Hizb al-Watani and from the Coptic community which for the first time showed common cause with the rest of the Egyptians. The Wafd Central Committee expanded to number seventeen members, while the rank and file rapidly grew to include almost the entire nation.

Although Zaghlul had very rapidly been chosen leader of the Wafd every step taken was planned collectively by the Central Committee, then penned in Arabic by Lutfi and in French by Ismail Sidqi. The original founders had chosen Zaghlul as leader of the Wafd for two reasons: first, he was the oldest in years and the most senior in position as a former cabinet minister and the elected vice-president of the Legislative Assembly; second, to forestall a man they disliked and mistrusted, Muhammad Pasha Said, from laying claim to the leadership of the party through seniority as a former premier.[11] In choosing Zaghlul the other members assumed that he would be first among

9. See Fahmi's own account in *Hadhihi Hayati*, p. 78.
10. Abd al-Rahman al-Rafii, *Thawrat sanat 1919* (Cairo, 1955), p. 100.
11. Told me by Ahmad Lutfi al-Sayyid.

equals, and indeed so he was during the early days of their agitation, but circumstances and Zaghlul's own personality were soon to change that.

To rouse public support the members of the Wafd took to public speaking and traveled around the countryside to galvanize the population behind them and give their movement legitimacy. Zaghlul, who was a forceful speaker in spite of a speech defect, as the judicial and political circles knew from experience, was thus thrust upon the public and his oratory put to good use in speaking to the masses. It was during his public speeches that Zaghlul came to realize his potential as an orator. It is true that in the Legislative Assembly he had been recognized as a persuasive speaker, but it was during his contacts with the people that he felt his power to sway them and win their support. When he spoke of freedom from tyranny, of independence, he seemed to dredge out of his atavistic recollection as a fallah themes and emotions that met a corresponding need in the collective fallah memory, and the coincidence of the two manifested itself in an instant response on the part of the masses, and in an instinctive adulation. Like Pied Piper, Zaghlul was followed by the people wherever he led, and as the nationalist movement grew, so did his awareness of his power and of his position in the Wafd. As he filled the post to the exclusion of anyone else, he came to regard himself as the quintessence of Egypt and to view the duty of the other members as simply to follow him. From a "lackey of the British," as Zaghlul's enemies had once called him, he came round full circle to become the personification of Egypt's future aspirations in the eyes of the population. Yet to the Wafd Central Committee Zaghlul remained one among several leaders, and the final struggle for absolute leadership of the party was to take place in Paris in 1920 when his colleagues came to regard him as a Frankenstein monster they had created but were no longer able to control.

The turmoil that Wafd agitation caused in the country, in spite of British orders banning public speaking, vexed and alarmed the British authorities in Egypt, and Milne Cheetham, the chargé d'affaires, resorted to force. On March 9, 1919, Zaghlul, Ismail Sidqi, Muhammad Mahmud, and Hamad al-Basil were arrested and deported to Malta. This event triggered a general demonstration in support of the Wafd, and when that was repressed by the authorities it caused an outbreak of violence, the revolution of 1919. There are those who question labeling these events a "revolution" since they do not fit the textbook requirements for a revolution. Yet to all Egyptians they

do stand for a revolution for they displaced one ruling elite to make
way for another and mobilized the masses. It was definitely a revolt
against the British presence in Egypt and in support of the Wafd and
its leaders and the principles for which they stood. By resorting to
repressive measures the British authorities catapulted a sick, sixty-
three-year-old man with a long history of collaboration with the British
into becoming a revolutionary and the leader, *zaim,* of his country.

March 10, the day following the arrest and exile of the Wafd
members, saw a massive but peaceful demonstration led by the School
of Law students and joined by the students of the Schools of Medicine
and Engineering. When the demonstrators refused police orders to
disperse, several hundred were arrested and imprisoned in the Citadel.
The secondary school students and those of the Azhar were not aware
of the demonstration until the end of the day; they then planned to
stage another demonstration the next day to protest the arrests and
were joined by the tram and taxi drivers. Transport communications
were paralyzed in the city. Shops closed down in sympathy with the
movement. This time the demonstrators were met with gunfire from
the police, and six students were killed and twenty-two wounded. The
demonstrations were renewed the next day, March 12, when the
largest number of those killed and wounded were students of al-Azhar.
Soon every element in the land went on strike and joined demonstrations: the Syndicate of Lawyers, all government officials—an act that
shocked the British, since bureaucrats had been an element of stability
from time immemorial—railway workers, even the women of the elite,
muffled to the eyes, paraded in the streets and shouted slogans in
favor of independence. Students carried the news of the uprising all
around the country and strikes and demonstrations broke out in the
cities, towns, and villages. Railway lines were cut and carriages destroyed to prevent the British forces from putting down the uprising,
so that in desperation General Bulfin, the acting commander in chief
of the Army, issued a warning that any further damage to the railways
would cause the nearest villages to be burned in retaliation. But the
warning did not stop the population, and railway communications
came to a standstill. British army personnel and officials were mas-
sacred in the rural areas.

On March 25, General Allenby arrived in Egypt as the new high
commissioner and he advised that Zaghlul and the Wafdists in exile
be released and allowed to present their case to the Paris Peace
Conference. The Wafd leaders were released on April 6 and allowed
to head for Paris, while the rest of the Wafd Central Committee

sailed for France to join their friends in Paris where they had hopes of pleading the Egyptian case before the Peace Conference. The turmoil in the country, however, continued unabated until the end of that year, and for a total of ten months, when the number of Egyptians killed by the British authorities was eight hundred and those wounded fourteen hundred.[12] In an effort to understand the cause of the unrest in Egypt, the British government formed a mission, headed by Lord Milner, which arrived in Egypt in December to investigate the situation. In Egypt the mission was met by a boycott of quasi-unanimity that lasted until their departure in March 1920. All their inquiries were met by directions to discuss Egypt with Egypt's representatives, the Wafd in Paris.

The frustration experienced by Milner's mission was nothing compared with that experienced by the Wafd in Paris. None of the representatives in the conference would talk to them. Desperate in the face of inaction, the Wafd members decided to seek help from Adli Yakan, the Minister of Foreign Affairs, and Zaghlul telegraphed him to come immediately. Adli responded with alacrity and arrived in Paris in April 1920. Through his connections he succeeded in opening the diplomatic doors, and the British government, under the influence of Milner's prodding, agreed to grant tne Wafd a hearing. Zaghlul, Adli, and a few other Wafd members went to England in June to begin conversations with the authorities, notably with Milner. The first of a seemingly endless round of Anglo-Egyptian negotiations over a treaty that would settle matters between both countries was thus begun, although the Milner-Zaghlul talks were to be conducted on the level of informal discussions.

While admitting the principle of Egyptian independence, the terms Milner offered Zaghlul limited that independence both internally and externally by a number of conditions which strengthened England's presence in Egypt, and more important, rendered it legal. In spite of these shortcomings Zaghlul's companions were willing to accept the terms of the agreement, but Zaghlul held out for more until in Milner's terms "an impasse was reached."[13] It is alleged that Zaghlul told an Egyptian journalist that as an Egyptian he was "surprised and delighted" by the terms offered by Milner, but as president of the Wafd "I find the recommendations unacceptable."[14] The rest of the

12. Great Britain, *Parliamentary Debates, Commons,* 1919, vol. 118, col. 1534.
13. See Zayid, *Struggle for Independence,* p. 96; also for the Milner Mission report see Lord Lloyd, *Egypt Since Cromer* (London, 1934), II, 367 ff.
14. Grafftey-Smith, *Bright Levant,* p. 76.

Wafd recommended that the terms be presented to the Egyptian public to test their reaction. Public reaction was distinctly cool, although had Zaghlul come out in favor of the talks in public, the people would undoubtedly have followed his lead.

During the course of his talks with Milner, Zaghlul grew to suspect that Adli had an ulterior motive in helping the Wafd and that he in fact was trying to make a bid for himself with the British.[15] Zaghlul knew French but no English and the conversations with the British officials took place in French; occasionally Adli would say something in English, which roused Zaghlul's suspicions. Whether these suspicions were founded or based on his resentment that Adli had succeeded where he had failed still remains to be established, although there seems to be a good case for justifying Zaghlul's suspicions. The fact remains that whereas the rest of the Wafd members were grateful to Adli in appreciation of his efforts on Egypt's behalf, even if they were self-serving, Zaghlul was not.

An autocrat by inclination, disease and age had reinforced Zaghlul's proclivities and made him impatient of opposition and argument. The frustrations he encountered in Paris had caused him to quarrel with every member of the Wafd, except Lutfi al-Sayyid who always managed to smooth his ruffled feathers and to avoid his biting tongue. Even more galling to Zaghlul personally was the admiration most of the Wafd members had for Adli, not only because he was a "grand seigneur," although they were also impressed by that, but because of his cleverness and his unfailing courtesy which contrasted favorably with Zaghlul's gruffness. But having become the leader of the Wafd, Zaghlul was not one to allow any other to displace him, especially a man like Adli who was his complete antithesis. Zaghlul the "fallah" was not going to be undone by Adli the "Turk."

Zaghlul was a fallah at heart, that is, an individualist who distrusted others and suspected their motives, who was eager for recognition and believed in his destiny. Tall and ascetic looking, with small but piercing eyes above a distinctive, bushy, white mustache, he had an elegance of bearing that was innate and impressive. He stood out in any crowd because of his height, his noble mien, and his quick wit. He looked a natural aristocrat but was a self-made man who had had to struggle long and hard to gain recognition and position in a society that valued birth and wealth but rarely talent. He was arrogant,

15. Charles Smith has made a good case for the truth in Zaghlul's suspicions in his forthcoming book dealing with the intellectual and political biography of Ahmad Husain Haikal.

vain, susceptible to flattery, and keenly intelligent. A man of the
people, he had scrambled to the top through sheer will power. He
was a political animal who, when he had to, could fight dirtier than
the next man, and when expedient had little compunction about
stabbing his collaborators in the back; but he could also be loyal. He
was an orator who made the people identify with him and his cause
so that *"Kulluna Saad,"* "We are all Saad," became the slogan of the
man in the street. He was therefore venerated by the fallah, the
student, the man in the street, the quasi-totality of Egypt as no other
leader before or after him, but he was also hated, feared, and
respected by his opponents.

Adli Yakan was totally the opposite. He was born an aristocrat but
looked more like a fallah than Zaghlul did because he was dark
skinned and had negroid features which some attributed to a Sudanese
ancestry. Yet he was related to the royal family, was immensely
wealthy, and never had to fight for survival or recognition. It came
to him by right of birth coupled with his undoubted qualities, especially his administrative talent. He was educated in France and Turkey
and attended French and German schools in Egypt. He first saw
government service when he became private secretary to Nubar Pasha,
and thus worked closely with Egypt's wiliest politician. In time he
became a cabinet minister and was associated with Rushdi Pasha in
whose cabinet he held the portfolio of Foreign Affairs. Adli was not
only an aristocrat: he was also honest, had dignity and self-respect,
ʿizzat nafs, a highly prized quality in Egypt. He would never stoop to
perform a mean act and would rarely accept becoming involved in
anything rougher than a gentlemanly political skirmish. He preferred
to resign rather than demean himself in his own eyes through involvement in a political brawl. A statesman, but not a politician, Adli was
always admired, but because of his aloofness, seldom loved. The
public scarcely knew him; he, in turn, rarely communicated with the
people and seldom, if ever, was influenced by them. Adli, however,
was a sensible man who could see both sides of the question and who
had respect for opinions other than his own.[16]

Zaghlul was by no means the cleverest politician in Egypt—that role
was reserved for Ismail Sidqi; nor was he the most profound thinker—
that role was Lutfi al-Sayyid's; nor was he even the most energetic,
for that was uncontestably Mustafa al-Nahhas's quality. Zaghlul was

16. Notes on the members of the new Egyptian cabinet, Great Britain, F.O.
371/11584, July 7, 1926. One of the functions of the Oriental Secretary was to compile
these notes, which today would more pompously be called "psychological profiles."

an old, sick man who suffered from diabetes, arthritis, and heart disease, all of which made him cranky and vulnerable, but he had qualities that outshone those possessed by all the other politicians in Egypt. He had the ability to lead and to make others follow blindly; he had the will to succeed despite all odds, and the wit to squirm out of difficult situations, allied to a firmly entrenched belief, shared by many leaders, that only he could lead his country to success. One may call such a belief the result of an egocentric personality, and it undoubtedly was; one may call it the result of charisma, that overworked term that has by now lost its original meaning; or one may call it greatness, for, though Zaghlul's behavior could be incredibly shabby, he was larger than life. He could be hated, but never ignored.

When the Milner-Zaghlul talks came to an end at the end of August, the Wafd returned to Paris to rejoin the rest of their comrades, and there Abd al-Aziz Fahmi suggested that since the unofficial talks with Milner had led to nothing concrete, Adli should lead a cabinet into official negotiations with the British government, and the Wafd should throw their support behind Adli. Nor surprisingly, Zaghlul opposed the scheme and was more persuaded than ever that Adli was scheming behind his back. He judged the plan as political "suicide" for himself.[17] One of the men, whose patience had been exhausted by Zaghlul's arrogance, fits of pique, and general tantrums, snapped that the Wafd was there to advance Egypt's cause, not that of Saad Zaghlul. Zaghlul reluctantly agreed to abide by the decision of the majority, which was the rule among them, but planned privately to dig Adli's political grave. The split in Wafd ranks was just beginning and was soon to widen into a break.

Zaghlul could and did make use of Adli, but when he judged his value at an end and potentially dangerous to his own position, he plotted Adli's undoing without the slightest compunction. He incited Nahhas, who always obeyed him blindly, to send a telegram to Cairo which was published in *al-Akhbar* and which said "Adli was a catastrophe for the nation." When the other Wafdists remonstrated with him for such behavior he said in justification, "I'll slit their throats before they slit mine."[18] Zaghlul was acting in quite predictable fashion, for the function of a rising political elite is to supplant the dominant one that Adli epitomized; in order to do so Zaghlul could not tolerate any deviationist group in the ranks, so that his next step was most surely to get rid of all the Wafdists who were in sympathy

17. Fahmi, *Hadhihi Hayati*, p. 114; also Lajin, *Saad Zaghlul*, p. 275.
18. Fahmi, *Hadhihi Hayati*, p. 114; Lajin, *Saad Zaghlul*, p. 318.

with Adli, leaving him in sole control of the party, surrounded by only those members who were in full agreement with his methods and aims.

On March 17, 1921, Adli was appointed to form a cabinet and to lead an official Egyptian delegation to negotiate a treaty with the British government. Despite Zaghlul's telegram, Adli planned to include him in the official delegation of leading Wafdists, and invited him along with the others. Zaghlul accepted on the condition that he lead the delegation. Adli seems to have agreed, but Lord Curzon, the British secretary of state, refused and insisted that the prime minister of Egypt should be the leader of the delegation.[19] Meanwhile the Wafd Central Committee in Egypt, in opposition to Zaghlul's wishes, had taken a collective decision in April to support Adli's government and his negotiations with Britain. They were taken aback when Zaghlul countered with a public statement that he would join the delegation only if he were at the head, and ordered the nation to oppose Adli's government, saying that any negotiations that it conducted would be unrepresentative of national demands, which only he had the mandate to carry out. On his return to Egypt Zaghlul had been greeted so deliriously by the population that it left him in no doubt as to his power over them. He then fully realized that the people were completely on his side, and that he could dispense with his early colleagues and behave as he pleased without fear of the consequences.

In reply Muhammad Mahmud, Lutfi al-Sayyid, Hamad al-Basil, and Abd al-Latif al-Mukabati published a letter in which they expressed their disapproval of Zaghlul's position, affirming that his distrust of the Adli ministry and his insistence on leading the delegation were based on personal grounds and went against the advice of the majority of the Wafd. They therefore repudiated his "arbitrary and isolated act."[20] On April 28, 1921, they resigned from the Wafd. Resignations by other members of the Wafd Central Committee soon followed until all the original founders of the Wafd but Zaghlul had resigned. Of the Central Committee of eighteen only a loyal court of five remained around Zaghlul. Alienated were all those who would have made the Wafd a party organized on collective lines rather than dependent on one man. The Wafd now came to be dominated by one man, utterly subservient to his commands. Zaghlul surrounded

19. Lord Curzon to Lord Allenby, March 24, 1921, F.O. 371/6293.
20. Lord Allenby to Lord Curzon, March 30, 1921, F.O. 371/6295; Lajin, *Saad Zaghlul*, p. 323.

himself with younger activists like Makram, Nahhas, and Nuqrashi; a few older and capable men like Wasif Ghali, Ali al-Shamsi, and his nephew Fathallah Barakat also remained with him, but all would carry out his orders without question.

He was the Man of the Hour. Any attempt at negotiating with England without him would therefore be doomed to failure, no matter the concessions obtained, for the Wafd would oppose it, and that was to be the pattern of Anglo-Egyptian negotiations and the reason for their failure until 1936 when the international situation forced on all parties a change of outlook.

The struggle for power between Zaghlul and the other forces in Egypt very early took on life-and-death dimensions. To discredit Adli and the dissident Wafdists, his main supporters, Zaghlul evolved a mystical concept of the Wafd and of his role in it, which was typical of the self-righteous attitude developed by most revolutionaries. To his memoirs he confided, "I must set myself the goal of being unique, *farid*, without partner. . . . I have no need to be delegated, *mawfudan*, or to be a party leader, it is enough that I represent a goal, *mumathil ghaya*, bearer of a principle. Should that principle gain supporters, well and good, otherwise I stand alone." In public Zaghlul said that the Wafd was not a party; it was a delegation empowered by the nation and expressing the will of the nation, exactly the terms used by Mustafa Kamil and applied to his party. "Anyone who says we are a party demanding independence is a criminal," said Zaghlul, "for this implies that there are other parties which do not want independence. The whole nation wants independence, we are the spokesmen of the nation demanding it, we are the trustees of the nation."[21] Here was the leading fallah expressing the desiderata of all the fallahin and awlad balad—the disinherited of Egypt—in their opposition to Adli Yakan and all the other dhawat who had despoiled them for centuries. As the voice of public opinion the Wafd, then, was the final arbiter for all decisions undertaken by whatever government was in power; it was the real authority in the land, for only the Wafd knew what the public wanted and only they could be trusted to safeguard public interest. It was a most adroit way of impugning the motives of any other party, which obviously did not have a popular mandate, and was to dominate the Wafd ethos until the demise of the party after the 1952 revolution.

On July 1, 1921, Adli went to London to begin negotiations,

21. Ibid., p. 328; Albert Hourani, *Arabic Thought in the Liberal Age* (London, 1960), p. 221.

probably realizing that his efforts were doomed from the start. Strikes
and demonstrations had broken out in Egypt, and Zaghlul, who
encouraged them, had described the negotiations as "George V negotiating with George V" thereby questioning Adli's patriotism and
loyalty to his country, and setting the stage for the immediate refusal
of whatever terms Adli was able to arrange.

Throughout the negotiations the British government seemed to be
motivated by a fear of being displaced in Egypt by some other
foreign power, especially if the Egyptian government were allowed
to appoint non-British advisors in the ministries and if the British
forces were withdrawn from the cities, both of which became vital
issues in the talks. When neither side seemed to be moving toward a
final decision, Lord Curzon jumped the gun and on November 10
presented Adli with a memorandum of clauses for a suggested convention between the two countries. The draft treaty provided for the
abolition of the Protectorate and for the drafting of a perpetual
treaty. Egypt was to have the free conduct of her foreign relations
but was not to enter into any political agreement with other foreign
powers without prior consultation with the British government. British
forces were to be maintained in Egypt to support Egypt in the defense
of her territory and to protect British imperial communications. The
British government was to continue negotiating with the Powers for
the abolition of the capitulations. The Egyptian Government was to
appoint a financial and judicial advisor and to undertake not to
appoint any foreign officials in her army or bureaucracy without the
prior concurrence of the British high commissioner. The terms were
generally similar to those of the Milner-Zaghlul talks, although more
restrictive of Egypt.

Adli refused the draft treaty on the grounds that it was invested
"with the quality of an actual deed of guardianship"[22] and sailed for
Egypt to be greeted by the masses as a traitor who had betrayed his
country by attempting to negotiate with the British without Zaghlul.
Adli immediately resigned and set a pattern for successive cabinets —
failure to negotiate with Britain followed by resignation.

While in exile in Malta in 1919 Zaghlul had set up an extensive
secret organization with the help of Abd al-Rahman Fahmi, about
which very few Wafdists were aware. This organization proved useful
in carrying out Zaghlul's program of agitation, for he called upon it

22. Zayid, *Struggle for Independence,* p. 103; see Great Britain, *Egypt,* 4 (1921),
cmd 1666, 8-10, for Adli's answer in full.

to organize massive strikes and demonstrations in his support and to illustrate his power over the population. Had Zaghlul had the Egyptian stage all to himself his agitation might have had a chance of achieving success, but he had to contend with two other major protagonists: the Egyptian Sultan and the British Resident, both of whom opposed him.

Sultan Fuad (king after 1922) was a fit match for Zaghlul. The sixth of the Khedive Ismail's eight sons, he had been brought up mostly in exile in Italy where he had served in the army. Subsequently the Ottoman Sultan appointed him military attaché in Vienna for two years. When Fuad's nephew, the Khedive Abbas, reached the throne of Egypt, he appointed Fuad chief aide de camp. In Egypt he was an impoverished prince with a reputation as a gambler and a womanizer. Fuad's contretemps with Zaghlul started across the poker table where he was often outbluffed by the Egyptian. He married Princess Chevikiar, a great-granddaughter of Ibrahim Pasha, but divorced her after her brother put a bullet through his gullet which was never removed and gave him a distinctive and disconcerting bark. His initial poverty caused him to set about amassing a very large fortune when the opportunity arose, and not by the most scrupulous means. Fuad was brought to the throne by the British authorities as a poor alternative when Sultan Husain, Abbas's successor, died and his son refused the throne. On becoming Sultan in 1919 he married the daughter of Abd al-Rahim Pasha Sabri, a descendant of the famous Colonel Sève, Sulaiman Pasha al-Faransawi, as he was known in Egypt, who bore him a son in 1920, Prince Faruq.

Fuad was a clever and unscrupulous man who believed, like Zaghlul, that he was marked by destiny for great things. He had hoped at one time to be chosen King of Albania, but when he was overlooked he regarded that as an omen of better things to come.[23] When he was appointed Sultan he grew into the role of monarch. Like his father Ismail, Fuad had charm and a very tortuous mind. A strong, handsome man with boundless energy, he had a love for both work and play. He had an arrangement with the King of Italy whereby they shipped mistresses to each other when they tired of them. He was fond of practical jokes and had once scandalized the respectable women of the foreign community by showing them a picture of what he termed a "beautiful beast" which turned out to be a nude and generously

23. Information told me by Bahi-Eddine Barakat (Pasha) along with the subsequent details.

endowed Dinka warrior. Fuad had a keen mind, was extremely well read, and had an excellent memory. Little that happened in his country escaped his attention, and he was equally well informed on international affairs. Above all, he was a determined man. His knowledge of the Arabic language was limited and his public speeches were greeted with derision by his loyal subjects for mangling their language, but he very rapidly mastered it, a remarkable achievement, and spoke Arabic well except for a quirk he had of describing things as *fawq al-ʿada kwayis,* a term that does not exist in Arabic and is a literal translation of "extra-ordinairement bien."

Upon attaining the throne he hesitated for a while over what policy to espouse and gave encouragement to the nationalists. Yet, throughout his entire reign he conspired to undermine parliamentary rule in Egypt and to render the constitution null and void, for he did not believe in the value of either. An able and intelligent man, he was marred by his refusal to consider sharing the government of Egypt with the Egyptians. (But then, as Machiavelli said, the thought of the palace is one thing and that of the marketplace another.) Those who at first mistook Fuad for a lightweight quickly reversed their judgment, and even his enemies developed a grudging respect for him. His success in battling constitutional life in Egypt was attributable to two factors. The first was British support, for whatever sins he committed in Egypt Fuad knew that in the last analysis he would be supported by the British government, which had brought him to the throne and was the guarantor of his continuing existence as a monarch. The second was that through his power as ruler Fuad could wave the dazzling post of prime minister before the eyes of any politician and win his cooperation.

The Residency, that other palace which overlooked the Nile at Qasr al-Dubara, frequently thwarted the moves of the men in the palace at Abdin when they became too obstreperous or ran counter to British interests. It was the real ruler of Egypt from 1882. The rise of the Wafd and the disturbances of 1919 had brought General (later Field Marshal) Allenby to Egypt as high commissioner. As a victorious military commander in the area, the man who had won the war in the Near East in the Palestine campaign, Allenby had an exalted reputation in Egypt and, more important, had the ear of the authorities in England, unlike his predecessor Wingate who could not influence the British establishment and was unfairly accused by them of encouraging Egyptian pretensions. Allenby, along with the British residents in Egypt and the whole foreign community, was disturbed by the agitation of the Wafd and suggested to the Foreign Office the wisdom behind such a move as "an early visit to Egypt of the vessels of the Mediterranean fleet." On June 17, 1921, just before the Adli-Curzon talks started, Allenby forwarded to Curzon a memorandum written by Sir William Hayter, the British legal advisor in the Ministry for Finance, which said that no Egyptian would consent to become a party to a permanent arrangement with Great Britain which fell short of securing complete independence for Egypt, and that since there was little prospect for the successful issue of the impending negotiations "some other solution must be found." Allenby then added that the British government must be prepared with an alternative policy "which they may have to enforce without preliminary agreement from the Egyptian side."[24] Allenby realized, like many Egyptians, that Adli would not be able to negotiate with any degree of success (because England was not willing to concede complete independence to Egypt), but he thought that some gesture should be made by the British government to show its goodwill and to encourage other Egyptians to cooperate with the British authorities. He also realized, however, that the gesture, whatever it was, would fall flat the minute Zaghlul held it up to scorn before the public as a pis aller, and that the only way to forestall this inevitable opposition was to take positive action and to send Zaghlul out of the country into exile until events settled down.

To put an end to Zaghlul's by now daily disruption of the public peace and to encourage more moderate politicians to cooperate with the Residency on December 23, 1921, Allenby arrested Zaghlul, his two nephews Atif and Fathallah Barakat, Mustafa al-Nahhas, and Makram Ubaid and exiled them first to Aden and then to the Seychelles.

Adli was opposed to sending Zaghlul into exile and insisted that should Allenby pursue such a course it be done after his resignation had gone into effect to avoid being accused of having fomented a plot against the Wafd leader. Two of Adli's friends, Abd al-Khaliq Tharwat and Ismail Sidqi, who had fewer scruples, were in favor of the exile, and as soon as Zaghlul was safely out of the way they set to work with Allenby. Together the three planned that "gesture of goodwill" to which Allenby had alluded in his despatches.

Ismail Sidqi had been a member of the Wafd delegation to Paris but he had been expelled when other members accused him and

24. Allenby to Curzon, June 17, 1921, F.O. 371/6295.

Mahmud Abu-l Nasr of revealing secrets. Sidqi was the son of a high government official and born to affluence. He was a man of very superior intellect, a brilliant but unscrupulous politician. He did not pin much faith to anything save his desire for power. One of his close friends remarked that there were three things Sidqi could never resist: the lure of power, the lure of money, and the lure of a woman.[25] In 1915 he was involved in a scandal with Yahia Pasha Ibrahim's daughter; when she committed suicide rather than face the scandal, he was dropped from the cabinet. Time and again, almost to the end of his very long life, he was to be the focus of scandals involving women and dubious financial transactions. Although he joined the Wafd, probably under the influence of his friends Lutfi al-Sayyid and Tharwat, and was later to help create the Liberal Constitutionalist and the Ittihad parties, he basically played a lone hand and was happier when operating without the trammels, or charade, of a party.

Sidqi was charming, cultured, and a brilliant conversationalist who captivated his friends and enemies alike, and the former, while well aware of his shortcomings, forgave him much because of those very qualities. He richly deserved to be called the cleverest man in Egypt. His close friends Lutfi and Tharwat were very different. All three had been friends from their student days in the School of Law. And while each man pursued a different, and on occasion opposing, political path they remained friends to the end of their days.

Lutfi and Tharwat had been connected with the nationalist movement practically from its inception under Mustafa Kamil. Lutfi had early broken away from Kamil and what he considered his too close commitment to the Khedive Abbas and had helped found Hizb al-Umma in 1907. Tharwat had remained a loyal friend of Kamil to the end. Where Sidqi was a politician and manipulator, Tharwat was a statesman.

Tharwat was perhaps the least appreciated of Egypt's public servants. He was honest, hardworking, and capable, yet he had a strain of weakness which led him to condone the most blatant jobbery on the part of his colleagues when he headed a cabinet. He always sought to avoid unpleasant confrontations, especially with his colleagues, and thus allowed his ministry to become a byword for corruption when he himself was scrupulously honest. Professionally he had the capacity to cut through knotty problems and present matters in a lucid and concise fashion. He was especially astute at negotiations and grasped subtleties

25. Information derived from Barakat quoting Tawfiq Doss (Pasha).

very rapidly, one reason that persuaded Adli to request his presence in Paris in 1920. Unlike Sidqi, Tharwat never lied, although on occasion he simply omitted any reference to certain matters. For that reason many of his countrymen called him foxy, while others said that he was like quicksilver.[26]

British officials liked and respected Tharwat. They described him in the reports sent back home as akin to an old-fashioned, English liberal politician, "disliking autocracy and demagogy," and had much admiration for the loyalty he showed to his English friends even throughout the most trying times.[27]

Tharwat and Sidqi take credit together for helping Allenby see the need for a gesture of friendship by the British government which would demonstrate a willingness to meet the Egyptians halfway. They believed it would defuse the Wafd and allow any Egyptian government that was formed to get on with the vital business of drawing up a constitution.

The outcome of their deliberations was that on Allenby's prompting, even bullying, of Lloyd George, the British government unilaterally issued the Declaration of 1922, which ended the Protectorate, declared Egypt independent, and raised Sultan Fuad to the rank of King of Egypt. Four points of contention were reserved at the discretion of the British government until it became possible "by free discussion and friendly accommodation on both sides to conclude agreements in regard thereto."[28] The four reserved points were: the security of the communications of the British empire in Egypt; the defense of Egypt against foreign aggression or interference; the protection of foreign interests and the protection of minorities in Egypt; the Sudan and its status.

These four reserved points robbed Egypt of anything more than a *de jure* independence, for they allowed the British influence on the Egyptian government to continue unabated and enabled Britain to use the reserved points as a lever for intervention; and they allowed British military presence to continue. The Declaration's only value was that it paved the way for a constitution and the establishment of parliamentary life. To Tharwat and Sidqi that very fact spelled a victory, but to Zaghlul and the Wafd, the Declaration negotiated by a dissident minority was a "national catastrophe," an abdication of

26. Barakat Memoirs, (1923), 14:84.
27. Notes on members of the Egyptian cabinet, July 7, 1926, F.O. 371/11584.
28. For full details see Great Britain, *Correspondence Respecting Affairs in Egypt*, no. 9.

national rights, and a betrayal of the nationalist cause. But since Zaghlul was in exile at the time there was little he could do save fire off telegrams of protest, most of which were not delivered, and fume at the "cowards" who had "betrayed Egypt" and him.[29]

Abd al-Khaliq Tharwat was appointed prime minister and a committee was chosen to draft a constitution and an electoral law. The British government was in favor of a constitution and an elected government that would conclude a settlement between the two countries. The Wafdists, however, felt that since they had refused to recognize the validity of the Declaration, any involvement on their part in the constitutional committee would be a tacit acceptance of the Declaration. They therefore objected to the constitutional committee and argued in favor of an elective constituent assembly as the only satisfactory vehicle for drafting a constitution. When their argument was refused they boycotted the committee, demanded the abolition of martial law, which had been declared in Egypt in November 1914, and the release of all political prisoners, especially Zaghlul. Their agitation was rewarded by mass arrests, stiff fines, prison sentences, and some were sentenced to death and then reprieved.

The constitutional committee was formed of thirty-two members including the leading legal minds of the time, men like Rushdi Pasha, and Abd al-Aziz Fahmi, and Husain Haikal; the religious minorities; and members of various interest groups like the bedouin Arabs who were represented by Salih Lamlum Pasha. Abd al-Aziz Fahmi, a purist, wanted to produce the perfect constitution, one that would guarantee the nation immunity from arbitrary actions on the part of the executive or the King. Husain Rushdi, a former premier who had headed the ministry during the war years, was more realistic as the result of his intimate knowledge of power circles. He knew King Fuad would never accept a constitution that stripped him of all his powers, so Rushdi set out to create a compromise between the ideal and the possible.[30]

The King was most displeased over the constitution which he rightly suspected would be too liberal and democratic, and he embarked on a policy of harassing the cabinet in an attempt to discredit Tharwat's ministry and delay having to sign a constitution. Fuad had always detested Tharwat because of his close friendship with Adli Yakan, who,

29. Mr. Scott, Acting High Commissioner, to Lord Curzon, Sept. 9, 1923, F.O. 371/8693.

30. Fahmi, *Hadhihi Hayati,* pp. 140-141.

aside from Zaghlul, was the only Egyptian capable of standing up to Fuad and on occasion even putting him down. The personal dislike that Fuad had for both men and for their friends by association deepened with his suspicion that the constitution was to be the major means they would use to limit royal prerogatives. Fuad therefore made overtures to the Wafd as a means of bringing down Tharwat's ministry.[31]

Meanwhile Adli, Tharwat, and Sidqi, who were aware of the King's intentions, set about to create a political party that would support Tharwat's cabinet and protect the drafting of the constitution. Several meetings to set up the party then took place in Adli's house, which Husain Haikal describes in his memoirs.[32] Ahmad Lutfi al-Sayyid, who had returned to a position in the government as Director of Dar al-Kutub, and who was another of King Fuad's *bêtes noires*, but who had been one of the founders of the party, could not join the party officially; he acted behind the scenes as its organizer and chose Haikal as editor for the party organ, *al-Siyasa,* which they were soon to bring out. Lutfi believed that Tharwat and Sidqi as Adli's right-hand men in the last cabinet should both be members of the party, but Muhammad Mahmud objected violently to the inclusion of Sidqi implying that he could not work with him, so Sidqi did not join the party officially. The speech that Adli delivered to a select audience in October 1922 announcing the creation of the Liberal Constitutional party, al-Ahrar al-Dusturiyyun, was written by Lutfi; it declared the party's program: support for an independent Egypt; constitutional rule; the protection of civil rights; free speech; and the establishment of social justice.

The membership of the new party was very similar in composition to the old Umma party. It was composed largely of dissident Wafdists, moderate politicians, young professionals, and large landowners. While they had all been involved in nationalist movements at one time or another, the leading members of the Liberal Constitutionalist party were characterized by their belief that advancing one step at a time toward complete independence was more constructive than attempting precipitate actions. They believed that a policy of moderation and of compromise with Britain would yield more rapid results than Zaghlul's intransigence had done. Meanwhile, they asserted that a constitution was of more immediate importance as a safeguard for

31. Barakat Memoirs (1923), 15:52; also Allenby to Curzon, Aug. 15, 1922, F.O. 371/7736.
32. Haikal, *Mudhakkirat,* I, 144 ff.

any government against the King, whom they all distrusted and whose autocracy was well known. Once more, as under Abbas II, a constitution was viewed as a panacea for many ills and parliamentary government as the first step toward independence, the rationale being that the British presence would eventually be withdrawn, but the King would always be there to interfere in the affairs of state. These men, as children of the Enlightenment, shared a belief that problems could be solved by rational discussion, and the British were credited with a rational approach to politics, whereas the Turkish King was believed to lack that quality and to be motivated by self-interest and personal feelings. It took them some time to realize the truth of Lord Palmerston's adage that countries are motivated by self-interest, not by reason.

The Liberal Constitutionalists had little following and were always to remain a minority party, but one whose importance outweighed its numbers because of the prestige of its members. This was the party of intellectuals who frowned on demogoguery, and of the elite who had little in common with the masses, who were without doubt wholeheartedly behind the opposing Wafd party. The Ahrar believed that they could govern rationally and fairly and that the masses would benefit from such a paternalistic attitude and in time see where their advantage lay. The party came to be known as the party of the aristocrats, dhawat, in contrast with the party of the people, probably not because of the degree of affluence of its members (the Wafd was richer as a party), but because of its aloofness from the day-to-day skirmishes of usual party life. There was less class distinction implied in the term for after all Muhammad Mahmud, Abd al-Aziz Fahmi, and Lutfi al-Sayyid were of fallah origin as was Zaghlul; the distinction was more one of attitude and of political approach. With acute perception the man in the street, without the benefit of having read Marx, realized instinctively that political models are directly related to social position, and the men of the Ahrar were representatives of the affluent bourgeoisie who thought with its mind and its ideology.

Adli Yakan, who usually held aloof from party politics, was persuaded to accept the presidency of the party.[33] In 1924, he resigned and the party leaders induced Abd al-Aziz Fahmi, who was not even a party member, to take over the position, which he did with reluctance, for he was a hypochondriac and at the time believed himself to be ill.

33. al-Rafii, Fi-aʿqab, I, 69.

When the Ahrar party was formed the opposition papers called its members "highwaymen and murderers," presumably because they had been formed in order to destroy nationalism, that is, the Wafd. Tactically the enemy had to be morally discredited in order to render it politically powerless. It was thus that Shafiq Mansur, who headed a terrorist group and was later hanged for the murder of the Sirdar in 1924,[34] plotted the assassination of Adli and Rushdi when they were due to attend a party meeting in November 1922. For some reason the meeting was canceled but two men, Hasan Abd al-Raziq Pasha and Ismail Bey Zuhdi, did not receive the cancellation notices. Both men bore superficial physical resemblances to Adli and Rushdi in girth and size and they were shot dead when they reached party headquarters. The cold war between the two parties had inexorably developed into a hot one. Ironically, Zaghlul knew nothing about the assassinations because he was in exile.

The support of a new political party did not help Tharwat much in the face of the King's displeasure and the popular demonstrations fomented against him by the Wafd, and he finally resigned. The succeeding cabinet, with Yusif Pasha Wahba as premier, was too weak to last for longer than three months before it too resigned, and for some forty days the country remained without a cabinet. Public security had by then become an acute problem with daily demonstrations and disruptions, and a wave of terrorism gripped the cities. Bombs were thrown at British military personnel and in their camps, and a number of officials were assassinated, allegedly by the Wafd secret organization. Egyptian politicians lived in terror of assassination and several attempts were actually made against Tharwat and Yusif Pasha Wahba.

In March 1923 a caretaker cabinet under Yahia Pasha Ibrahim was finally formed. Zaghlul and his men were released from imprisonment in the Seychelles and allowed to return to Egypt. Other political prisoners were freed. The constitution was proclaimed in April and a few days later the electoral law was passed.

The constitution as promulgated differed widely from the one first drafted by the committee and was in fact a compromise, which the committee only accepted on the assumption that a defective constitution was better than none, and with the knowledge that Fuad, presumably backed by the British government, was ready to fight tooth and nail to save his prerogatives. The new constitution was a much

34. See chapter III, below.

more authoritarian one, which vested legislative power in the king and
a bicameral parliament. The king had the right to choose and appoint
the prime minister (art. 38), the right to postpone parliamentary
sessions (art. 39), the right to dismiss the cabinet and dissolve parliament (art. 49), the right to appoint the president of the Senate and
two-fifths of its members (art. 78).[35] Every one of these articles in time
was to be used by the King to undermine the cabinet and parliament.
Despite its defects, the constitution was hailed by all groups save the
Wafd. Having boycotted the constitutional committee, the Wafd was
in no position to praise its achievement. Indeed, Zaghlul on his return
from exile in the Seychelles described the 1922 Declaration of Independence as "the bitterest catastrophe which ever befell the nation,"
and the constitutional committee as *lajnat al-ashqiya*, "the committee
of delinquents." Yet, quite ironically, when the constitution was
suspended by the Ziwar government in 1925, Zaghlul and the Wafd
valiantly fought to have it restored, for the constitution was the only
means of insuring Wafd supremacy. As the majority party they dominated parliament and their strong position allowed them to head
cabinets or harass them into resignation.

Martial law, which had been one of the sharpest thorns in the side
of the Wafd because it hedged their freedom to call public meetings
and circulate round the countryside, was to end. Lord Curzon had
agreed that martial law must be abrogated but he insisted that its
maintenance was necessary to the British government until the Act of
Indemnity to cover the measures taken during the war years had been
passed and legislation enacted for the enforcement of the peace treaty.
On March 30, 1923, the Yahia Ibrahim cabinet passed the Indemnity
Law, and martial law was lifted on July 5. That same month a law
was passed allowing all foreign officials serving the Egyptian government to retire within a year or to continue to serve the country
provisionally until 1927. The retirement of these officials and their
compensation for termination of service were later on to cause considerable friction between the British Resident and the Egyptian government, as we shall see.

When Zaghlul was released from exile he seemed to be in a more
chastened mood for before he arrived in Egypt in September 1923 he
announced his willingness to collaborate with anyone who would work
with him "for the full realization of Egyptian aspirations," and added
that he only wished to serve "King and country."[36] He paid a visit to

35. For full details see al-Rafii, *Fi-a'qab*, I, 116 ff.
36. Barakat Memoirs (1923), 15:11.

the King on his arrival and it seemed as though a period of amity and goodwill was about to begin. The coming elections absorbed everyone's attention.

One can thus choose 1924 as a convenient date with which to begin a new phase in Egyptian history, one that constituted a break with the past in legal though not in any other terms. Egypt had been officially recognized by Britain as an independent sovereign state having a hereditary form of monarchy, a constitution, and a parliamentary system of government. That was the theory. But in practice, to name a few outstanding issues, Egypt was still saddled by the presence of an army of occupation and of British advisors in the army and the administration; the government was handicapped by the capitulations which continued to exempt the most affluent residents from its juridical and financial jurisdiction; and the problem of the Sudan was still unsolved. Egyptian independence was therefore regarded by many nationalists as a legal farce, a sop thrown to them to keep them quiet. On the other hand more moderate politicians believed with equal justification that de jure independence was a step in the right direction which could only end in a de facto recognition of Egyptian rights.

That same year a British official in Egypt writing to a friend in England described the Egyptian scene and predicted the future political pattern in astute terms. He said that at present the British authorities in Egypt are on good terms with all parties because they know that (a) whatever party is in office will be attacked for being too servile to the Residency; (b) the Opposition will make overtures to the Residency to secure help in upsetting the government; (c) the government will openly curse the Residency while covertly relying on its support; and (d) everyone will urge the complete evacuation of Egypt and the Sudan. But, he added, none of the British were worried because they knew that the Egyptian army had been neutralized, "all their ammunition is in the citadel with a perfectly good British battalion sitting on it."[37] Cynical, but a most apt comment on the shape of things to come.

The outcome of the elections held in January 1924 was a foregone conclusion and even the most optimistic among the opposition could hardly have expected anything short of a landslide for the Wafd. The results justified all Wafd hopes with a total of 151 seats, with only 7 seats for the Liberal Constitutionalists, 2 for Hizb al-Watani, Mustafa Kamil's old party which was still agonizing on, and 15 Independents. All the leading members of the Ahrar and their sympathizers, men

37. Mr. Murray to Mr. Ingram, Dec. 26, 1923, F.O. 371/8963.

like Abd al-Aziz Fahmi, the "Father of the Constitution," Ismail Sidqi, and Mahmud Abd al-Raziq, were defeated. The only one among the Ahrar leaders to win a seat was Muhammad Pasha Mahmud, and his election was invalidated by the Lower House in April 1924 in retaliation for an attack made by the opposition press on the election of a Wafdist. The Wafd was now legally in power. Their claim to represent the majority of the Egyptian electorate was fully vindicated, and none dared contest Zaghlul when he claimed to speak for the whole of Egypt. Although the people were behind him all the way, Zaghlul was opposed by the Palace and the Residency, both of whom could not view him as other than a demagogue and a rabble rouser. Above all he represented a danger to their interests, which did not necessarily coincide with those of the Egyptian public who were dismissed as too ignorant to have any worthwhile opinion or even any opinion at all. Herein lay one of the basic flaws in future political behavior, the inability to accept the implications behind a democratic election, to wit, to allow the peoples' representatives to govern the land untrammeled. In consequence every Egyptian cabinet was denied a free hand and was inevitably tampered with, either by Palace or Residency or both together.

In one of his many speeches Zaghlul described the 1919 revolution and said that its most important results were the Egyptianization of the economy; the abandonment of the veil by the women and their participation in the national movement; the destruction of the pasha class; the seizure of power by the fallahin; the disappearance of the Turkish element from Egyptian politics.[38] Aside from the reference to the veil, that speech sounds very much like a speech Gamal Abd al-Nasir might have made some thirty years later. Had nothing changed within those thirty years?

Although the economy had begun to Egyptianize under the impetus of Talaat Pasha Harb when he founded the Misr Bank in 1920 and its affiliates in the next decade, the process was a very slow one and it was only subsequent to the 1952 revolution when Nasir passed the decrees that nationalized the economy in 1960 that one could say that it was now in Egyptian hands. Before that time the economy was controlled by the foreign elements in Egypt, who because of the capitulations did not pay taxes and were not subject to Egyptian laws. The large majority of labor was also non-Egyptian. Many foreigners were later to claim credit for developing Egyptian industry; the fact remains that the economic development of Egypt at the hands

38. Hourani, *Arabic Thought in the Liberal Age*, p. 216.

of foreigners benefited them more than the Egyptians. The ones who did benefit were three-quarters of a million alien residents in Egypt and three-quarters of a million Egyptians who were the first to westernize.[39] The population remained unaffected and the bulk of the profits generally went abroad so the argument that the country was benefiting did not apply.

Women had indeed abandoned the veil and had participated in the nationalist movement in an active fashion. Although their tale has yet to be told in detail it was a well-known local fact that women in society played a key role in the organization and logistics of the nationalist movement. They organized and supervised boycotts of English goods, they agitated, they smuggled pamphlets to outlying areas of the land, and they carried on when their men were exiled or imprisoned. Later on the same women carried out a massive campaign of social work in the country, and through the twin organizations of the Mubarat Muhammad Ali and the Mar'a al-Jadida they established a network of hospitals, schools, dispensaries, orphanages, and rehabilitation centers that were more widespread and much more efficient than those established by the Ministry for Social Affairs, which often appealed to them for assistance.

But, had the fallahin seized power? Had the Turkish element and the pasha class disappeared? The Turkish element in Egyptian politics was but a shadow of a once frightening situation that had existed in the past century. Like some remote star millions of light years away which continues to send its beam toward earth long after its dissolution, little remained of the old Turkish elements except the royal family and a few others like Adli and Ziwar. By then the Turkish elite had become Egyptianized, and the Egyptians, even Zaghlul, were married to Turks. The issue of the Turco-Circassian elite which had exercised Urabi and his followers was of little real consequence in 1919, until one remembers that Zaghlul and many of his older colleagues were the last of the generation that had had to suffer from Turkish superiority and discrimination against native Egyptians. Memories die hard and for decades after the waning of Turkish power, Egyptians remained obsessed by it. The only effective Turkish influence that survived was concentrated in the monarchy and little could be done about that until 1953 when Egypt became a republic.

Zaghlul had mentioned the destruction of the pasha class, and yet he was himself a pasha — and was it in fact a class? The answer must be in the negative for the title cut across class lines; while it might have

39. Charles Issawi, *Egypt in Revolution* (London, 1963), p. 265.

described a class in past centuries, it now simply described the elite of the country, an elite of politicians, intellectuals, and bureaucrats and frequently one of wealth, although that was not necessarily the case, which had continued to perpetuate itself with new blood by turning the upcoming politicians and the new ruling group into pashas. The irony was that when Nasir in the upheaval of the fifties castigated the pashas he was referring to the very men who in their youth had railed against the old pashas. Nasir's treatment of the pashas was much more radical and really destroyed them since he canceled the title and shunted its privileges and appurtenances to his new government elite, the technocrats.

What Zaghlul meant to convey by his words was the gradual displacement of an elite wholly dependent for survival on either palace — Abdin or Qasr al-Dubara — by another elite of fallah origin which was not wholly identified with the Palace, but which rose from the people and depended for its backing on the people. The new bourgeoisie that had led the 1919 revolution had its roots in the rural society but had developed into lawyers, intellectuals, and bureaucrats who wanted a share in the governing process in the natural fashion of all rising groups. The sons of those who in the past had been called *pis-fellah* by their Turkish overlords were now their equals if not their superiors. Although the new parliament was composed largely of landowners and men of rural origins, Zaghlul's reference to the seizure of power by the fallahin was, one suspects, not a general reference to power by the people but a specific reference to himself and his colleagues, to all the members of the new elite who were fallahin and exulted in their newfound psychological independence from the shackles of a long, bitter, aristocratic domination by the Turks.

Zaghlul ended his speech by saying "external independence has no value unless there is also an internal liberation," which supports the above interpretation although it also applies as poignantly to the British presence as to the capitulations. Internal liberation was to be made secure by a constitution, the one bulwark that lay between the fallahin and the last Turkish bastion in the land, the monarchy.

Egypt waited with bated breath for a new era to commence, the era promised by Zaghlul in all his speeches, the era for which it had dearly paid in dead and wounded for the nationalist cause. A truly popular elective parliamentary assembly for the first time in the entire history of Egypt was going to rule that country.

III

The King of Hearts

SAAD ZAGHLUL'S new cabinet was an odd mixture of loyal Wafdists and veteran politicians such as Muhammad Said and Tawfiq Nasim, former premiers, and Ahmad Mazlum, president of the last Legislative Assembly. The inclusion of such men in the first nationalist cabinet was curious. Said was an unscrupulous politician whom many distrusted. He had agreed to form a cabinet after the Rushdi ministry resigned in 1919, a gesture that was regarded as inimical to the Wafd and to the nationalist cause, but he had a strong following in Alexandria. Nasim was a respectable man who had served as the King's chef de cabinet but who had been one of the first to welcome Zaghlul back from exile and to pave the way for his meeting with the King, so he was the obvious bridge between the new ministry and the palace. Mazlum was neutral. The main reason for Zaghlul's choice of these men was his belief that they would carry out his orders, yet they had enough prestige to serve as a link with the past and with the monarchy.[1] The rest of the cabinet was Wafdist, among them two Copts—Morcos Hanna and Wasif Ghali—then Hasan Hasib, Najib al-Gharabli, Fathallah Barakat, and Mustafa al-Nahhas. The last two men had accompanied Zaghlul on his exile to the Seychelles.

Barakat was Zaghlul's nephew and right-hand man and had been a prominent member of the Legislative Council. It was his organizing talent that enabled the Wafd to acquire grass roots support all over the Delta. As an affluent peasant and a member of the *ayan*, as well as a clever politician, Fathallah knew how to appeal to fallah and ayan alike, and it was he who planned the campaign and toured the Delta

---

1. Abd al-Khaliq Lajin (*Saad Zaghlul: Wa dawruh fi-l siyasa al-Misriyya* [Beirut, 1975], p. 359) points out that some of them were foisted onto Saad by the King.

73

village by village to rally support for the Wafd. Fathallah was a sensible and courageous man who was completely devoted to his uncle; he was, however, handicapped by his ignorance of a foreign language at a time when relationship with England was a vital element in Egyptian political life.

Nahhas was a former judge who had been a member of Hizb al-Watani, but when the parties agreed to cooperate in 1919 he joined the Wafd. He was dedicated to Zaghlul and to the Wafd but was regarded by some of them as having an unstable personality, and by others as being not quite sane.[2] Zaghlul judged him to be hasty, stubborn, and lacking in manners. Together they had shared a long exile and Zaghlul had grown to admire his talent for getting things done efficiently, a talent that had proved very useful in organizing student demonstrations in 1919 and 1920.[3] For while Mustafa Kamil had been the one to initiate the use of students in political activities as a form of pressure, the Wafd had refined it into a potent instrument, thanks to Nahhas's efforts. Nahhas inevitably fell under the influence of a stronger personality—in the beginning Zaghlul and later Makram and Nuqrashi.

Wasif Ghali was the son of Butros Pasha Ghali, the premier who had been assassinated in 1911. He was an intelligent and cultured man, something of a poet. Having married a Frenchwoman, he was regarded as Francophile. When his father was killed, he created a sensation in Coptic circles by allegedly saying that he sided with the murderers of his father against the murderers of his country. Nevertheless, save in that one instance, he was not given to making such emotional statements and was viewed by both British and Egyptians as a level-headed and wise man.

The cabinet began its term of office bathed in the warm glow of entente. The King was cordial. Upon receiving Zaghlul as prime minister young prince Faruq walked into the room waving an Egyptian flag and shouting *"Yahia Saad,"* "Long live Saad,"[4] a calculated move on the part of the King who knew how susceptible Zaghlul was to flattery. Unfortunately, the entente was not to last for long and within the brief period of four months Zaghlul resigned twice, in obviously tactical moves. Each time he drove to the Palace to tender his resignation he was accompanied by a mass of demonstrators who

2. A. K. Clarke Kerr, Acting High Commissioner to Ramsay MacDonald, Jan. 5, 1924, F.O. 371/10020.

3. Barakat Memoirs (1925-1926), 17:19.

4. Clarke Kerr to MacDonald, Oct. 24, 1924, F.O. 371/10022.

stationed themselves under the palace windows and shouted *"Saad aw al-thawra,"* "Saad or the revolution." Zaghlul was very secure in the knowledge of his popularity in the country. One one occasion he said with pride "If he [Fuad] is the King of Egypt, I am the King of their hearts."[5] The demonstrations were visible and audible proof of that claim.

Many of Zaghlul's grievances against the King were fully justified, for the latter acted on his own initiative aided only by his camarilla, headed by Hasan Pasha Nashat. Nashat was to become the most hated man in Egypt, after the King, and a thorn in the side of every cabinet for his interference in all executive matters, whether on orders of his master or on his own. The conflict was therefore vital to the future political life of the country for it was to set a precedent and determine whether the King or the cabinet was to be the stronger branch of the executive, that is, the true ruler of the country.

The first duel between King and Premier occurred over the nomination of the senators to the new Upper House. Article 74 of the constitution decreed that two-fifths of the members of the Senate be appointed by the King. Fuad assumed that he had the sole authority to appoint whomever he wished without consulting his executive. Zaghlul insisted that the proper constitutional interpretation was that the King appoint the senators after due consultation with his government since articles 60 and 62 of the constitution laid full responsibility for the government of the country on the cabinet. A constitutional crisis arose, and both parties agreed to appeal to the Public Prosecutor of the Mixed Courts, the Belgian Baron Van den Bosch, for a decision. In his memoirs Van den Bosch described the incident as the conflict between a king intent on hanging on to his personal prerogatives and a premier intent on establishing the authority granted him by the constitution. The Belgian heard Zaghlul say in a menacing tone, "If the people were consulted . . ." leaving no doubt in anyone's mind as to the outcome. The man who ruled Egypt heart and soul could rouse the masses to terrible anger. Van den Bosch requested a few minutes to allow him to collect his thoughts and then said that the spirit of constitutional government ruled in the sense that responsibility lay with the cabinet and that any appointment of senators would have to be effected through the cabinet.[6] For the time being the King accepted his defeat with good grace and the crisis was over.

5. Barakat Memoirs (1925-1926), 17:7.
6. Baron Firmin Van den Bosch, *Vingt Années en Egypte* (Paris, 1932), p. 75. Saad Zaghlul's version is that he had convinced Van den Bosch that legally he was right (Zaghlul Memoirs, 47:2789).

On March 15, 1924, the first parliament was inaugurated, and Zaghlul read his Speech from the Throne. Although the new cabinet lasted for less than a year, it set the behavior pattern for successive cabinets. To begin with, the Wafdists encouraged the spoils system of party patronage whereby Wafd supporters were appointed to government posts and their opponents dismissed from office. Zaghlul announced that he wanted a government that was "Zaghlulist, flesh and blood" from the lowest umda to the top bureaucrat.[7] Although the spoils system is common to most political parties the world over, when carried to an extreme it is disruptive to the orderly transfer of power and especially was this the case with governments that were to rise and fall with giddy rapidity as in Egypt. Every government that came to power thus followed the Wafd example and replaced the opposition men by its own. Umdas were the first to be replaced, for the umda was the man who delivered the votes at election time. Provincial officials were replaced or transferred, and even government bureaucrats who could not be dismissed were transferred to rural positions on the periphery of power to eat their hearts out in idleness until the ministry fell and they could be recalled by their party to the urban sphere of action. Many men who were unsuited for any public office received appointments on the basis of their loyalty to the Wafd rather than on merit. Even a dedicated Wafdist like Barakat confided to his memoirs the jaundiced comment that every man seemed preoccupied with promoting his relatives to public office, regardless of their worth.[8]

The promises that Zaghlul had made to the nation so vehemently were conveniently forgotten or set aside. The unpopular Law of Associations, which had been passed by a prior government in 1923 after the abolition of martial law and aimed at the Wafd, and vociferously attacked by it, now became an instrument in Wafdist hands to be used in muzzling the press. The freedom of the press which the Wafd had so earnestly upheld when they were out of power was forgotten and the harassment of opposition papers like al-Siyasa pursued.[9]

Meanwhile internal unrest continued. Even though labor was still exiguous, comprising barely 10 percent of the population with industrialization still in its infancy, large-scale strikes were organized

7. Ibid., p. 2770, where Saad talks of ridding the administration of "dirt" although he quickly chides himself for language unbecoming a popular leader.

8. Barakat Memoirs (1923), 15:74.

9. Haikal, Mudhakkirat, I, 190 passim.

TO ALL WHOM IT CONCERNS.

Britannia (to Egypt). "I GAVE YOU LIBERTY. SEE TO IT THAT THE THINGS DONE BY YOU IN HER NAME DO NOT MAKE ME REPENT MY GIFT."

Source: *Punch,* 167 (Dec. 3, 1924), 631.

throughout 1924 by the workers for better working conditions. Most of
the workers were concentrated in Cairo and Alexandria. Any agitation
on the part of labor therefore could not fail to embarrass the government of the day. Even though workers had joined in the 1919 uprising,
they had not really played a prominent role in the activities, in part
because of their small number and in part because much of labor
was non-Egyptian. Zaghlul and the Wafd did not feel at ease with
labor because they suspected them of Bolshevik tendencies. The charge
had been leveled at a union founded in 1920 by a Russian Jew who
certainly was a socialist and a fellow traveler.[10] Continued labor
strikes finally convinced Zaghlul that the Wafd should take a hand in
organizing labor along party lines, and a labor union was duly created
under Wafd guidance. As we shall see the union did not have much
success. The basic reason was that Zaghlul with his rural upbringing
did not understand or even sympathize with labor, nor, for that
matter, did any of the other leading figures of the day, so that
labor faced an uphill fight until some of its demands were granted a
decade later.

Unrest was rife among the rest of the population as well. The
heaviest blow to popular hopes was dealt when their *zaim*, Zaghlul,
failed to negotiate a treaty with Ramsay MacDonald's Labour government in England in the summer of 1924. High hopes had been roused
in Egypt when the Labour government came to power that year, for
most Egyptians were convinced that it was less imperialist than the
Conservative government and therefore more responsive to Egyptian
wishes. The same belief had held sway over the past four decades when
the advent of every Liberal cabinet was hailed as presaging a reversal
in British policy from the Conservative one. Each time Egyptian hopes
proved vain, for, although the Liberal government under Sir Henry
Campbell-Bannermann in 1906 had accepted Lord Cromer's resignation, Eldon Gorst, Cromer's successor, did not encourage the nationalist cause. And it was Lloyd George's Liberal cabinet that had twice
exiled Zaghlul from Egypt. MacDonald, however, was an old friend of
Zaghlul's, and his party, while in opposition, had advocated a policy of
independence for Egypt—but when a party in opposition comes to
power it behaves quite differently. MacDonald had a small majority
in the House of Commons and was not willing to jeopardize his cabinet
in order to meet Egyptian demands, not even halfway, since he knew
the House would refuse them out of hand.

10. See chapter VII, below.

NILODRAMA.

Egypt. "AH! MY LONG-LOST CHE-ILD! COME HOME TO ME."
John Bull }
Soudan } together. { "WE DON'T THINK."

SOURCE: *Punch,* 167 (July 9, 1924), 31.

Before his departure for England that summer of 1924 riots had broken out in the Sudan. Zaghlul made a speech to the Egyptian Lower House in which he referred to the riots and expressed his disapproval of any British act that tended to separate Egypt from the Sudan. This was countered by a statement made by Lord Parmoor in the House of Lords which expressed British intentions not to abandon the Sudan. Zaghlul immediately tendered his resignation to the King, who refused to accept it.[11]

By then Zaghlul was beginning to suspect that the British authorities condoned his leading a cabinet as a lure to weaken his patriotic fervor through power and position. Should Saad the politician behave in any way differently from Saad the nationalist leader, the people could be told that their leader was nothing but an adventurer, a man who craved power and who on attaining it forgot his previous patriotic statements.[12] Zaghlul's naturally suspicious nature strengthened his belief that the impending negotiations were to be a test of his standing as a patriot and a means of forcing him to accept the terms of the 1922 Declaration as the basis for negotiations. His stand was therefore firm and irrevocable, naturally unacceptable to the British. The British position was equally uncompromising.

The Egyptian demands that Zaghlul carried to England were: withdrawal of British forces from Egypt; union of Egypt with the Sudan; and Britain's relinquishment of its claim to protect foreigners and minorities in Egypt,[13] which was one of the four reserved points. But no British cabinet would consider the protection of the Suez Canal as anything less than a cardinal point in imperial defense policy, and Britain's Committee for Imperial Defense had counseled against a withdrawal of British forces from Egyptian cities.[14] As for the Sudan, the scene of recent anti-British demonstrations (which the British assumed were fomented by the Wafd), Britain had no intention of abandoning it ever.

Even if Zaghlul's stand had weakened, it is highly doubtful that MacDonald would have been in a position to offer Egypt concessions. His government was extremely shaky and indeed fell a month later after the failure of the negotiations.

11. al-Rafii, Fi a‘qab, I, 168.
12. al-Aqqad, Saad Zaghlul, p. 154.
13. Zaghlul Memoirs, 45:2704 ff.
14. E. W. P. Newman, The Mediterranean and Its Problems (London, 1928), p. 285.

Although Zaghlul failed to obtain any concessions from Britain he was undaunted and returned to Egypt in a victorious spirit, announcing that though he had won nothing he had also lost nothing, that is, he had given none of Egypt's rights away and had shown that in or out of power his position regarding Egypt's independence was exactly the same. He said, *"du⁽aina li nantahir fa abaina,"* "We were invited to commit suicide and we refused."[15]

On his return to Egypt Zaghlul faced an internal crisis, for Fuad had interpreted his failure to negotiate a treaty differently from Zaghlul. He thought that the premier's position had weakened and that the Conservative cabinet which had followed on the heels of the Labour government would not support Zaghlul and might even be pleased to see him go. To that end Fuad incited the Azhar against the Wafd, and Zaghlul heard Azhar students shout "La zaim illa al-Malik," "No leader save the King," after their constant cry had been "La zaim illa Saad," "No leader save Saad."[16] To make matters worse, the King, without consulting his government, appointed Hasan Nashat, Egypt's *bête noire,* to the position of sous-chef de cabinet and bestowed upon him the highest decoration in the land, the Grand Cordon of the Nile, in order to grant him precedence in protocol over the rest of the government. When Zaghlul was confronted with the two problems, especially that of a refractory Azhar, and knew full well the prime mover who had roused them, he again tendered his resignation to the King on November 12, 1924. Meanwhile a public uproar developed, as was expected, and the cry *"Saad aw al-thawra,"* "Saad or revolution," assailed the King's ears while Saad was still closeted with him. The members of the Upper and Lower Houses of Parliament sent delegations to the King pointedly expressing their faith in the cabinet, and the King was forced to back down and ask Zaghlul to withdraw his resignation. Zaghlul accepted but only after he extracted from the King the understanding that in the future all appointments to the royal household and all decorations be countersigned by the cabinet, that is, become subject to the approval of the executive.

Barely three days elapsed when a violent incident occurred which was to create a crisis of even greater proportions and bring down the cabinet. On November 19, 1924, the Sirdar or commander in chief of the Egyptian army, Sir Lee Stack, was assassinated. High Commissioner Allenby and the rest of British officialdom in Egypt blamed

15. al-Aqqad, *Saad Zaghlul,* p. 158.
16. al-Rafii, *Fi a⁽qab,* I, 181.

the incident on Zaghlul. Allenby believed that Zaghlul tacitly encouraged the mob and the acts of violence including assassination directed against the opposition which had been carried out over the last two years (and which had caused the murder of Ali Pasha Abd al-Raziq and Ismail Bey Zuhdi), even though Zaghlul was at that time in exile. His reaction was therefore brutal and extreme. Without waiting for approval from the Foreign Office, Allenby delivered an ultimatum to the Egyptian government which demanded an indemnity of £E500,000, and included two clauses that were designed in purely punitive vein; the first demanded the withdrawal of all Egyptian army units stationed in the Sudan to retaliate for the anti-British demonstrations in Khartoum; and the second informed the Egyptian government of an intention to increase the cultivation of land in the Sudan by 500,000 acres, to punish the Egyptians economically with the threat of a rival cotton crop in the Sudan.

Zaghlul was deeply shocked by the assassination of Stack. On being told the news he said "We are lost."[17] He believed that it spelled the end of his career, and rightly, for he was never again allowed to lead a government. Although he had encouraged and manipulated the mob he had never condoned assassination, and had not known that such a move was being planned. He signed the indemnity check forthwith but refused to accept the clauses concerning the Sudan which he recognized as insulting and vindictive. When British forces occupied the customs house in Alexandria, Zaghlul resigned. Ahmad Ziwar was appointed premier by the King and accepted all the terms of the ultimatum. Parliament was dissolved a month later after having sat in session for a total of nine months.

Allenby's severe terms were deliberately designed to crush Zaghlul once and for all, but they were strongly disapproved by the Foreign Office who regarded them as childish and unbecoming. They asked Allenby whether the going rate for the assassination of a general was now £E500,000, in reference to a recent incident when the same amount had been extracted from the Greek government by the Italians for the death of General Tellini.[18] To mark that disapproval, an announcement was made that Nevile Henderson was to be minister plenipotentiary in Cairo "while employed at the Residency."[19] Allenby

17. Zaghlul Memoirs, 49:2826.
18. Grafftey-Smith, *Bright Levant*, p. 88.
19. Ibid., p. 89.

assumed this implied a lack of confidence in him and resigned as high commissioner. He was succeeded by Sir George Lloyd (who became Lord Lloyd).

The Wafdist government had not acted in an entirely unproductive manner during its brief stay in office. It had modified the electoral law from a two-stage process to one of direct suffrage, which was admittedly a move in their favor, but it had also created a General Accounting Office, Diwan al-Muhasaba, and to give Egyptian bank notes greater autonomy from the British currency, had altered the means by which they were issued. Lastly they had refused to pay the expenses of the British army of occupation which the Egyptian government had been forced to pay since 1882.[20] The most substantial action it had taken was to offer to sell the Domains lands, a move that was only to add to the ranks of large landowners, for the lands were parceled off in such large tracts that no small farmer could afford them and they were therefore bought up by the affluent people.

When those who were implicated in the Stack assassination were brought to trial several months later, the chief planner turned out to be an embittered former Wafdist lawyer, Shafiq Mansur. Zaghlul had always distrusted Mansur and had dashed his hopes for the post of director General of Public Security. Mansur had created a secret society which planned to murder prominent persons in a wave of terrorism that was supposed to advance Egypt's national demands, but which in fact weakened the Wafd position — perhaps Mansur's ulterior motive in setting up the organization. Two important figures in the Wafd were implicated in the plot: Ahmad Mahir, Minister of Education, and Mahmud Fahmi al-Nuqrashi, Under-Secretary of State for the Interior.[21] Their guilt was never established. Mahir was cleared, and, although Nuqrashi was released for insufficient evidence, there was little doubt in British minds that he was implicated, as we shall see later.

Ahmad Ziwar, the new premier, who was affiliated with no party, had the singular distinction of being the fattest man in government. He was a jolly, fun-loving man whom nobody took very seriously. He was disrespectful to everybody, a trait that endeared him to some, but he antagonized the more serious of his colleagues by his insouciance.

20. Rafii, Fi aʿqab, I, 157.
21. Lajin (Saad Zaghlul, pp. 430-431) claims that Hasan Nashat had incited Mansur to commit the assassination in order to embarrass the Wafd government.

His language was extremely immoderate; he referred to the King as "Le Maquereau d'Abdin" and to the King's men as "I Carabinieri."[22] Of an indolent nature in keeping with his girth, he was nonetheless, when he set his mind to the task, an astute politician as befits a student of the Jesuits. He realized that any election would return a Wafd majority to power and immediately laid plans to inflict a "crushing defeat on Zaghlulism, if Egypt is to hope for decent administration, good order and friendly relations with us [the British]."[23] As Allenby reported to London, Ziwar had been chosen by the King with the intention of carrying on "open war" against the Wafd and this he planned to do with the cooperation of the Liberal Constitutional party, who would relish such a plan.

The Liberal Constitutionalists had suffered much at the hands of the Wafd and through what they considered to be the tyranny of parliament under Zaghlul.[24] Some of the Ahrar had misgivings at joining a cabinet that was obviously going to cave in to British pressure. Tharwat refused to join the cabinet, but his friend Ismail Sidqi had no such scruples and accepted the portfolio of Minister of the Interior. The two-stage electoral process was reinstated and a new party created at the King's instigation, the Ittihad, Union party, headed by a King's man, Yahia Pasha Ibrahim, in January 1925. While the elections were still running, on March 10, 1925 Saad made the following comments in his diary, comments that show how lucid his analysis of general problems was, but also reveal his monumental ego.

> If the Wafd wins the elections that is a sign of the strength of the nation and of her resoluteness . . . but there are many things which prevent the Wafd from fully gaining control. In the first place the Wafd needs thinking minds, working hands, and faithful hearts, all united in their task. In the second place we need to see that the palace problem is settled and that he [King] reigns but does not rule. In the third place we need to deal with the British so that they stop their opposition and that is very difficult, seeing what they have seen from us these days. Thirdly [sic] we need to settle our

22. Profile of Egyptian personalities drawn up by Robert Furness, Oriental Secretary, May 25, 1927, F.O. 371/12388.
23. Allenby to Curzon, Dec. 5, 1924, 371/10022.
24. Haikal, *Mudhakkirat*, I, 214.

internal affairs, for the administration thinks only of salaries,
are lazy, apathetic and inclined to corruption.[25]

For all these reasons Saad envisaged a change in the bureaucracy
as the only solution, but saw at the same time the impossibility of such
a suggestion, because, he continues, the country does not contain a
sufficient number of capable men. Reforming the morals of those in
charge is very difficult. It might be better, he concludes, if the Wafd
did not get a majority of votes but enough votes for it to enter into a
coalition cabinet as the junior partner. "The cabinet needs a great
man to lead it," he muses. "How can the Wafd accept a coalition
cabinet whose leader is not a Wafdist? . . . Who is to lead? As for me
I refuse and will refuse, but who is there beside me as prime minister?
It is a dilemma."[26]

Saad's soliloquy lays bare the man's political soul. He despised his
colleagues and the opposition equally, albeit for different reasons.
Basically Saad was a believer in absolute rule—his rule—and the
dilemma was how to put that into effect, and not who was there to
lead the country. How Saad was to become premier in spite of the
opposition from palace and residency was the real problem he faced.

During the elections provincial authorities were told to see to it that
government-sponsored candidates won the elections. Governors were
ordered to coerce umdas and umdas to coerce fallahin into voting
accordingly. In spite of all efforts to the contrary, and because most
of the umdas were Wafd appointees, the Wafd won out with 116 seats
out of 214, and Zaghlul was elected Speaker of the House over his
opponent Tharwat. The Residency sent the King an ultimatum demanding that parliament be dissolved.[27] Ziwar tendered his resignation, but the King begged him to reconsider and Ziwar acquiesced. He
agreed to dissolve parliament and to rule solely with the King's
support, by decree. The new cabinet was formed of Ittihadists, Independents, and the Ahrar; it encouraged absolutism at the expense of

25. Zaghlul Memoirs, 47:2792.

26. Ibid.; also Lajin, Saad Zaghlul, p. 446.

27. Abd al-Aziz Fahmi, Hadhihi Hayati (Cairo, 1952), p. 151. Zaghlul claims that
Abd al-Malik Hamza, editor of al-Balagh, told him that he had been chosen president
of the House by a secret agreement between Ibrashi, the King's man, and the Wafdists
but Nashat had found out and told Allenby who ordered the King to prorogue the
House, much to the King's anger. Zaghlul did not entirely believe the story but all the
same he decided to sign the court register on the King's anniversary (Zaghlul Memoirs,
50:2862).

constitutional authority, so that the constitution was undermined by
the very people who had sworn to nurture and protect it, including
Fahmi, the "Father of the Constitution." Rule by decree meant the
absolute reliance of the cabinet on the Palace or on the Residency for
survival. But the machinations of the King and his man, Hasan
Nashat, were soon to reveal the stresses in the cabinet and destroy that
coalition of parties in favor of a wholly palace-dominated cabinet.

As the King's evil genius, or willing tool, Hasan Nashat used his
position to peddle titles and decorations, ostensibly in order to finance
the new Ittihad party.[28] Worse still, he arrogated to himself the right
to attend cabinet sessions, to disagree with ministers, and even to veto
their decisions if they ran counter to what he alleged were the King's
wishes.[29] The members of the cabinet knew that Nashat was acting
unconstitutionally, for no provision allowed the sous-chef du cabinet
royal to attend the Council of Ministers, but since the whole cabinet
was in session extralegally, having suspended constitutional rule, they
had to swallow their pride and rage and put up with Nashat's bullying
as the price for royal support.

During the summer months, when Ziwar was away on one of his
cures in Vichy, Nashat decided the time had come to oust the Ahrar
ministers from the cabinet and make it totally Ittihadist, thus more
malleable. He therefore fomented an intrigue aimed at the Ahrar and
centering on a recently published controversial book by Shaikh Ali
Abd-al-Raziq. The family of the shaikh were strong Ahrar leaders and
therefore presented the perfect target to use against the party. The
book in question, *al-Islam wa usul al-Hukm*, Islam and the Funda-
mentals of Government, argued that since Muhammad had come as a
prophet and not as a statesman the caliphate was not essential to
Islam and could be dispensed with. Muslim rulers were thus mere
heads of state and not caliphs bearing any religious connotation in
their office. The ulama of al-Azhar were disturbed by these allegations,
and the King, who had his eye on the caliphate, and who had
befriended the Azhar to that end, egged them on.[30] The Supreme
Council of al-Azhar announced its determination to revoke the Shaikh's

28. Grafftey-Smith, *Bright Levant*, p. 100.

29. St. Antony's Papers, Stanley Parker Memorandum regarding Lord Lloyd in
Egypt. Parker was the London *Times* correspondent in Egypt and this information was
given him by Ali Bey Ismail at the request of Ziwar Pasha who wished Parker to send
a telegram to *The Times* explaining that the cabinet crisis was attributable to Nashat's
behavior.

30. Rafii, *Fi-a‘qab*, p. 227.

university degree and to divest him of his functions as qadi in the sharia courts.

The minister of justice, Abd al-Aziz Pasha Fahmi, who was then also president of the Ahrar party, was expected to sign the decrees revoking Abd al-Raziq's degree and dismissing him from his functions. He read the book carefully and found in it nothing of an offensive nature to Islam, as the ulama had alleged. Moreover he regarded the action of the ulama as illegal, for the Supreme Council of al-Azhar had no authority to carry out either decision, and refused to sanction it. The Palace, angry at Fahmi for having opposed a deal whereby the King offered to exchange a piece of property he owned, Zaafaran, for another piece of property owned by the government, Taftish Bashbish, which was worth four times as much,[31] urged Fahmi's removal from office. Acting Prime Minister Yahia Ibrahim, the palace man in the cabinet, requested Fahmi's resignation. Fahmi, a peppery man, refused as a matter of principle. Ibrahim then transferred his functions to the Minister of Awqaf "pending the appointment of a Minister of Justice." The other two Liberal Constitutionalists in the cabinet, Tawfiq Doss and Muhammad Ali Alluba, resigned from the ministry.

The cavalier dismissal of a cabinet minister who was also leader of the major coalition party was a clear expression of the palace decision to rule through a completely Ittihadist ministry, a tool in the hands of the palace. Worse was to follow.

The new cabinet passed a new, strong Law of Associations which made all assemblies and political party meetings subject to government approval. The new law was rapidly put to use to muzzle the opposition. On November 13 the Wafd called a meeting of its members in their headquarters, the Saadist Club, but the government prohibited the meeting and surrounded the club by a police force. When the members insisted on entering their club premises a scuffle ensued on the pavement between Wafdist senators and members of parliament and the police. Two days later Zaghlul delivered a speech in which he demanded that parliament meet on its own initiative on November 21 as was stipulated in the constitution, even though not summoned by the King.[32] This time the Ahrar sided with the Wafd and approved his proposal. The government countered by issuing a prohibition against the proposed assembly and a warning that the police would

31. Ibid., p. 228.
32. Historical Summary of Events in Egypt 1925-26, March, 1927, F.O. 371/12344.

prevent such a meeting by force of arms if necessary. The government also issued a warning to the students to refrain from any political activity. The houses of parliament were cordoned off by troops and a police guard placed outside Zaghlul's house to insure that no popular manifestations reached his house and that no meetings took place there.

On November 21, 1925, at the Continental Hotel 134 deputies and 50 senators gathered. They declared themselves a parliament in session. Zaghlul was elected president of the Lower House, and the members took an oath to defend the constitution. Protesting the unconstitutional behavior of the Ziwar cabinet they passed a vote of nonconfidence in it. For the first time adversity and a common danger had made all the political parties, Wafd, Ahrar, and even Hizb al-Watani, bury their animosities and political differences and unite in a joint endeavor to save parliamentary life from extinction and to oppose absolute rule. It was one of the many ironies of Egyptian political life that those who had been the most violent opponents of the constitution, the Wafd, had now become its most ardent supporters. The students went on strike in defiance of government orders.

Lord Lloyd, the new high commissioner in Egypt, was then preoccupied with the negotiations concerning the oasis of Jaghbub in the Libyan Desert. The Italians, who were in occupation of Libya, and the Egyptians both claimed the oasis as part of their territory. Jaghbub, which had been founded by the Grand Sanusi, was a sufi haven and therefore revered by all Muslims. The negotiations were of a delicate nature, and the public disturbances going on in Egypt were threatening to disrupt the negotiations. Lloyd was anxious to bring the talks to a rapid end for fear that the Italians would unilaterally annex the oasis, which "would have involved us [Great Britain] in a quarrel with a friendly power,"[33] on Egypt's behalf. Lloyd therefore paid a visit to the King and warned him that he personally would be held responsible if the negotiations failed. The King fully appreciated the nature of the warning and immediately issued orders to the cabinet to desist. The cabinet was then reshuffled. The heavy-handed Minister of the Interior, Hilmi Issa, was replaced by the more subtle Ismail Sidqi who could keep firmer control on events. A few days later the negotiations were concluded and an agreement signed between Egypt and Italy by which Jaghbub was ceded to the Libyan authorities. The three opposition parties were outraged at the agreement which delivered a sufi

33. Lord Lloyd, *Egypt Since Cromer* (London, 1934), II, 150.

center into the hands of the Italians, and in a joint manifesto they condemned the deal.

With Jaghbub out of the way Lloyd was now free to turn his attention to internal affairs. He knew that Hasan Nashat was a source of friction and would have to go, for his open interference in affairs of state was fast becoming scandalous. Lloyd put pressure on Fuad to dismiss his favorite. Fuad demurred at first and then, much against his will, agreed to dismiss his henchman who was promptly gazetted minister plenipotentiary to Madrid as the price of his ouster.

Lloyd at first believed that the internal turmoil could be calmed if the Ahrar were wooed away from the Wafd and induced to cooperate with the Ziwar cabinet, but that proved impossible. New elections would have been another possible solution, but that was ruined as an alternative when the Ziwar cabinet passed a new electoral law on December 8, 1925, which stipulated financial requirements for both electors and candidates. It was obviously aimed at disenfranchising the mass of Wafd supporters, the fallahin, who were destitute. The opposition declared the law unconstitutional and announced a joint decision to boycott the elections. They also gave open encouragement to the umdas to boycott the elections and thus to paralyze the whole electoral process which was largely dependent on their authority. Thirty-six umdas who supported the boycott were brought to trial by the government, twenty-seven among them were discharged, and the rest, who had resigned office, were fined.

On February 8, 1926 a tea party given at the Saadist Club was attended by seventy-two Ahrar, Wafdist and independent senators who passed a number of resolutions warning the government against the use of an illegal electoral law in defiance of the terms of the constitution. Elections, they said, should be carried out in accordance with the law. They argued for the necessity of restoring constitutional government by convening the last parliament that had been elected according to the "will of the Nation." Ziwar's cabinet inquired to which of the three electoral laws did the senators refer? They replied, the law of 1924 which had established direct suffrage.

Lloyd, fully aware of the general animosity toward the Ziwar cabinet which had swept Egypt, advised Ziwar to suspend the new electoral law and to announce forthcoming elections held under the terms of the electoral law of 1924.

A Wafd victory at the polls in May 1926 was regarded as a certainty. The Wafd returned 144 seats, Liberal Constitutionalists, 28, Watan, 5, Ittihad, 7, and Independents, 17. The major problem facing both

LIBERTY AND LICENCE.

Britannia (*to Young Egypt*). "I GAVE YOU PLENTY OF ROPE, BUT IF YOU'RE GOING TO USE SOME OF IT TO BIND THE HANDS OF JUSTICE I SHALL HAVE TO TAKE IT BACK."

[The British President of the Cairo Assize Court has resigned as a protest against the acquittal by that tribunal of a number of Egyptians implicated in political murders and other crimes.]

Source: *Punch,* 170 (June 9, 1926), 607.

the Residency and the Palace was how to keep Zaghlul from returning to power as prime minister. Like Allenby, Lloyd chose to blame Zaghlul for all the disturbances in Egypt, but unlike Allenby who ignored Zaghlul out of power but treated him honorably in power,[34] Lloyd was convinced that Zaghlul was inextricably wedded to a policy inimical to British interests, and so did his best to keep him from returning to power as prime minister.

Zaghlul, who knew that he could not become premier against British wishes and because he was sick at the time, decided that a coalition cabinet headed by Adli Yakan would be the best plan to follow, and he promised Adli cooperation and a free hand. In the interim, the murder trial of the Sirdar came to an end. Mahir and Nuqrashi were acquitted, but the British Judge Kershaw resigned in protest at the verdict acquitting Nuqrashi and dubbed it a grave miscarriage of justice.[35]. The Residency accepted Kershaw's version and remained unconvinced of the innocence of both men, but they could do little save to oppose the political advancement of the men in question, not reverse the acquittal. Both men, who had run successfully for parliament, duly took their seats. Many years later, in the 1940s, both were to become premiers and were to die by assassins' bullets within a few years of each other. The tragedies set tongues wagging that he who lives by violence dies by violence, for there were also many Egyptians who were not convinced of the innocence of both men.

Gradually Saad began to change his mind. His change of heart is recorded in his memoirs. On May 7th Adli visited Saad and Saad promised him his support. After Adli left Saad mused over his reluctance to become premier and over allowing his erstwhile opponents to step into office. Would it not be wiser to take on the burden, "but I fear ill health."[36] Later in the month, Gerald Delaney, Reuter's correspondent, visited Zaghlul and hinted that Lord Lloyd, who had never called on Saad or even met him, wanted a written reassurance from Saad that he would not become premier, which made Zaghlul very angry. Delaney also pointed out the fact of the King's opposition. Zaghlul snapped back "If the King does not respect the constitution then we'll depose him." Delaney then arranged for a meeting at Saad's

34. St. Antony's Papers, letter from Lord Allenby to Sir William Hayter, dated The Residency, Cairo, May 1924.

35. Lloyd, *Egypt Since Cromer,* II, 166.

36. Zaghlul Memoirs, 52:2976 ff.; 2996.

house between him and Lord Lloyd. Saad was beginning to feel physically healthier and under the influence of the acquittal and the prodding of the extremist Wafdists — Nahhas, Makram, and Nuqrashi — he decided to accept the premiership.

He spent a sleepless night wondering what he was going to tell Lloyd and Adli about his change of heart and decided to say that the Wafd members objected to Adli as premier because he did not lead the majority and so his choice would be unconstitutional.

The meeting between Zaghlul and Lloyd took place on May 30th and Zaghlul records the conversation in detail as did Lloyd and Delaney, who was present, although Lloyd's version is different from that of the other two men. Lloyd (whom Zaghlul wrongly and continuously refers to as Lloyd George) told Zaghlul that British public opinion would not stand for having him as premier. Zaghlul said his Wafdist colleagues would not stand for Adli as premier, but were he, Saad, to become premier then he would take both Adli and Tharwat into his cabinet. Lloyd expressed his disbelief and Zaghlul said, "Vous pouvez vous renseigner." Lloyd took offense at that sentence and said, "How dare you talk to me in that fashion! What if I told my government?" Zaghlul apologized and said that he did not mean to offend him; he simply wished him to find out from Adli the facts, and they parted on amicable terms, or so Zaghlul thought.[37] But he was wrong for Lloyd was bent on teaching him a lesson.

Lord Lloyd was a right-wing Tory imperialist who wanted to show the Egyptians who was master in Egypt. Fresh from India, where he had served as governor of Bombay, Lloyd was determined to interpret the four reserved points in the strictest sense.[38] Where Allenby on occasion had listened to the Egyptians, Lloyd had little patience with views other than his own and brooked no argument. At the slightest provocation, he was inclined to resort to strong-arm tactics and call out the gunboats. Sir Laurence Grafftey-Smith in his delightful book of reminiscences writes that when he was assistant Oriental secretary at the Residency Lloyd said: "When I see those jacarandas in bloom, I know it's time to send for a battleship."[39] He believed that the hot khamsin winds of spring unsettled the Egyptians and provoked them. But to investigate the cause of the provocation or to seek an amicable

37. Ibid., pp. 2992-2994; Barakat Memoirs (1925-26), 17:46 ff.; Lloyd, *Egypt Since Cromer*, II, 164 ff.; also F.O. 371/12344.

38. Memorandum written by Gerald Delaney, Reuter's correspondent in Egypt, St. Antony's Papers, Sept. 1970.

39. Grafftey-Smith, *Bright Levant*, p. 102.

solution was alien to Lloyd's nature, and he preferred a show of imperial force even though force no longer yielded any lasting returns.

Lloyd did call out a gunboat on that occasion and Saad became apprehensive. On June 2d he suggested to Muhammad Mahmud that either Mahmud or one of the other members of parliament request that he refuse the premiership. On the following day at an official tea party Makram Ubaid suggested that the *zaim* relinquish the burden of premiership to healthier shoulders and accept the leadership of the House.

At the time Zaghlul's alienation from power had seemed a judicious choice to Lloyd, but was it in fact?

In an account of a meeting which Lord Lloyd subsequently had with Delaney and which Lloyd forwarded to Secretary of State Sir Austen Chamberlain, Delaney expressed his belief that better results might have been achieved through friendlier relations between the Residency and Zaghlul. Zaghlul could be induced to work on terms of friendly cooperation with Lloyd. Because of Zaghlul's position in the country, Delaney believed it was impolitic to ignore the "strongest factor in Egyptian politics," however much they disapproved of his earlier record.[40] Delaney even doubted the wisdom of refusing to consider Zaghlul as prime minister for there was some advantage to dealing with him directly than to leave him as the power behind the scene where he could not be held responsible.

There was wisdom and perspicacity in Delaney's remarks, not only insofar as they pertained to Zaghlul's position but also vis-à-vis the healthy development of parliamentary life in Egypt. It is customary in constitutional governments that the leader of the majority be chosen to head the government, but the British authorities, by refusing to consider Zaghlul, had condoned if not encouraged the infraction of that basic tenet. Thus the King's disrespect for constitutional practice was allowed to develop into overblown proportions later on, for he now had a precedent sanctioned by Qasr al-Dubara to refer to in the future. Adli set another harmful precedent by discussing the members of the cabinet with Lloyd. In the past it had been common procedure for the Residency to interfere in the appointment of cabinet members, but with the advent of constitutional government that precedent had been broken. It was now reestablished by Adli who sought Lloyd's approval before announcing the members of his coalition cabinet of Wafd and Ahrar.

40. Delaney Memorandum, also account of a talk between Gerald Delaney and Lord Lloyd sent to Sir Austen Chamberlain, Sept. 7, 1926, F.O. 371/11584.

Adli had also sought Zaghlul's approval of his cabinet and had even presented him with the speech from the throne before its publication.[41] The appointed ministers were Tharwat for Foreign Affairs, Muhammad Mahmud for Communications, Zaki Abu-l Suud for Justice, Fathallah Barakat for Agriculture, Morcos Hanna for Finance, Najib al-Gharabli for Awqaf, Ahmad Khashaba for War, Uthman Muharram for Public Works, and Ali Shamsi for Education. A perfect entente seemed to animate both factions who just a year earlier had been sworn enemies. The only sour note came from Abd al-Aziz Fahmi whose aversion for Zaghlul had not abated and who had resigned the leadership of the Ahrar party on the eve of the entente in order to avoid any contact with Zaghlul, a position he pursued relentlessly to the end of his days. Fahmi's irascibility, however, was well known to his colleagues, who sooner or later fell into his bad books, so they ignored it.

For the first few months Adli's ministry went very smoothly. Zaghlul kept the parliament in line and was an excellent leader in the House. His methods for keeping order were effective albeit unorthodox; his ferociously barked *"uskut,"* "Be silent," which cut off speeches made by the long-winded bores with which every parliament is blessed, became a byword. He scolded the deputies whenever they failed to make an appearance, shooed them out of the corridors and into the chamber to vote, and acted as nanny, scold, and headmaster all in one. The deputies, many of whom were rural notables not yet familiar with parliamentary procedure, were taken aback by such abruptness, but all had a fervent desire to avoid a tongue lashing, and so were forced to take their parliamentary duties more seriously than they were inclined to do. Zaghlul was disappointed in the deputies. He expected them to behave like parliamentarians the minute they set foot in the building, and overlooked the fact that such procedures are not instinctive to mankind, but develop only with experience and over a long period of time. Zaghlul was disappoointed in his own followers the most. He told Fathallah that Nahhas was rash, stubborn, and rude, *mutassari*, *salib al-ra'y wa ghair muhadhab,* that Wissa was too easygoing, and that he could find none amongst them who was worthy of leading an important ministry, that they surfaced only when there was booty to split, *tataqasam al-ghana'im,* and that Adli and Tharwat were much more capable men, *afka'.*[42]

41. Barakat Memoirs (1926), 5:54.
42. Ibid., (1925-1926), 17:21.

King Fuad did not scruple to hid his contempt for parliament and its members, especially when they opposed a number of his financial plans, like the Zaafaran deal, or the financing of his new Royal Entomological Society, and above all the budget for the religious institutions. The government was well aware that much of the King's influence over the religious institutions stemmed from his control over their purse strings, and that he was inciting them against the government with promises of material *bien être*. Fuad called the deputies a "bunch of cowardly slaves."[43] The choice of epithet clearly revealed how steeped he was in the antiquated notions of a nineteenth-century autocrat concerning the rights of an absolute ruler, and how little understanding he had for the role of a twentieth-century constitutional monarch in which his people had cast him. He told Acting High Commissioner Nevile Henderson that should Adli's government fall he would like Morcos Hanna to become premier. His reasons were simple and unvarnished. Hanna was more cowardly and as a Copt would be more disliked by the people, therefore completely malleable.[44] But when Adli's government showed no signs of collapsing Fuad tried to goad it and Zaghlul into an indiscretion that would topple the ministry. Royalist newspapers like *al-Ittihad* launched provocative attacks on the cabinet and the parliament.[45] These attacks were calculated to create unease in a coalition cabinet and to nurture suspicion mutually between the two factions.

The first near crisis occurred in September 1926 over the publication of another book, this time Taha Husain's work *Fi-l shiᶜr al-Jahili,* "Pre-Islamic Poetry." Husain questioned the validity of certain tenets concerning pre-Islamic poetry which had been accepted unquestioningly and which had been used in interpreting the Quran. Husain's doubts therefore were viewed as an attack on religious beliefs and on their authenticity, and roused the ulama to even greater furore than Ali Abd al-Raziq's book had done. There was some justification in their reaction for Husain was opening a Pandora's box of religious doubts by questioning the validity of the Quran. A resolution was therefore passed in parliament which stated that the book should be confiscated on the grounds that it was subversive to religion, and that Husain's post as university lecturer should be suppressed and he himself prosecuted. Adli, who on several other occasions had had cause to

43. Nevile Henderson, Acting High Commissioner, to Sir Austen Chamberlain, Sept. 8, 1926, F.O. 371/11584.
44. Ibid.
45. Lloyd, *Egypt Since Cromer,* II, 180; also Barakat Memoirs (1926-27), 6:15.

complain of the interference of deputies in matters of government, regarded the resolution as a more obvious act of interference with the executive by the legislature. The interference of the deputies in the administration had created friction on several other occasions, for the deputies espoused the cause of their constituents so wholeheartedly that regardless of the merits of a case, they took it upon themselves to issue orders to the executive. Some *mudirs,* the provincial governors who bore the brunt of the meddling by the deputies, laid the blame for the increase in crime on their interference and the support they gave to their "men."[46]

Adli firmly announced that if the resolution was passed he would consider it a vote of nonconfidence, and obviously the government would fall. Zaghlul, enraged by the attacks which had redoubled in the press and which implied that he was afraid of a dissolution of parliament, accused Adli of challenging the rights of parliament. Several members of both parties expended a great deal of effort to cool the rage of the two leaders and the resolution was finally withdrawn. The government could chalk up a victory, but not for long.

Adli was uneasy. He suspected that the Palace was intent on overthrowing his cabinet and that the Residency would cooperate with the King and create an incident at an opportune moment. He would have liked to resign but feared that that would once again place the country in the critical position of being ruled by a cabinet that had no popular backing.[47]

Adli had gauged correctly the Residency's growing displeasure with his cabinet. Ahmad Mahir had been elected president of the Comptabilité Committée in parliament and Nuqrashi had been elected secretary of the Education Committee. Lord Lloyd received the election of these two men, whom he regarded as murderers even though the court had acquitted them, as a "dangerous incident," and an indication that Wafdist extremists were gaining influence over Zaghlul.[48] British officials in Egyptian service were to be terminated in 1927. Despite Egyptian decrees, Lloyd believed that British officials should continue to serve the Egyptian government and that Egypt should not hire non-British officials in advisory positions. If the government refused to obey, then he believed that an ultimatum should be delivered.[49] Lloyd

46. Barakat Memoirs (1927), 8:48-49; also Historical Summary of Events in Egypt 1925-26, F.O. 371/12344, and Lloyd, *Egypt Since Cromer,* II, 183.
47. Barakat Memoirs (1926-1927), 6:13 and passim.
48. Lloyd, *Egypt Since Cromer,* II, 191.
49. Ibid., p. 185.

persisted in acting as though he were still the governor of a subject province completely overlooking the fact that Egypt was now an "independent" country. His arrogant attitude and his high-handed tactics made any discussion of the issues impossible. Two further matters were to add to the cabinet's problems and bring matters to the danger level.

The first concerned a project for an umda's law and the second concerned the army. Minister of War Khashaba had a project to increase the size of the army. Adli refused to consider the project and suggested that he take it up with the King. The King likewise refused to consider the project. An acrimonious dispute between Adli and several Wafdists, notably Makram Ubaid and Nuqrashi, erupted; the latter insisted that they would see to it that Wafdist-sponsored projects were passed in parliament and Adli announced that in that event he would resign. On learning of the Khashaba project Lloyd told Ali al-Shamsi that Khashaba was "bête," stupid, and accused the entire Egyptian nation of ignorance,[50] language that was certainly less than diplomatic. The whole cabinet bridled at Lloyd's intemperate language, which Shamsi had hastened to communicate to his colleagues, and several among them planned to resign. In a rare display of anger, Tharwat, who was invariably calm and courteous even in the face of provocation, lost his temper during a cabinet meeting and accused Lloyd of mendacity and of being mad, especially on the subject of British advisors in Egyptian service.[51]

The second matter concerned a Wafd-sponsored project for a law whereby umdas would be subject to direct election and not to government appointment. They claimed that the passage of such a law would be a step toward local self-government. But since all those who were enfranchised for a parliamentary election could vote for the umdas, that is, the fallahin, the law would lead to a Wafd hold on the rural areas which was stronger than ever. Once the umdas had been elected through the Wafd efforts, they would see to it that the village consistently voted Wafd in any election. The fact that villagers, unless otherwise pressured, were always inclined to vote Wafd, seemed to have been paramount in the minds of the opponents of the law. They well knew that unless the umdas remained government nominees and therefore subject to manipulation and pressure by the Ministry for the Interior, no party save the Wafd would ever come to power.

50. Barakat Memoirs (1927) 7:25, 34; for Lloyd's account of the incident, April 22, 1927, F.O. 371/12355.
51. Barakat Memoirs (1927) 7:25; also (1927) 9:26.

The extremist members of the Wafd believed that prevalent conditions were favorable for precipitating a crisis. They calculated that the British government, which was facing political difficulties on the home front and was also beset by unrest in China, would not relish a crisis in Egypt just at that time and would therefore bow to Wafd demands in order to avoid a confrontation. They thus planned to heckle Adli in parliament to force his resignation. In Nahhas's words, they expected Adli "to go to the Devil," *"yastaqil fi dahiya."*[52] Adli was fully aware of how strongly the Wafd would support the bill; he was firmly set against its passage and threatened to resign if it were to pass. Moderate Wafdists like Barakat and Shamsi were not at all happy with the way Makram, Nuqrashi, and Nahhas were forcing the pace; they hoped to persuade Adli of the value of a compromise and so save the cabinet, of which they were members.[53] Zaghlul, a victim of arteriosclerosis and just recovering from a bout with pneumonia, was physically very weak, short tempered, and easily tired. He was therefore particularly susceptible to hints of his weakness vis-à-vis Adli which Makram and Nahhas were skillfully pouring into his ears. He agreed to the plan to heckle Adli and turned a deaf ear to the moderates, an attitude that Barakat noted in his memoirs, having earlier commented that Zaghlul hated to hear anything that disagreed with his opinions.[54]

The following few weeks brought a change in attitude. The King was planning a trip to Britain; the Wafd immediately suspected that their monarch was plotting something with the British government at their expense and tried to come to an understanding with him before he sailed. Fathallah Barakat was the author of a rapprochement with the Palace and had taken the first step by sending the King a telegraph of good wishes for the month of Ramadan. Fuad was equally desirous for an understanding with the Wafd.[55] He wanted to leave a friendly press behind and to get some of his pet schemes approved in the budget. He feared that a change in the British cabinet, which looked imminent, might spell the return of a Labour cabinet that would befriend the Wafd and leave him out in the cold. For all these reasons the King graciously responded to Barakat's message with one of his own, signed "Fuad." Both the King and the Wafd suspected that Adli would like to resign because of the two projects concerning the army and the umdas, but the King thought that he could moderate the

52. Ibid., 8:54; also see Lloyd's account to London, April 22, 1927, F.O. 371/12355.
53. Barakat Memoirs (1927), 9:3 ff.
54. Ibid., (1926-27), 6:41.
55. Lord Lloyd to Sir Austen Chamberlain, April 22, 1927, F.O. 371/12355.

Wafd extremists and persuade them to defer a showdown. The Wafd, on the other hand, hoped that if the government fell the King would accept their proposition for another coalition cabinet, which would still keep parliament safe from dissolution and thus retain them in the seat of power.

The hardening of Wafd positions, the constant carping of Wafd deputies in parliament, and their interference in the administration, added to Lord Lloyd's intransigence and Palace intrigues, all encouraged Adli to look for a good reason to resign. The opportunity came in April 1927. During a parliamentary session a motion was made by one of the deputies that the government be tendered a vote of thanks for the financial assistance it had given the Misr Bank whereupon a Wafdist deputy embarked on a long harangue the gist of which was that the government had done nothing to deserve a vote of thanks. The motion was rejected. It gave Adli the excuse he was seeking—he immediately interpreted the vote as an implication of nonconfidence in his cabinet and promptly resigned.[56]

The Wafdists were taken aback at his sudden resignation even though they had been trying to maneuver just such an event for a month. They became even more disturbed when the King blandly suggested that a caretaker government be formed. They were now hoist with their own petard. The younger Wafdists, having incited Zaghlul to say that Adli could resign with his blessings, *maʿa alf salama*,[57] now faced an angry Zaghlul, who recovered his senses and his health and suspected Fuad of having something up his sleeve. Barakat, who prudently refrained from saying "I told you so," was accused by Zaghlul of having pushed him into a mess, unjustifiably, since the pushers had been Nahhas and the others. Barakat suggested that Tharwat be chosen to replace Adli.[58] Tharwat accepted on the condition that the deputies put an end to their heckling and provocative interpellations, and that the umda and army projects be suspended.

King Fuad warned Lord Lloyd that Tharwat would "filch concessions" from the British government "in spite of themselves" and that from a British point of view he would be a dangerous choice because, in his opinion, Tharwat had "political courage born of an intense natural cowardice."[59] However, the King added, Tharwat was not likely to last for long because he was universally detested and especially by Zaghlul who blamed him as the author of the 1922 Declaration.

56. Barakat Memoirs (1927), 9:7.   57. Ibid., p. 3.
58. Ibid., p. 19.   59. April 22, 1927, F.O. 371/12355.

Fuad finally brought the conversation around to his main point which was that the ministerial crisis showed evidence of the growing discontent of the Egyptians with the parliamentary system. Parliament, he said, was like bleating sheep who blindly follow their leader nowhere. The leaders were corrupt, the followers ignorant, the opposition incompetent, and the whole spelled a policy of futility. He was sure, he added, that the British government would soon realize that the Egyptian constitution was a "dishonest farce."[60] Lloyd for once held his peace and declined to comment.

Having condoned treachery in his ranks toward Adli, Zaghlul had to pay the price of being saddled with Tharwat whom he detested even more than Adli. In 1922 Zaghlul vowed never to have any dealings with Tharwat for the part he had played in sending Zaghlul into exile and for stage-managing the 1922 Declaration. But when Tharwat accepted a post in Adli's cabinet he insisted that the Ahrar ministers act in conjunction with Zaghlul, saying that the Ahrar had formed a pact, *mu^cahada*, with Zaghlul.[61] Together with the changing political circumstances and Tharwat's attitude toward him, Zaghlul was forced to treat Tharwat more honorably than he had treated Adli, and was even placed in the position of having to entreat Tharwat to accept the post of premier.

A major crisis was to greet Tharwat just weeks after he had formed his new cabinet in April 1927. The incident was triggered during a parliamentary discussion of the budget. Minister of War Khashaba Pasha (called "stupid" by Lloyd) had a parliamentary subcommittee draw up a report on ways to be considered for improving the army. The report suggested among other items that the size of the army be increased, that an air force be formed, that the position of Sirdar, which had remained vacant for the three years since Sir Lee Stack's death, be annulled, and that the post of inspector general, at present occupied by another Englishman, Spinx Pasha, not be an ad hoc member of the Army Council. Lord Lloyd got wind of the report and before it could be presented to parliament he precipitated a crisis, which he then proceeded to mishandle in true imperialist fashion.

Lord Lloyd was continually exercised over what he believed to be a "steady erosion" of Britain's position in Egypt. Especially was this so in the army where he saw Egyptians displacing British influence in local appointments. According to Lloyd the process of Egyptianization was

60. Meeting between the King and Lord Lloyd, April 26, 1927, F.O. 371/12355.
61. Barakat Memoirs (1927), 7:30; also (1928), 13:62.

radicalizing the army. "The objective of the extremists was now becoming more clear . . . they desired an anti-dynastic revolution, and they were screening this ultimate purpose behind the popular demand for complete independence."[62] The process of thought that had led Lloyd to his conclusion was not clear; what was perfectly clear was that Lloyd wanted to nudge the Foreign Office into action. It had long been an axiom of British imperial policy in Egypt, set by Lord Cromer, to disregard any nationalist manifestation as long as a British army of occupation was present on Egyptian territory. If British influence were to wane, then the Egyptian army might be induced to join the ranks of the national lists and turn a public manifestation into something much more serious.

When Khashaba brought forth his proposal Lloyd concluded that the Egyptians under Wafd incitement "would not hesitate to launch these combined forces in assault against the Monarchy."[63] The policy he suggested to London was consequently based on the urgency for compelling the Egyptians to give up their project and for sending a man-of-war to threaten them. He wrote that Zaghlul intended to "use the Egyptian army question as a pretext for hostile outburst against England."[64]

Contrary to Lloyd's allegations, Gerald Delaney, the Reuter's correspondent in Egypt, said that he had persuaded Zaghlul to agree to a British military mission which would take in hand the training of the Egyptian army, provided that the mission was led by a British general of some standing, which would thus solve the army issue. Delaney communicated the whole conversation to Lloyd (Lloyd never conversed with Zaghlul) and assumed that the matter had been amicably settled. Much to his dismay he subsequently learned that Lloyd had made no mention of Zaghlul's suggestion to the Foreign Office.[65] Even over Foreign Office directives to Lloyd that he not precipitate a crisis, that he collaborate, Lloyd persisted in heavy-handed efforts at compulsion, rather than striving at a mutual agreement.

Lloyd was sponsored by Winston Churchill and therefore felt secure enough to act any way he pleased. Austin Chamberlain, the foreign secretary, did not wish to create difficulties with Lloyd because he feared Churchill would side with his friend and bring down the

62. Lloyd, *Egypt Since Cromer*, II, 200 ff.
63. Ibid., p. 202.
64. Lloyd to London, May 20, 1927, F.O. 371/12355.
65. St. Antony's Papers, Delaney Memorandum.

cabinet. When Lloyd requested a gunboat in May 1927 for the second time in as many years, Chamberlain allowed him to have his way and considered the issue not important enough to precipitate a crisis within the British cabinet.[66] Once again Egyptian affairs took second place to British interests.

Throughout that period Tharwat protested that matters dealing with the Egyptian army were internal in nature and did not constitute one of the reserved points. Lloyd insisted that the army issue was a negation of the reserved points. Tharwat bowed to the inevitable and to Lloyd.

For the duration of the crisis over the army Zaghlul played fair with Tharwat and gave him constant support and loyal collaboration. Any complaints that Tharwat had were directed against the Wafd rank and file, not against their leader. Indeed, Tharwat came close to resigning in May when some Wafd deputies tried to pressure him in a matter concerning the umda of Dairut. Tharwat was outraged at the rank interference with the executive by the members of the legislature.[67] Many suspected that though the outrage was genuine his talk of resignation was motivated by his frustration over the army crisis and Lloyd's intransigence.

None of the Egyptian politicians had much respect for Lloyd. They accused him of ignoring the facts, of being untruthful—a trait that shocked them in an Englishman who was also the high commissioner. They said he was inconsistent—like a weathervane—that he constantly changed his mind and then denied whatever he had previously asserted. They considered that he meddled too frequently and unjustifiably in internal affairs.[68] Adli thought him rash and bent on pursuing a basically unsound policy. Even Tharwat lost his equanimity and used bitter terms when he talked about Lloyd.[69]

Lloyd's British colleagues said much the same thing about him: Delaney, that he was inclined to conceal from the Foreign Office "developments or trends conflicting with his own personal policy";[70] Grafftey-Smith, that he had had to invent a "weekly review of the Egyptian press" to make sure that important material that Lloyd was likely to keep back from the Foreign Office did reach London by this

66. Ibid.
67. Barakat Memoirs (1927), 9:53.
68. Ibid., p. 42.
69. Ibid., p. 26; also (1928), 12:24.
70. Delaney Memorandum, St. Antony's Papers.

devious means.[71] Lloyd was therefore held responsible for embittering the Egyptians toward England by his arrogance and his misplaced assumption of authority. He was trying to out-Cromer Cromer three decades too late when Egypt was in theory an independent sovereign state and no longer a veiled protectorate.

During the summer of 1927 King Fuad and Tharwat went on a state visit to England. During a talk with Tharwat, Chamberlain was so impressed by the other's common sense that he insisted that together they embark on Anglo-Egyptian negotiations, and a draft treaty was hurriedly drawn up. Lloyd, not consulted or even kept informed about the negotiations, later commented sourly, "To enmesh Sarwat Pasha at this juncture in the net of treaty negotiation was to render his political downfall inevitable."[72] But that was wisdom long after the act and savored of sour grapes at having been left in the dark during the proceedings. Had Zaghlul remained alive during the period of negotiations, there was a good chance that the treaty might have been signed. The treaty was, however, turned down by the Wafdist parliament. Unfortunately Zaghlul died on August 27, 1927, at the age of seventy. With his death an era of Egyptian political life came to an end.

Zaghlul was venerated by his countrymen and respected by his opposition, both British and Egyptian. His influence over Egyptian political life was unique and not always beneficial. He had encouraged ministerial autocracy, exemplified in his behavior when he came to power; he had continued to use a system of patronage and personal influence in government; he had perfected a system of violence in strikes and demonstrations as a weapon against the opposition and as a means of exerting pressure in the name of public opinion. He had surrounded himself by men of worthy talents but alienated the truly brilliant minds of the time. Zaghlul had sowed and nurtured the seeds of many of the political ills that beset political life for decades to come, for while he could dominate the scene through sheer force of personality and thus camouflage the flaws in the system, his successors who were lesser men in every way merely accentuated the defects of the system. Yet Zaghlul did much for Egypt. He had galvanized and united the nationalist movement until he became synonymous with it, and because of that everything else was forgiven him.

The British authorities in Egypt obviously saw Zaghlul from an

71. Grafftey-Smith, *Bright Levant*, p. 105.
72. Lloyd, *Egypt Since Cromer*, II, 230.

altogether different perspective. Oriental Secretary Robert Furness
described him as

> at bottom a demagogue, vain and jealous of all authority that
> does not emanate from himself, a bitter and relentless parti-
> san, confusing obstinacy with firmness and opportunism with
> foresight. He seems to be unable to construct. First and
> foremost he seeks the promotion of his own influence and
> popular applause. He is a past master of oratory spiced with
> invective and humour, and always sways Egyptians with his
> eloquence. To Adli Pasha and others of his early colleagues,
> he has at various times now forgotten behaved shamelessly . . .
> so rarely do outstanding personalities appear in this country,
> so skillfully does Zaghlul Pasha exploit the sympathies of his
> friends, so legendary is his demigod influence throughout the
> country; there is no doubt that his passing would unite all
> Egypt in real and heartfelt mourning. For he is a man to
> whom, for the sake of the cause which he inflamed, much
> has been forgiven, and the fact remains that with all his many
> faults he is today the only Egyptian apparent, with real
> personality and power. He is a highly typical Egyptian, which
> is perhaps the real reason why they like him so much. What
> are the adjectives? Vain, weak, tyrannical, capricious, un-
> trustworthy, sentimental, vindictive, malicious, sensible in
> flashes, quick in temper and long in resentment, not devoid
> of kindness and affection. He excels most of his compatriots
> in activity of mind—a narrow mind—perseverance and per-
> suasive eloquence of speech, and many of them in financial
> honesty.[73]

All who knew Zaghlul well realized that he was responsive to kind
words, even susceptible to flattery, but that he would invariably return
violence with violence. By treating Zaghlul with hauteur, Lord Lloyd
succeeded only in setting the politician against him. Had he succeeded
in befriending Zaghlul, they would certainly have achieved more
constructive rapport. While it is futile to speculate on what would
have happened had different personalities behaved differently, Egyptians wistfully wonder out loud what would have happened had Fuad
been less an autocrat and more inclined to reign as a constitutional

73. Lord Lloyd to Sir Austen Chamberlain quoting Furness, the Oriental Secretary,
May 23, 1927, F.O. 371/70371.

monarch, had Zaghlul been less tyrannical, and had the British government been less intransigent. Might not the Anglo-Egyptian treaty finally negotiated in 1936, or even a more favorable treaty, have been negotiated at a much earlier date? Might not Egyptian constitutional government have had time to develop strong roots?

Unfortunately for the Wafd, and consequently for Egypt, the choice of a successor to Zaghlul was a very poor one and revealed clearly the conflicting currents that dominated the Wafd. To many moderates the obvious choice of Zaghlul's successor was his nephew, Fathallah Barakat. Fathallah was a clever politician, adroit at handling people and at organizing the rural population, but he was not westernized and knew no foreign language, a handicap on the international level. The extremist Wafdists opposed his candidacy on the theory that Wafd leadership was not a hereditary fief to be passed down to Zaghlul's heirs. Their opposition was sustained by Madame Zaghlul who had little liking for Fathallah on purely personal grounds. Other candidates were Wasif Ghali—who really did not want the honor and would have been opposed on the basis of his religion which was not representative of the majority—and Mustafa al-Nahhas, secretary of the party, whose candidacy was pressed by the extremists who knew that he would be more malleable than the cautious, canny Barakat, and would allow himself to be guided by them. Moreover, Madame Zaghlul was much taken by Nahhas who flattered her and catered to her whims. Nahhas was therefore chosen to succeed Zaghlul as leader of the Wafd. Acting High Commissioner Nevile Henderson, commenting on the various candidates, wrote that Nahhas's candidacy could be "heavily discounted" because he was recognized as "mentally unbalanced."[74] Zaghlul himself had regarded Nahhas as too volatile, but Makram, Nuqrashi, and Mahir threw their weight behind him, and Nahhas then also became president of the lower chamber.

Tharwat was disconsolate over Zaghlul's death because he realized that the negotiations he had reached with England now had no chance of success. So that they could reap the full glory, Nahhas and his supporters would sanction only negotiations that came to fruition through their sole efforts. Their approach was entirely consistent with Zaghlul's early tactics, but Zaghlul had mellowed in his last years and might have accepted the terms negotiated by another politician had the terms been fair. Nahhas and his advisors were trying to make their

74. Henderson to London, Aug. 23, 1927, F.O. 371/12355. The same opinion was shared by Furness, May 23, 1927, F.O. 371/12388.

mark on Egyptian politics, and therefore would not allow any victory that was not attained through them.

The King, too, was in for a hard time from the Wafd. The new leadership was determined to prove to the monarch that a change of leader did not imply a change of party policy, and that no matter who the party leader was they were firmly committed to fight royal autocracy and make him respect the constitution.[75] The other parties, not to be outdone by Wafd vigor, showed a tendency to harden their positions. The coalition, which had worked successfully for the past year owing to Zaghlul's loyalty to Tharwat, was falling into shreds. The Wafd extremists egged Nahhas against Tharwat in parliament, hoping thereby to unseat the cabinet and install Nahhas in the seat of premier, or, if that was opposed by the Residency, to promote Muhammad Mahmud, then Minister of Finance and vice-president of the Liberal Constitutionalists, to the premiership. Many among the Wafd were convinced that Muhammad Mahmud was a Wafd sympathizer and some even considered choosing him to succeed Zaghlul as head of the Wafd party. Muhammad Mahmud would have been pleased to see Tharwat's cabinet fall because he assumed that he would then be chosen as premier of another coalition cabinet. The rest of the cabinet felt the conflicting crosscurrents. Fathallah Barakat and Ali al-Shamsi, who represented the moderate Wafd faction, resigned their positions after a quarrel with Nahhas. They later withdrew their resignations to save the cabinet from falling, realizing that if the cabinet did fall through Wafd machinations they would be accused of having fomented the intrigue.

The Liberal Constitutionalist party also showed a split in leadership. Many were suspicious of their vice-president's behavior and of his increasing friendliness toward the members of the Wafd at a time when the party organ, *al-Siyasa,* was attacking Nahhas, suspicious also of their leader Mahmud's opposition to Tharwat, who was supposed to be on his side. Some therefore busily searched for a president for the party, knowing that if they did succeed in nominating a president,

75. Nevile Henderson, Acting High Commissioner, reported to London, Oct. 31, 1927, F.O. 371/12355, on "growing determination on the part of politically conscious Egyptians that their King shall be a constitutional and not an autocratic monarch. These feelings which were only found amongst the Liberals are now openly shared by the popular Wafd party." While the statement is not entirely true—unless the Liberals he refers to are the former Umma party, for the Wafd from the beginning stood for constitutional rule—nonetheless, the statement does describe the feelings of all aware Egyptians.

Muhammad Mahmud would resign from the Liberal Constitutionalist party and very likely join the Wafd party.[76]

Tharwat did not know what to do and showed an ever increasing indecisiveness and tendency to do nothing, a personality defect that Zaghlul had commented upon before his death. In a conversation with Gerald Delaney, Zaghlul had criticized Tharwat for not providing the leadership expected of a prime minister in the Chamber of Deputies when it was most urgent. It was not forthcoming, and Tharwat showed his indecision and weakness to the Wafd, which only strengthened their resolve to be rid of him.[77]

The King found the opposition ripe for an intrigue. According to the terms of the constitution two-fifths of the Senate were to be nominated by the King. Under Zaghlul the government insisted that nominations were to be drawn up with their approval, and after a showdown the King had acquiesced. Now five seats were vacant, and the King refused to nominate anyone unless he could have total freedom to choose whomever he wished.

The Wafd cautiously sounded out King Fuad on his feelings about a cabinet headed by Nahhas, and Fuad signified his assent.[78] The King assumed that with the demise of Zaghlul he could easily control the Wafd. He was also convinced that any cabinet headed by Nahhas would inevitably produce chaos and would fall within a very short time, giving the King his chance to choose a cabinet to his own liking. Lord Lloyd could see what the King was planning, for throughout the year the King had made very plain his desire to rule without the handicap of either parliament or constitution; he conveyed a warning that the King was not to tamper with the constitution and was to behave in a strictly constitutional fashion.

The rest of the country could not help but mirror the indecisiveness and intrigues of their political leaders. Student demonstrations broke out, and, while most of them were encouraged by the Wafd, some students who joined in the strikes were undoubtedly expressing their general frustration with the political scene. The demonstrations soon escalated into riots and on March 8 students and police clashed violently in Cairo and thirty students were wounded. Similar incidents occurred in Tanta and Asiut. Tharwat finally stopped procrastinating

76. Lloyd to Chamberlain, Feb. 6, 1928, F.O. 371/13114.

77. Delaney Memorandum, St. Antony's Papers; also Lloyd to London, Jan. 2, 1928, F.O. 371/13114.

78. Lloyd to London, Feb. 19, 1928, F.O. 371/12355.

and presented his treaty terms to the government. The terms were
rejected and he resigned. Nahhas Pasha was entrusted with the formation of a new cabinet.

At first the Liberal Constitutionalists would not continue their
collaboration with the Wafd, but Muhammad Mahmud pointed out
that if their party refused to join the coalition and if conflict arose
between the Egyptians and the British government, and if parliament
was subsequently dissolved, the blame would be placed squarely on
them. The party would be accused by the people of treachery and
intrigue, especially if in consequence they agreed to form a government. Reluctantly the Ahrar agreed to collaborate with the Wafd and
a cabinet was formed on March 18, 1928.

In spite of a majority in parliament, Nahhas Pasha was destined to
last as premier for only three months. The issue once more focused on
the project for a Bill of Assembly, the modification of a previous bill
passed in 1923, which the Wafd was determined to push through
parliament. Lord Lloyd was equally determined to block the passage
of the bill, the terms of which he considered posed a danger to foreign
lives and interests in Egypt, since it would deprive the police of all
rights to interfere with or prevent public meetings, or to disperse a
meeting that had become disorderly. Lloyd said the bill was a direct
incitement to disorder and a deliberate attempt to discourage officials
from doing their duty.[79] Those in favor of the bill viewed it as a means
of preventing future clashes between police and students, and of
prohibiting the executive from quelling public manifestations of
disapproval as had happened under the Ziwar government.

Lloyd once more claimed that after Zaghlul's death the Wafd had
"reverted to a condition of irresponsible extremism very nearly resem-
bling that of the old murder campaign days. Their legislative activity
since the previous summer had been confined to measures designed
quite clearly to suppress nonpolitical authority among the officials, to
bring the Mudirs and Omdehs in the provinces under party influence,
and to tie the hands of the police in dealing with political agitation in
the towns."[80] Lloyd could not forget that Mahir and Nuqrashi had
been involved in the Sirdar Case, and could not remember that they
had been legally cleared of the charges, and thus suspected that any
plan in which they were involved spelled murder and violence. The
Foreign Office instructed Lloyd to issue a verbal warning to Nahhas on

79. Lloyd, *Egypt Since Cromer*, II, 257-258; also Lloyd to Chamberlain, March 1,
1928, F.O. 371/12355.
80. Lloyd, *Egypt Since Cromer*, II, 271.

April 18/19 against the passage of such a bill and, if the warning was disregarded, to issue a strongly worded, written ultimatum, which he did ten days later, demanding an undertaking in writing that the measures mentioned above would not be carried out.

The King was delighted at the Wafd's discomfiture and insisted that Nahhas reply to the memorandum, which caused Lloyd to comment acidly that the King was up to his old tricks of pushing Nahhas into a showdown with the British authorities so he could quash both Wafd and constitution,[81] but Lloyd also overlooked the fact that an answer was necessary. The Egyptian government then replied that it did not recognize the right of Britain to intervene in Egyptian legislation but "professed conciliatory statements" and an intention to postpone the bill since parliament was near the end of its session.[82] Lloyd was dissatisfied with the answer and suspected that the bill would be brought back during the next session, but the British government was content to leave well enough alone.

King Fuad, finding that the Bill of Assembly had not brought the cabinet to grief, looked around for other means with which to discredit the cabinet. He approached Muhammad Mahmud and intimated that he would like him to form a cabinet once the present one had fallen.[83] The present cabinet, however, was reluctant to fall. Elections for provincial councils and umdas were due to take place during the summer and the Wafd wanted to remain in power long enough to supervise the elections to their advantage. It was a well-known axiom of Egyptian political life that the provincial councils and the umdas were the keys to success in any election. But when Nahhas sent a message of thanks to the British government for its conciliatory attitude during the recent crisis, the cabinet tottered although it did not fall. An interpellation arose in parliament questioning the need for gratitude on the part of the Egyptians over the recent ultimatum. The Ahrar showed their teeth in the House and Makram Ubaid, defending the government position, and Abd al-Hamid Said, a Liberal Constitutionalist opposing it, flew at each other's throats. For a minute the floor of the House threatened to become the scene of a sidewalk brawl but cooler minds prevailed to restore order and dignity to the Chamber. The rift between the two parties was hurriedly patched up to prevent the fall of the cabinet until the summer had passed. But on June 17 Muhammad Mahmud abruptly resigned from the cabinet.

81. Lloyd to London, April 3, 1928, F.O. 371/13118.
82. Lloyd, *Egypt Since Cromer*, II, 273.
83. Mahmud to Lloyd, May 26, 1928, F.O. 371/13121.

Two days later his reasons for resigning became known when a public scandal erupted which concerned the probity of the prime minister and his professional conduct.

The press published the text of an agreement purporting to be concluded among Nahhas Pasha, Wisa Wasif, and Jaafar Fakhri, three lawyers representing the mother of Prince Saif al-Din in a court case. Saif al-Din, who had been declared insane when he tried to kill Fuad, his then brother-in-law, was enormously wealthy and his estate had been left in the King's hands. The lawyers undertook to take the estate out of the King's hands and turn it over to the Prince's mother in return for the enormous fee of £E130,000. On the date the agreement was allegedly written, Wisa Wasif and Nahhas were vice-presidents of the Chamber. Had Nahhas's guilt been established his political career would no doubt have ended over the implied conflict of interest. In time he was declared innocent of the charges but the incident allowed the King to seize the opportunity of Nahhas's public disgrace to dismiss him summarily from office on June 25, 1928. Muhammad Mahmud was entrusted by the King with forming a new cabinet and the new ministry promptly requested His Majesty to dissolve parliament and postpone elections for a period of three years. The King had thus succeeded in engineering a second coup d'etat against the constitution and parliamentary life, and in this intrigue he was aided and abetted by the Liberal Constitutionalist party, by the men who had designed and drawn up the constitution. Fuad seemed to be right, that constitutional life was a farce as he had once told Lloyd, for its suspension was plotted and executed by its very authors.

IV

The Iron Grip

IT IS one of the imponderables of human nature that those who claim allegiance to certain principles are able to set them aside and behave in a fashion diametrically opposite in the name of safeguarding those very principles. Egyptian politics are fraught with irony, but the bitterest one of all was that the party calling itself al-Ahrar al-Dusturiyyun, Liberal Constitutionalist, felt constrained, or opted, to rule in a manner that was not liberal, to set aside the constitution and govern by decree through a cabinet which to most of their countrymen became notorious as *al-qabda al-hadidiyya,* the Ministry of the Iron Grip.

Muhammad Mahmud was l'enfant terrible of the Ahrar. He was the son of an extremely wealthy landowner, Mahmud Pasha Sulaiman, a former vice-president of the Legislative Council, who owned extensive estates in Upper Egypt. The family had originally stemmed from the Hijaz but had long been settled in Egypt. Stocky, with swarthy features, a broad flat face, and thick lips, Mahmud looked a typical fallah from the Said, but he was decidedly not typical of anything, and certainly not of an Egyptian fallah. He was educated in Egypt and in Balliol where he took honors in history. He then entered government service and was very rapidly promoted to mudir of Fayyum province and later mudir of Buhaira province. He was retired from the latter post for using methods deemed too autocratic. As a mudir he was disliked by both the British and the Egyptian officials as well as by the local notables all of whom he treated in an arrogant manner. He was one of the original five founders of the Wafd and had been deported with Zaghlul to Malta in 1919 for his activities. He broke with Zaghlul in Paris in 1920 but Ali Mahir later induced him to act

111

as an intermediary in talks between Zaghlul and Lord Milner,[1] and was one of the four delegats sent back to Egypt to explain the terms of the Zaghlul-Milner talks. In time he became one of the pillars of the Liberal Constitutionalist party, and when Abd al-Aziz Fahmi resigned as leader of that party in 1926 Muhammad Mahmud became vice-president and acting leader. After Nahhas was dismissed from office in 1928, he was chosen to lead a new cabinet and became president of the party.

Because of his Balliol background Muhammad Mahmud was regarded by the English officials in Egypt as someone who could talk their language. It was alleged, however, that Mahmud had become embittered toward the English when he was called a "nigger" or a "dago"[2] in a railway carriage in England during his student days. Whether the story was true or apocryphal, it was always dragged out to explain how it was that Mahmud had become involved in the nationalist movement while still retaining strong pro-British sympathies. Like most colonial officials, the British in Egypt could not understand that personal sympathies had nothing whatever to do with political principles, and while many Egyptian nationalists liked the English individually they did not relish their rule in Egypt and wanted an Egypt that was ruled entirely by and for the Egyptians. Mahmud was ambitious and was convinced that he was the only man clever enough to govern Egypt properly without the assistance of the British. Once again that trait of conviction of personal superiority which seems to be the hallmark of most politicians, dominated.

Mahmud's friend, Oriental Secretary Robin Furness, in the character sketches he sent to the Foreign Office about the major Egyptian personalities, described him as "influential, intelligent, energetic, arbitrary, sentimental, fidgety, moody, jealous, naive, disappointed, on the whole likeable. He is very responsive to the personal touch, friendliness, flattery and firm advice, and equally quick to take offence at any imagined rudeness or slight. . . . He loves intrigue and deeply plots, has some courage and is said to be kind-hearted. He is utterly unreliable."[3]

Muhammad Mahmud was one of the architects of the coalition between the Wafd and the Liberal Constitutionalist party in 1926. He thought of succeeding Zaghlul as leader of the Wafd—for he had been

1. Notes on the members of the new cabinet, July 7, 1926, F.O. 371/11584.
2. Waterfield, *Professional Diplomat*, p. 150.
3. May 23, 1927, F.O. 371/12388.

led to believe that he would be quite acceptable to the rank and file
of the Wafd, a clear indication of how similar both parties were on
matters of principle and of how their differences were mostly a matter
of the personalities involved. Mahmud, however, unhesitatingly re-
nounced the coalition when the post of prime minister was dangled
before his eyes by the King, for which the Wafd dubbed him a
traitor, although when offered the same opportunity they behaved in
the same fashion.

Fathallah Barakat disliked Muhammad Mahmud and described him
in his memoirs as an intriguer and a liar who would do much in
order to become premier.[4] The rest of the Wafd were soon to call
Mahmud worse names.

The new cabinet under Mahmud was filled with astute and capable
men. Ali Mahir, older brother of Ahmad, much more conservative
and devious though every bit as clever as his brother, was Minister of
Finance. Hafiz Afifi, a former pediatrician who had been a member of
Hizb al-Watani and had joined the Wafd along with Nahhas in 1919
when all the parties were coming together, was a brilliant man who
was to become Director of the Bank Misr group and to prove to be a
fine economist, was Minister of Foreign Affairs. Afifi was a soft-
spoken man who gave the impression of gentleness but could be hard
and determined as a negotiator. Abd al-Hamid Sulaiman, an engineer
trained in England, was Minister of Communications, while Ahmad
Lutfi al-Sayyid was Minister of Education. Lutfi had not wanted to
join the cabinet because of his political principles. He had written
a series of articles in al-Jarida to explain to the Egyptians what he
called "constitutional behavior," to teach them their rights and duties
toward the government, to teach them to fear tyranny and autocracy,
and to strive for independence. He did not believe that a constitution
should be set aside out of convenience, but Mahmud was an old and
dear friend who appealed to him saying, "Would you desert me in my
hour of need?" Lutfi, surely in a moment of weakness, laid aside his
political principles in the name of a principle that to Egyptians is
greater, that of loyalty to one's friend, and accepted the post in the
cabinet.

Most of the men in the cabinet were men of integrity and honesty,
and by their lights they were certainly moderate liberals, especially
when compared with the more extreme Wafdists. They accepted the

4. Barakat Memoirs (1928), 13:13, 62; Zaghlul Memoirs, 52:2975. Even Adli had no
admiration for him.

suspension of the constitution and of parliament in the belief that a few years of nonpartisan government would restore political equilibrium in Egypt, and allow parliamentary government to reformulate itself in a more moderate and temperate fashion. In reasoning thus, the Liberals were taking a page out of British imperialist policy. The British parliamentary system and form of government were admired by the Egyptian Liberals. Yet the British who ruled their country in a democratic fashion could deny democracy to other peoples under their dominion, notably the Egyptians, because they had set a double standard for political behavior. The Liberals purloined that standard and applied it to their own political situation. So long as the Wafd retained its hold on parliament, they believed, nothing constructive could be achieved there, and parliament would continue to degenerate into what it had become under the leadership of Nahhas, a forum for demogoguery and the rule of the mob. And yet had parliament been as bad as all that? One might on the contrary say that parliament had been too idealized to be effective. As Professor Jacques Berque put it in his inimitable manner, "Le parlement Egyptien est modèle plus que fonction. Qu'il reste trop en deçà ou s'élève trop au-delà de ce rôle, il en vient à décevoir ce que les citoyens (et l'historien peut-etre) attendaient de lui."[5]

It was true that over the past year the deputies had angered every member of the executive by their interference in administrative matters on behalf of their friends and electorate, but much of that zeal could be attributed to the inexperience of the deputies and to their ignorance of proper parliamentary procedure. Much of it could also be attributed to the principle of helping one's friends in time of need, a virtue that in Egypt frequently developed into a vice. After all, the elections of 1924 had been the first genuine elections the country had ever known, and disciplined parliamentarians have to develop through a long tradition of precedents and procedures which the total life span of the Egyptian parliament of nine months plus a second spell of one year and a half had not had time to nurture. Parliamentary errors, were it not for the special position of the institution in Egyptian minds, could thus be overlooked and chalked up to experience. Much of the recent behavior of the Wafd deputies could be attributed, however, not so much to lack of sophistication with parliamentary procedures as to their desire to heckle and obstruct the opposition in order to prove that nothing in Egypt could be achieved without assistance, indeed

5. Berque, *L'Egypt*, p. 395.

the permission of the Wafd. It was that attitude that embittered the opposition against the Wafd deputies.

Under Zaghlul's leadership bills instituting the general accounting office were passed in 1924, a budget for education was approved, a bill for the division and the sale of the Domains lands was passed. When parliament reconvened in 1926 it decided to help the new Bank Misr enterprises by depositing government funds in the bank, which spelled the beginning of effective Egyptian initiative in the industrialization of the country. Parliament passed bills dealing with loans to the cotton growers (for many of the deputies were themselves cotton growers), with the control of cotton cultivation, and with the creation of cooperatives. An act regulating elections for the provincial councils was passed, as was an act setting up a new state university (with Ahmad Lutfi al-Sayyid as its first rector). That was a fair record for an infant parliament and most of the credit for it was attributed to Zaghlul's handling of the deputies.

Nahhas was a different Wafd leader. His handling of the deputies from Zaghlul's death in 1927 through 1928 lacked firmness and direction, and that allowed parliament to degenerate into a sorry show of partisan obstruction. He was too influenced by the men who had furthered his candidacy as president of the Wafd to be able to control them. In brief, Nahhas as a parliamentarian was inept and as a leader disastrous.

Muhammad Mahmud therefore planned to suspend parliament for a period of three years, to be renewed if necessary, during which time he hoped to get his social, industrial, and agrarian reforms well under way internally, and to reach some sort of settlement with the British government externally.[6] The slogans his cabinet used were a *"Wizarat istiqrar wa nizam,"* "Ministry of stability and order," and *"ʿAdl wa islah,"* "Justice and reform." Mahmud had explained to Cecil Campbell that his dissolution of parliament was dictated by a need to redirect Egypt's energies away from obsession with Anglo-Egyptian relations and toward internal development and reform, which was certainly urgently needed in the country. Campbell reported to the Foreign Office that Mahmud would restore the constitution "not from a matter of political expediency but from a passionate personal conviction that the constitution was Egypt's only permanent safeguard against the tyranny of a despotic monarch."[7] It was up to them, the

6. Haikal, *Mudhakkirat,* I, 294.
7. Cecil Campbell to J. Murray, Aug., 1929, F.O. 371/13844.

elite, Mahmud and his party reasoned, to teach the people by example of good government how a parliamentary state should be run.

All the Ahrar leaders were moderates who believed in the value of reason, as intellectuals and professionals invariably do. They believed that a problem could be solved through discussion, and found demagoguery distasteful and harmful because it was irrational and based on emotion, whereas they were seeking the rational solution. They did not suspect that they would become enmeshed in the same traps that had caught the previous governments and that they would have to contend equally with royal tyranny and British interference, for to date no Egyptian government had had a free hand in governing. They were also to face the obstacles of lack of funds, lack of cooperation, and above all lack of time, which beset all cabinets in Egypt, since not one ever lasted its allotted time. This cabinet was to last for the average life-span of a cabinet, that is for sixteen months, before it resigned under British pressure.

Mahmud's efforts during the first few months of the cabinet were spent mostly in skirmishes with the King. Fuad was only too pleased at Mahmud's request to dissolve parliament and he hoped to tamper with parliamentary life even further and more decisively. Having brought Mahmud to power on the heels of an unpopular but successful parliamentary coup, he hoped that Mahmud would become more isolated from his political backing and therefore come to rely on the King as his sole means for survival, which would place him in the position of having to follow royal directions without question. The King therefore refused to sign the appointment of Ismail Sidqi as state auditor after having initially accepted the appointment. He even refused to confer grades and decorations on the ministers, hoping to use that as a bribe to force the cabinet into signing an amended form of the constitution which the palace was drafting.[8] When Lord Lloyd showed no sign of interfering in any of these maneuvers, Fuad assumed that the British government cared little about protecting the constitution and had chosen to regard the issue as an internal matter. This strengthened the King's belief that he was the only constant in Egyptian political life, that he could play fast and loose with parties and pit them against one another with impunity, a belief that did little to develop a sense of confidence in the politicians or of stability among the rest of the bureaucracy.

Mahmud was finally forced to complain to Lloyd that the King

8. Ibid.; also M. Anthony to W. Selby, June 9, 1929, F.O. 371/13843.

would not rest until he had an Ittihad cabinet in power, that is, a cabinet subservient to the palace. To that end Fuad was busy wooing Ali Mahir from the cabinet side to his and was trying to drive Tawfiq Nasim, his principal private secretary, into resignation so that Mahir could take his place and help the King in his plans and plots. For Mahir, said Mahmud, "would forward Fuad's aim and reduce the government to a state of impotence."[9] One wonders, then, why Mahmud had chosen Mahir for his cabinet in the first place? Was it to placate the King or to defuse Mahir?

Lest the King assume that he could count on British backing were he to try and upset the cabinet, Lloyd paid him a visit and expounded at length on how well the present government was doing. Fuad immediately got the hint and desisted from tampering with the cabinet until a more propitious time in the future.

In October of that year, 1928, Tharwat Pasha died suddenly. Tharwat had been a remarkable man, the man who extricated country and government from difficulty. One newspaper dubbed him "L'homme des heures difficiles." In spite of all the epithets his opponents hurled at him, Tharwat was a genuine nationalist who devoted his considerable energies to achieving the possible. His moderation and suppleness obviously irked the more extreme nationalists who accused him of compromise. He was, indeed, a great believer in the value of compromise and in the policy that half a loaf was better than none. He was proud of the role he had played in bringing about the Declaration of 1922, the constitution, and in the advances made in the Draft Treaty of 1927. For through these achievements he had pushed Egypt by small steps nearer the goal of independence from foreign rule and from royal tyranny, in spite of the opposition of the Wafd and the obstructionist tactics of the King. Whatever defects of character he had—though he was incorruptible in 1922, he allowed his administration to become a byword for corruption through a reluctance to remonstrate with his colleagues and a tendency to let well enough alone—he was not petty and always overlooked slights and injuries. Cool and unruffled, Tharwat baffled many of his more emotional countrymen who did not appreciate him save in time of crisis.

The Mahmud cabinet never enjoyed popularity in the country. The opposition disliked it on principle, as is the function of any opposition. They accused it of being dictatorial, and it was. The response that

9. Nov. 18, 1928, F.O. 371/13124.

the Ahrar made to that accusation is notable. Haikal, the editor of
al-Siyasa, the party organ, allegedly retorted that he supported dictatorship as long as it remained in the hands of the Ahrar,[10] for there
it was in good hands and used only for the good of the country. The
constitution would be restored, the Liberal Constitutionalist party
assured their incredulous opponents, as soon as the necessary reforms
had been implemented. But that argument smacked too much of
Britain's apologia for remaining in Egypt to be convincing. It was an
argument that had also been used by the Ziwar cabinet when it had
ruled by decree, so that the Egyptians could be pardoned for doubting
the sincerity of such motives, and for assuming that the high, prin-
cipled rhetoric of the Ahrar was so much empty talk.

The Mahmud government did try to introduce social and economic
reforms, but the opposition dismissed them as a form of bribery to
allay the discontent of the masses with the rule of dictatorship. When
the government carried out a worthwhile project of filling in swamp-
lands, the opposition press drew a cartoon in which the frogs who had
inhabited the swamps croaked loudly that even they had been rendered
homeless by the government. The implication that every government
project had backfired was not only unfair but also untrue. The Liberal
Constitutionalists had attempted something necessary in internal affairs, for example, improving the lot of the workers, which no other
government had hitherto seen fit to do, but it got little credit for its
efforts which were deliberately misconstrued and represented to the
people not as a genuine attempt at reform but as a smoke screen to
make absolutism more palatable.

Throughout the twenties the Bank Misr group had started a series of
industrial projects which by the end of the decade had supplied jobs
for nearly 1.5 million laborers. Labor's importance was thus becoming
more apparent to political leaders: for example, labor had played a
hand in the 1919 revolution by joining in the demonstrations and
organizing strikes and had agitated throughout 1922 and 1924. The
Wafd leaders came to believe that much of their agitation was inspired
by socialist leadership.[11] To neutralize that influence the Wafd had
organized a labor union, the General Association of Egyptian Labor

10. Bahi Eddine Barakat (Pasha), personal communication. "Nahnu nuʾayyid al-
diktaturiyya ma dumna nahnu al-diktaturiyyin" was the alleged retort made orally
to a friend.

11. *Abd al-Adhim M. Ramadan, Tatawur al-haraka al-wataniyya fi Misr* (Cairo,
1968), pp. 527 ff.; see also *The Times,* Jan. 3, 1920.

Unions, which by 1924 allegedly had 150,000 members.[12] Unfortunately for labor, the Wafd was then out of power, but even when it was in power it did little for the workers. The Liberal Constitutionalists, who could not count on the popular support of rural areas, attempted to woo urban labor. Muhammad Mahmud's cabinet was the first ministry to show interest in the workers and set up the first housing project for workers in Sayyida Zainab quarter. In 1928 the Ahrar also attempted to form a labor association under their auspices, but the association did not have much support. The workers were alienated by the fact that the Ahrar as a party represented capital in the extreme and they did not feel secure in a union that was controlled by management. The Ahrar leader of the union was therefore ousted, and, supreme irony, the post was offered to a member of the royal family, the Nabil Abbas Halim. Halim, who looked and behaved more like a German Junker than an Egyptian prince, was the black sheep of the family and delighted in accepting the leadership of a labor union because it would annoy them and, in fairness to the man, because he was interested in trade unions. Trade unions then had so bad a name through socialist and communist associations in the past that the monarch deprived Halim of his princely title. Ahrar attempts to win the working classes therefore did not meet with any success.

Much of the popular feeling against the Liberal Constitutionalists sprang not so much from a rational response as from an emotional one. Popular opposition to the government welled from a deep sense of loyalty to the Wafd and from their identification with that party. When Grafftey-Smith was touring the countryside he was told, "Le Wafd est ancrée dans le coeur du fellah."[13] When a Wafdist government came to power, though, that feeling of loyalty receded in the face of Wafd incompetence and general mismanagement and because of the Egyptians' basic mistrust of any government in power. But under the Wafd banner the fallah was made to feel a member of the majority, someone who was needed by the Wafd and to whom the Wafd appealed.

Under the government of the Liberal Constitutional party the psychological gap between the rulers and the ruled widened. There was no common ground between them and there was no attempt to bring the people into the system as a partner, even if only in name. An elitist group manned by intellectuals and professional men who have no éclat and nothing of the common touch is never popular; it is

12. Muhammad Anis, *Dirasat fi thawrat sanat 1919* (Cairo, 1963), I, 20.
13. Grafftey-Smith to London, Nov. 3, 1929, F.O. 371/13841.

رأس الصفحة الأولى في أحد أعداد مجلة ((الشرق الأدنى))

What Our Leaders Do!!
(While the fallah toils in the fields, the leaders lie indolent. Mu-
hammad Mahmud wonders whether they love him, love him not;
Ziwar is happy in his affluence.)
SOURCE: *Al-Sharq al-Adna*, March 19, 1929, front page.

especially detested when it manifests indifference to popular opinion.
Zaghlul had been a giant among men, and Nahhas, for all his
ineptness, was a man of the people who needed contact with the masses
and who thrived and caught fire from their adulation. Most of the
Ahrar believed that it served no purpose to go to the masses for that
was pure fraud on the part of the rulers. There was obviously some
measure of truth in the criticism directed at both Wafd and Ahrar
parties: the Wafd conned the populace with rhetoric and hollow
promises; the Ahrar was too paternalistic and aloof. As one wit put it,
even the transcendence of the Almighty needed to be mitigated by a
knowledge of His immanence, but the Ahrar would not acknowledge
that there was a drawback to aloofness, and instead translated all
political issues into administrative problems which seemed to make
them logical and liable to some solution.

Of more consequence were the economic reasons behind the unpop-
ularity of the Ahrar as a government. The world was then, in 1929,
beginning to feel the grip of the worst economic crisis it had known in
recent history, and the fallahin who formed 82 percent of the population felt the repercussions of the depression most acutely, as did all

cultivators of cotton. From the time Egypt became a one-crop economy, cotton had been the major index for the economic condition of
the country, and since agricultural land bore the brunt of taxation any
fall in cotton prices was immediately felt throughout economic Egypt.

Egyptian agriculture had experienced a postwar boom in 1919 and
1920 which was followed by a decline. Another boom occurred in 1923
which lasted until 1926 when it was succeeded in 1929 by a depression
that lasted until 1933 and then made a slow recovery up to 1939. The
crop area had risen from 7,717,000 faddans in 1912 to 8,474,000 in
1938, with cotton, rice, and onions the main export crops. Although
cotton absorbs much more labor and capital than cereals, it is the most
profitable crop, hence the most prized. Improved drainage and the
intensive use of fertilizers and of insecticides had increased the cotton
yield by almost 50 percent in two decades.[14] The government thought
that it could raise the price of Egyptian cotton by restricting the cotton
acreage in the depression of 1921-1923, 1926-1929, and 1931-1933,
but that plan proved a failure since cotton prices were linked to the
world market, and all it did was render the cabinets that had imposed
the restrictions odious to the cotton growers, and especially to the
fallahin whose meager surplus came from the cotton profits. A fall in
the price of cotton was a rural disaster and, rightly or wrongly, was
blamed on the government of the day, in 1929 the Ahrar.

The Egyptian parliament was strongly dominated by its landowning
members. Two and one-quarter million small landowners possessed
over half the cultivated area, 3,171,632 faddans, whereas 22,016 large
landowners owned 2.5 million faddans. Of the second group 61 people
controlled more than 300,000 faddans; thus half the land was controlled by 2 percent of the population.[15] On his accession to the throne
in 1917 Sultan Fuad owned 800 faddans; by 1936 he had acquired
20,000 faddans and enjoyed the revenues of 45,000 faddans of waqf
land. When King Faruq abdicated in 1952 the royal estates covered
an area of 100,000 faddans. Thus it was the large landowners who
controlled parliament; and in its few years of existence from 1924 to
1928 (even up to 1952) that body did little for the fallah. The
perception of an individual is defined by his place in society, and the
perception of the affluent umda or the ayan was quite different from
that of the poor fallah, who inevitably got short shrift. With a

14. Charles Issawi, *Egypt in Revolution* (London 1963), pp. 126 and 143.
15. Ayrout, *Egyptian Peasant,* p. 17 and table 3.

parliament dominated by landowners it was impossible for any legislation that encouraged the formation of rural labor unions to succeed,
and it was a very long time before legislation that set a minimum
wage for agricultural workers could ever get through, let alone legislation that limited landholding. Saad Zaghlul at one time actually had
formulated a plan for limiting landownership to a maximum of 50
faddans per individual, but in the face of the opposition it met in the
ranks of his party, the proposal was shelved, not to be revived until
1952, and then only in modified form.

While no minimum wage was fixed for the agricultural laborers,
whose wages were thus dependent on the law of supply and demand,
many wages between 1912 and 1929 had gone up 15-20 percent,
increasing from 35-50 milliemes to 40-70 milliemes. In 1914 wages
had been 25-30 milliemes, in 1920 they were 60-80 milliemes, then in
1928 they fell to 40-45 milliemes, and in 1933 they fell even lower to
what they had been in prewar years, 25-30 milliemes.[16] By that time
money wages had fallen 50 percent between 1920 and 1930 whereas
the prices of food staples and clothing had risen. Since the fall in
wages in 1928 occurred during a non-Wafd government it was natural
for the Wafd to blame the economic decline on the government of the
day, and equally normal for the population to follow suit. The "face"
or omen of government is regarded by the people as one that bodes
either good or evil, and since the government of the Ahrar and the
depression had come one upon the other, even simultaneously, the
people in the street reasoned that the Ahrar were ill-omened, a
conclusion no doubt inspired by the Wafd. The man in the street
coined a slogan, *"Nar al-Wafd wa la janat dul,"* "Better the fires of
the Wafd than the paradise of the Ahrar."

On coming to power, had the Liberal Constitutionalists effectively
practiced what they preached, had they in fact introduced good
government into the country, the judgment of history might have been
less harsh toward them than was the judgment of their contemporaries.
Once in power the Ahrar behaved toward the members of the Wafd in
exactly the same vindictive manner as the Wafd was wont to behave
toward their opponents when they were in power.

There are those who claim that early in his ministry Mahmud had
fallen seriously ill and for a long time was unable to deal with matters
of any importance, that during his absence Mahmud Abd al-Raziq,

16. Issawi, *Mid-Century,* p. 131.

the vice-president of the Ahrar who had refused to accept a cabinet position, had taken over from Mahmud and had disbursed patronage to Ahrar supporters, perhaps not as openly as under the Wafd—but then they had less supporters to reward—and penalized Ahrar opponents.[17] And while that may explain some things it does not explain the repressive policy followed by the cabinet and condoned by Mahmud. Although paying supporters the rewards of office when a party comes to power seems to be normal behavior the world over, it sat ill on a group who had preached a holier-than-thou gospel of political action and who had prorogued parliament for the same reason. Especially irksome were government attempts to muzzle the papers of the opposition. In the past Haikal, the Ahrar editor of *al-Siyassa*, had raised a tremendous outcry against what he alleged was the "persecution" journalists had suffered at the hands of Zaghlul and the Wafd. Ahrar journalists had indeed been harassed by Wafd bullyboys who had wrecked the newspaper premises, and they had had to cope with a series of petty lawsuits instituted against *al-Siyasa* by the government as a means of intimidation. The shoe was now on the other foot and those who had been the loudest to cry for freedom of speech and freedom of the press passed a law which prohibited government employees from giving interviews to the press, or even from talking with reporters, and which prohibited government employees from voicing political opinions and from joining political parties.[18] Another law was passed which prohibited the students of higher institutions of learning from joining political groups and from demonstrating over political issues. A third law prohibited litigation against any government employee arising from administrative cases, so that no one could sue a government employee for abuse of power or for the miscarriage of justice. These attempts to lift the bureaucracy above the realm of partisan politics may have been laudable had they rested on positive motives, for a partisan bureaucracy was certainly detrimental to the continuity of government and to its efficacy and efficiency. But the laws were also seen as an attempt to end freedom of speech, which by and large was inimical to the government. The attempt to deradicalize the students and return them to their books might also have had some virtue, save that it was common knowledge that the Wafd and the Ahrar were both buying support from student leaders with vast sums

17. Rex Hoare to A. Henderson, Aug. 12, 1929, F.O. 371/13845.
18. al-Rafii, *Fi-aᶜqab*, II, 83.

of money. The motives of the Ahrar government in passing these laws were therefore extremely suspect, in spite of the inherent positive or negative aspects of the laws themselves, and served the opposition as an extra weapon with which to belabor those "liberals" who were resorting to absolute rule.

Demonstrations against the government were therefore rife, and they were repressed by the police in brutal fashion, so that on one occasion the passersby were assaulted along with the demonstrators.[19] The incident allowed the King to remonstrate with Mahmud and led the opposition to spread the rumor that the Ahrar were collaborating with the British authorities, hence their apparent disregard for public opinion.

In February 1929 a verdict was reached in the Saif al-Din case clearing Nahhas of any wrongdoing.[20] The defense proved that some terms of the letter used as evidence had been erroneously translated from the Turkish original, leading to semantic misunderstanding. The defense was able to prove that witnesses had been suborned into giving false testimony. The case was an altogether disgraceful attempt on the part of the Palace to tar an innocent man with the brush of bribery and of abuse of authority in order to destroy him as a political opponent. The Ahrar government who would have enjoyed seeing Nahhas discredited forever, was most discomfitted by the verdict, which was a clear victory for the Wafd. (Ironically, Nahhas was to be accused of the same sins—bribery and abuse of authority—many years later, this time with justification. In the interim he married the beautiful and greedy Zainab al-Wakil who was some thirty years younger than Nahhas and who amassed an enormous fortune through peddling her influence, allegedly cornering the cotton market, and various other unsavory practices. Her greed was largely instrumental in earning the Wafd the reputation for corruption that in time it acquired, for Wafd cabinet ministers who witnessed her rapacity emulated it and joined in the booty.)

The suspension of parliamentary life—a way of life that Mahmud regarded as a sine qua non for good government—was fast becoming irksome to the former Wafd deputies. Not overly impressed by Mahmud's promise of an eventual return to parliamentary life, they took a page out of the events of 1925 and planned to reconvene parliament on their own initiative in accordance with article 96 of the constitution.

19. Haikal, *Mudhakkirat*, I, 299.
20. al-Rafii, *Fi aᶜqab*, II, 87.

Since the parliament houses had been cordoned off by the police, 125
deputies, mostly Wafdists, met in the offices of the party newspaper,
al-Balagh, and issued a statement that condemned the dissolution of
parliamentary life and voted nonconfidence in a government that
had contravened the constitution. They stated that any commitments
into which such a government entered were to be considered null and
void. The government confiscated the printed declaration so that its
terms were spread solely by word of mouth. Eventually some of the
recommendations were printed in Syrian and Lebanese newspapers.[21]

Mahmud was soon to place a feather in his cap when the Nile
Waters Agreement was signed in May 1929. The Agreement was hailed
by the British press as a great achievement for it opened the gates to
a flood of projects dealing with irrigation, plans of electrification
works, supplies of clean drinking water, labor legislation, and settled
relations with the Sudan regarding the waters. But if Mahmud thought
the Wafd was going to praise him for the Agreement he was sorely
mistaken. The opposition accused Mahmud of having played into
British hands by severing the Sudan from Egypt economically.[22] They
contended that before the Agreement, Sudanese irrigation was supervised by the Egyptian Minister of Public Works, but the Agreement
had put an end to that arrangement by placing the administration of
the Sennar Dam in the hands of the Sudan government. They claimed
that the entire Agreement was in accord with the British policy of
driving a wedge between Egypt and the Sudan.

Mahmud was planning to sail for England during the summer
months and intended to raise three matters with the British government. The first dealt with the Capitulations, the second with Egypt's
desire to enter the League of Nations, and the third with the British
army barracks at Qasr al-Nil.[23] The last was a series of ugly buildings
spanning half the distance between the Qasr al-Nil and the Zamalek
bridges overlooking the Nile, and facing the present Ministry of
Foreign Affairs. They were a festering sore in the side of Egyptian
national pride as an ever present reminder of a foreign occupation.
Mahmud, however, had no intention to push for a general settlement
with Britain just yet.

At first the British government was favorably impressed by Mahmud's plans for internal reforms, but with time they began to realize

21. Ibid., p. 86.
22. Recapitulations of Events in Egypt, June 27, 1929, F.O. 371/13843.
23. Ibid.

the shortcomings of a ministry that ruled by decree, the more so when the Egyptian population blamed the British government for everything. The public assumed that any Egyptian cabinet lasted in power only for as long as the British authorities allowed it to do, and therefore assumed rightly that Mahmud was in power with British blessings. In the interim, however, England held general elections and in 1929 the Labour government once again came to power led by Ramsay MacDonald. The first repercussion of the change in the British cabinet was felt in Egypt when Lord Lloyd resigned his post, at the request of the new government. The only people sorry to see him go were the members of the British colony in Egypt who had strongly approved of Lloyd's brand of neocolonialism which had strengthened their hand and furthered their economic interest in the country. The rest of Egypt heaved a sigh of relief to see the last of him.

The British Resident had been disliked and distrusted by the majority of Egyptian officials for his continued carping and his constant interference in internal affairs. Above all, his narrow interpretation of the Four Reserved Points and his insistence on British interests had roused antagonism to a great extent and had exacerbated incidents where a suppler policy would have been more profitable and would have removed the need to call out the gunboats for every single year of his term of office. Lloyd wanted to follow in Cromer's footsteps; the very title of his apologia for his policy in Egypt, *Egypt Since Cromer,* confirms such a belief. But he had overlooked a most important detail. Egypt, twenty years after Cromer, would have accepted "friendly advice" but jibbed at "intervention" and resented the gunboat diplomacy that Lloyd inflicted on it unnecessarily. Lloyd's policy in Egypt had done much to keep Anglo-Egyptian relations bubbling on the front burners to the detriment of any sound internal reforms. In the face of the intransigence he showed and of his frequently unreasonable demands of pushing British interests above Egyptian ones, as in the case of the British officials in Egyptian service, or the army issue, Egyptian politicians could only concentrate on making regular a situation that would, in the future, safeguard them from imperialistic pretensions on the part of other British Residents.

The manner of Lloyd's dismissal and the statements later made in the British House of Commons concerning the policy he had pursued in Egypt in contradiction to the directives of the former Secretary of State roused high hopes in the hearts of the Egyptian politicians that a change of local government might be contemplated by the British government.[24] Once more a Labour government was believed to be sympathetic to Wafd claims, and the Wafd were buoyed up by its advent.

Mahmud was in England when Lloyd's resignation was announced and when Arthur Henderson, the new foreign secretary, showed an inclination to open the subject of Anglo-Egyptian negotiations, Mahmud agreed. At first Mahmud was reluctant to embark on any negotiations and feared, as he told Haikal, that it might force his cabinet into resigning before it had had time to carry out its projected reforms. Haikal pointed out that Mahmud could not afford to refuse to negotiate and remain in power, that he had no choice but to embark on the talks and either negotiate a treaty or resign after having tried to negotiate one.

The new British premier Ramsay MacDonald believed "the present Egyptian government is the most capable from the internal point of view and the most moderate in external affairs which has yet held office."[25] The terms finally reached by Henderson and Mahmud were therefore fairer than any terms previously offered by Britain. The chiefs of staff were overruled and the British army of occupation was to evacuate Cairo for the Canal Zone. The Egyptian government was to take over responsibility for the protection of foreigners and minorities. The Sudan question remained untouched but the assumption was that when the negotiations went through, Britain would make some concessions to Egypt.[26]

It seems that Mahmud was not only busy negotiating terms for a treaty with Britain but was also preoccupied with the matter of amending the Egyptian constitution, or so Haikal informs us in his memoirs. While Haikal used the term *ta{c}dil* to mean "reform" or "amend," others considered the term to mean "abrogation," which is a very different matter, and they have inferred that the plan came subsequent to a conversation Mahmud had with Cecil Campbell and Gerald Delaney. The conversation with both Irishmen had nothing to do with the constitution but did with the negotiations: they told Mahmud that he should keep the King informed of the negotiations. Mahmud therefore went to Paris and told the King that negotiations were well

24. Barakat Memoirs (1930), 14:28.
25. July 23, 1929, F.O. 371/13844; Waterfield, *Professional Diplomat*, p. 149.
26. Ibid., p. 150.

under way. Then when he returned from Paris he asked Haikal for his opinion regarding a change in the constitution, and some historians have construed that as a sign that Mahmud had been swayed in favor of the King's pet scheme for annulling the constitution. We realize now, though, that that was to totally miscontrue Mahmud's feelings toward the King and toward the constitution which he believed to be the sole guarantee against the King's tyranny.[27]

While the British and Egyptian negotiators seemed to be close to a final understanding there remained one fly in the ointment, but a somewhat inconvenient one, namely Mahmud's lack of popular support in the country. Any election would return a Wafd majority to parliament so that whatever agreement Mahmud had reached with the British government would not be acceptable to a Wafd parliament who would refuse to ratify it. Others more optimistic in England believed that once the terms of the treaty were published they would be recognized as so favorable to Egyptian demands that it would silence the opposition, who could not hope to negotiate for better terms.[28] The optimists, however, reckoned little with the ingenuity of the Wafd in inventing fences on which to sit and with their ability to oppose any terms of whatever degree of benefit to Egypt which were not of their own doing.

The British government then decided that Mahmud had better take the treaty terms back to Egypt and put them to a popular vote, that is, Egypt was to return to parliamentary life. Mahmud planned to return in the autumn, modify the electoral law of 1924 in favor of one that would be of less benefit to the Wafd by disenfranchising many of their supporters, and then submit the terms of the treaty, which were to be kept secret till then. Unfortunately for Mahmud's plans, the terms of the treaty were leaked by the Foreign Office to Makram Ubaid who was in England at the time, in spite of their promise to Mahmud to keep them secret. On August 9 Hugh Dalton, the parliamentary undersecretary for foreign affairs, who disliked Mahmud, announced publicly that treaty negotiations were conditioned on a return to constitutional government in Egypt and on no change in the electoral law.[29] Mahmud was thus given what in common Egyptian parlance is known as the *khazuq*, the banana peel. The only way out then seemed

27. Haikal, *Mudhakkirat*, I, 302-304; compare with the interpretation given by Berque, *L'Egypte*, pp. 429-430.

28. J. Murray to R. Hoare, July 23, 1929, F.O. 371/13844.

29. For details of incident, see Waterfield, *Professional Diplomat*, pp. 152-154.

to be to resort to a coalition government, to which Mahmud was agreeable, but the Wafd saw no necessity for a coalition when a general election would put them in power.

The new British high commissioner, Sir Percy Loraine, had reached Egypt by September 2, 1929. A handsome career diplomat possessed of private wealth, Loraine at first was greeted with approval as a sign that sanity was returning to Egyptian political life after the merry-go-round come tug-of-war of the Lloyd era, although that feeling was not to last for long. Loraine believed that Mahmud's cabinet should be given support for that was better than having the Wafd in power, "a party which has shown a rather contemptuous indifference to the offer and desiderata of H.M.G. as publicly announced."[30] Both Loraine and the Residency staff were sure that no treaty negotiated by Mahmud would be acceptable in Egypt, although Mahmud would be "chivalrous and patriotic enough to efface himself if it became clear that his personality was a bar to the acceptance of the treaty."[31] On the other hand, they opined, Nahhas and the Wafd were incapable of thinking in nationalist terms, as opposed to merely playing party politics. "The Wafd," Loraine wrote in a letter to his wife, "refuse to express any opinion on our treaty proposals and merely want to have Mahmud kicked out, to have elections, to get a big majority, form a Wafdist Govt. & then perhaps talk about a treaty, and *condescend* to start a fresh negotiation over the whole field of our proposals! It is really quite preposterous."[32]

The Labour government was so anxious to settle the treaty question that Henderson finally gave Loraine instructions to get rid of Mahmud, who was by then feeling bitter at this betrayal by the British government, and on October 1 he was relieved to resign and end his humiliation. Adli Pasha Yakan stepped into the breach with a neutral, nonparty cabinet and organized the elections.

Once more the Wafd party returned to power with an overwhelming majority of 212 seats out of a total of 235. By then, after the 1927 census had been taken, the number of deputies had increased. Mahmud, still feeling bitter, had prevented the Ahrar party from entering the elections. Having organized the elections, Adli Pasha then resigned and on January 1, 1930, Mustafa al-Nahhas was called upon for the second time to become premier. Parliament sat in session ten days

30. Ibid., p. 158.
31. F.O. 371/13845.
32. Waterfield, *Professional Diplomat,* p. 160.

later. The Wafd party, with the greatest majority recorded in the brief history of Egypt's parliamentary life, was confident of their ability to negotiate a conclusive treaty with the British government at the earliest opportunity. Internally, they felt that they had the situation well in hand, having replaced government officials, both high and low, with Wafd supporters, in what by then had become the characteristic pattern for every cabinet and the cause of instability not only on the cabinet level, which is to be expected, but on the lesser bureaucratic and administrative levels. In the worse days of Egyptian government under the despotism of the Mamluks, there had always existed a certain degree of administrative continuity, and, although the top echelons changed rapidly through assassination or other mishap connected with high office in those days, government affairs continued to function through a bureaucracy which remained at their posts by virtue of tradition and a sense of social responsibility. The village communities continued to have the same leaders, no matter who the provincial governor was or how often he was replaced. The guild heads continued in office, so that administrative life went on unaffected. Modernization had destroyed the discrete society with its decentralized functionaries that had been Egypt and had replaced it with an elaborate bureaucracy that lay at the mercy of volatile governments and was highly susceptible to power fluctuations. The village umda was now changed with every cabinet shuffle, and the new umda dismissed all his predecessor's appointees and appointed a new set of village officials, from the ghaffir up or down. In his satirical *Yawmiyyat naʾib fi-l aryaf*, Tawfiq al-Hakim has drawn a striking picture of the disruption caused in village life every time a change of umda took place. The telephone, the symbol of the umda's civic authority and his link with the *hukuma*, was carried out of the deposed umda's house followed by a phalanx of the ex-umda's women wailing as though at a funeral, to be escorted in a village procession to the house of the new umda, where the instrument was greeted by the new umda's women ululating in joy as at a wedding ceremony. When one remembers how rapidly cabinets rose and fell in those days, the average life of a cabinet being around sixteen months, one can begin to estimate the element of chaos which the transfer of power injected into public life with the adoption of such nefarious practices. These were not only limited to the village level but continued all along the administrative line. On reaching office the Wafd dismissed forty umdas and when it was threatening to resign had not yet appointed new ones.[33]

33. Barakat Memoirs (1930), 14:96.

The Wafd's return to power soon aroused the inevitable opposition by its clumsy handling of the administration and of the treaty talks with Britain. Even Wafdists like Fathallah Barakat, who had a deep sense of party loyalty in spite of his dislike for Nahhas and his men but who was also a patriot, criticized in his memoirs the behavior of the Wafd leaders. He complained that Nuqrashi, minister of commerce in the new cabinet, had become the "strong man" of the Wafd, that he was dictating what to say to the rest of the cabinet, and that he was vetoing any Wafd policy with which he disagreed, even when it was accepted by the majority of the Wafd members.[34] Barakat accused Nahhas and his men of setting up a dictatorship which he likened disparagingly to that of Kemal in Turkey and Mussolini in Italy.[35] Fathallah asserted that no one in the cabinet dared oppose Nahhas or argue with him.[36] Even if one takes into account Barakat's animosity toward Nahhas, these were serious accusations to make, even if only to his own diary, but succeeding events vindicated Barakat's complaints.

Nahhas had begun treaty negotiations with Henderson, but they were not going as well as the Wafd had hoped. Much to British dismay, Nahhas categorically refused the terms that had been offered regarding the Sudan. Even while Nahhas was still negotiating in England the rest of the Wafd back in Cairo received the ominous news that Nahhas was proving to be tiresome and talkative.[37] Fathallah Barakat alleged that Cecil Campbell said that Makram was playing a "despicable" role and was secretly trying to undermine the treaty negotiations because he believed that any treaty would be contrary to Coptic interests in Egypt. Makram certainly played a part in scuttling the negotiations, but whether on orders of the Coptic community or otherwise is not clear.[38] On the other hand Campbell praised Ahmad Mahir's efforts and his superior intellect, which came as a pleasant surprise to the British authorities who expected to deal with a "murderer." Campbell also told Abd al-Rahman Azzam, who relayed the conversation to Barakat, that the Wafd delegates had not played fair over the negotiations. They had begun the negotiations on the understanding that they would accept the terms that had been offered Muhammad Mahmud, and throughout the negotiations Makram had assured the British delegates that they intended to return to Cairo with

34. Ibid., 12:91.
35. Ibid., p. 94.
36. Ibid., 14:84.
37. Ibid., p. 11; also 17:34.
38. Ibid., 14:119; Waterfield, *Professional Diplomat*, p. 176.

the treaty signed and that any changes the Wafd requested would be changes in wording, *ta'dilat lafdhiyya*,[39] a statement that seems to be in direct contradiction with what Loraine had earlier expressed as the Wafd position. Then Nahhas requested the right of unrestricted immigration by Egyptians into the Sudan and the opening of negotiations to discuss the political status of the Sudan a year later. Nahhas claimed that at first Henderson accepted the terms, and that when Henderson received a telegram from the British Governor of the Sudan warning him that he could not admit any Egyptian soldier in the Sudan and could therefore not advise in favor of the treaty, the negotiations fell through.

The British version differed from Nahhas's. They claimed that they regarded the Sudan as potentially an independent state, and they certainly did not recognize Egypt's claims to sovereignty over it. The error made by the negotiators was that they did not tell the Egyptians from the beginning how they stood on the question of the Sudan, and their reticence aroused in the Egyptians the suspicion of double-dealing because throughout the negotiations they were led to believe that some compromise was likely to be reached.[40] The majority of the Wafd had been convinced by Nahhas that Henderson had promised a deal and then had reneged on his promise, when his cabinet refused the terms. For that reason Fathallah attributed the failure of the negotiations to the fact that the Wafd had put their faith in a Labour government, thinking that its aims were different from those of a Conservative government. As far as he was concerned Barakat preferred to deal with the Conservatives, who *"yuqaddirun li-karama-tihim haqqan wa wajiban khilafan li-l 'ummal,"*[41] "valued their dignity and sense of duty unlike Labour." As far as Fathallah was concerned, as long as the terms of the 1899 agreement remained in force, any new terms that were offered by the British, even had they accepted the right of unlimited immigration into the Sudan, made the Sudan nothing but a legal protectorate, a clear demonstration of the gulf that lay between the British and the Egyptian governments over the matter of the Sudan.

On the other hand Muhammad Mahmud was convinced that the British government had ended the negotiations with the Wafd because

39. Barakat Memoirs (1930), 17:78.

40. Ibid., 16:25-26; Waterfield, *Professional Diplomat,* p. 181; Zayid, *Struggle for Independence,* p. 133; *The Times,* May 9, 1930.

41. Ibid., 14:28.

they were convinced of Nahhas's perfidy, *su'nafs*.[42] Others believed that the British delegates, bored by the long-winded rhetoric and pointless quibbling, had tired of hearing Nahhas and Makram talk. Barakat claimed that most of the members of the Wafd with whom he had talked were agreed that Nahhas showed flashes of lunacy and delusion, *junun wa hawas*, and blamed him for the "catastrophe" that had befallen the country, notably the dead end to negotiations. Wisa Wasif said that while Nahhas was a "truthful and honest man" he was also "obstinate and woodenheaded" and was therefore unfit to lead any negotiations or even to lead any cabinet. As for Makram, Wasif opined, though he was intelligent and capable, he was an *arriviste* with all the defects that the term implied.[43] Still others, like Wasif Ghali and Najib al-Gharabli, were not even convinced of Nahhas's truthfulness and accused him of changing his story to suit his political needs. For instance, Nahhas had made a speech to the Wafd in which he extolled the excellence of his relations with English; then, when the negotiations failed, he claimed that the Palace and the British were to blame. Which, they wondered, was the true version?[44]

The King was gratified that once more a cabinet had floundered on the rocks of negotiations. He hoped that it would fall so he could be rid of a man he regarded not only as extremely unstable but also as a very dangerous threat to the King's own position. The immediate source of conflict with the King stemmed from a bill that the Wafd cabinet proposed in order to muzzle the opposition and also in a spirit of vindictiveness: to bring to trial any cabinet minister accused of having undermined the constitution. This move was obviously aimed at engineering Mahmud's impeachment for suspending the constitution, and was opposed naturally, by the Ahrar and by the King for quite different reasons. At the time the King claimed to be ill, therefore unable to discuss the bill or to come to any decision about it until he had recovered his health. Rumor had it that the King was procrastinating until Sir Percy Loraine arrived from abroad when he would be able to gauge how much support he was likely to get.[45]

In the interim, to cover his flank, the King made overtures to Muhammad Mahmud and granted him an audience that lasted for two hours, which belied his alleged indisposition and revealed it as nothing more than a diplomatic feint.[46] Nahhas thereupon threatened to

42. Barakat Memoirs (1930), 17:34.   43. Ibid., p. 65.
44. Ibid., 15:7.   45. Ibid., 14:59.
46. Ibid.

resign, saying that in 1928 he could not contemplate resignation
because the issue was between his government and the British government, but in 1930 the issue was between him and the umma on one
side and the King on the other, and unless the umma received satisfaction he would resign.[47] Not since the early days of Zaghlul's regime,
had Fuad been threatened with the "wrath of the umma," but Nahhas
was now reviving that specter, and in no uncertain manner. In
parliament Abbas Mahmud al-Aqqad, a talented writer and journalist
who had become a fervent Wafdist and the mouthpiece of the party
of a particularly virulent variety, had harangued the chamber and
said that the House was ready to crush the highest head in the land in
defense of the constitution. The Speaker of the House immediately
objected to the use of such inflammatory language within the walls of
the House and ordered that the words be struck from the record. But
all the members of the Assembly had clearly heard the speech, and
just as clearly had realized who the threatened heads were.[48] The
Liberal Constitutional paper, al-Siyasa, promptly reported the incident
to the public.

Threats against the King were not restricted to the lower echelons
of the Wafd; they were current among the active leadership. Ahmad
Mahir, in a conversation with Fathallah Barakat, said that should
circumstances force an issue between the Wafd and the King, the
Wafd would at once request the Assembly to depose King Fuad. In
horror at such revolutionary talk, Fathallah placed his hand across
Mahir's mouth and begged him not to be so rash.[49] But Mahir meant
every word of it. The King realized full well that Nahhas was using
the project on ministerial responsibility to the constitution as an excuse
to accuse the King of anticonstitutional behavior, and Ahmad Mahir
assured Fathallah that that was just what Nahhas was doing.[50] Although the king was very anticonstitutional, he did not wish that
to be the reason for his ouster and therefore planned to get rid of
Nahhas before his temerity led him any further.

There seemed to be several valid reasons that made it expedient to
dispense with Nahhas.[51] In the first place, the Anglo-Egyptian negotiations had failed lamentably, in spite of Wafd assurances that they
would return with a treaty in their pockets. In the second place, the
economic and financial situation in the country was well-nigh disastrous—as it indeed was in other parts of the world. The Wafd could do

47. Ibid., p. 71.   48. Ibid., p. 98.
49. Ibid., p. 97.   50. Ibid., 15:8.
51. Ibid., 14:87.

little to alleviate it, save for the passage of an important bill which
dealt with customs tariffs as a means of protecting Egypt's infant
industry and which did much to help and encourage the development
of industry. But industry was still a minute factor in the Egyptian
economy, and the major factor, the agricultural sector, was overwhelmed by the world crisis. As usual, the government of the day bore
the blame for the economic difficulties. In the third place, Nahhas was
implicated in a scandal with a European woman of dubious reputation
named Vera, but Nahhas seemed to be very much taken by her, and
almost seemed to take pride in parading their liaison in the public
eye.[52] The newspapers published numerous pictures of the couple
attending functions and inflamed public opinion against what was
regarded as loose morals on the part of their national leaders. Safia
Zaghlul even alleged that Nahhas resigned because the King had
threatened to oust him over his affair with Vera.[53] Last, there was the
odium with which the King by now viewed Nahhas. Nahhas, on the
other hand, did not fully appreciate the currents of opposition around
him and accused the King of sabotaging all the projects that his
cabinet put forward.[54]

Nahhas had presented several projects, but none had been accepted,
except a bill dealing with tariff reform which was passed in February
1930, and which had done much to encourage industrialization.

Other projects presented by Nahhas but turned down were a bill
regarding ministerial responsibility (which had triggered the crisis) and
a bill aimed at founding a Cour de Cassation, Mahkamat al-naqd wa-l
ibram; he had presented a list of nominations to the rank of ministers
plenipotentiary and president of the court of appeal, Mahkamat
al-istiʾnaf. Ali Mahir told a friend later that Nahhas was entirely to
blame for the failure of his projects. In the first place, he had been
guilty of gross discourtesy in presenting to the King a draft of a law on
ministerial responsibility without giving him prior warning, and then
in refusing to accept the King's excuse of sickness. He said that the law
project had not been presented to the Judiciary Committee, Lajnat
al-tashriʿ, as it should have been; that there were clauses in the project
for the Cour de Cassation which were patently there to enable the
Wafd to appoint their own men to the court; and that the diplomats
and the president of the court of appeal whom Nahhas had chosen
were totally unsuited for the posts.[55]

Be that as it may, the rest of the Wafd blamed Nahhas most of all

52. Ibid.   53. Ibid. (1931), 21:86.
54. Ibid. (1930), 14:100.   55. Ibid., 15:8.

for the failure of the negotiations with Britain. And, as usual in time of crisis, they appealed to Adli to help them out, to act as a mediator between them and the King. They promised that if the King agreed to sign the law, they would promise to shelve it until the next session.[56] But the King had no intention of signing that law then or ever, and he refused.

Next, Fathallah suggested to Adli that the King should ask Nahhas to form another ministry and, if Nahhas refused, the King should invite him to suggest a successor or call in the leading Wafdists and ask them to convince Nahhas of the error of his ways. Here we note how Fathallah and his group thought they could continue to act in a constitutional manner and that the King would abide by the practice common in Western countries, for in spite of the King's past behavior they pretended to believe that he would not behave so once more or resort to autocratic methods. Adli countered Fathallah's arguments with a terse, "And who will convince the King?" for in his conversation with King Fuad Adli realized how violently the King felt toward Nahhas. "The British," of course, was the answer. Both men bitterly agreed that in the final analysis nothing could force the King's hand save the British authorities.[57]

Nahhas resigned in a fit of pique a mere six months after coming to power, assuming that the public outcry would force the King to recall him to power. But, once again, Nahhas was not Zaghlul. No public outcry ensued and Nahhas was censured by his party for resigning in so precipitate a manner and against the proffered advice of the rest of his cabinet and of his colleagues in the party.[58] More important, Nahhas received no support from the British authorities. On his return from London in May, 1930, Nahhas was convinced that though he had failed to negotiate a treaty, he had nevertheless forged such strong links of friendship with the members of the British government that they would render him their full support.[59] He therefore expected that the British government would restore him to power over the King's objections — a very unrealistic estimation.

His Majesty's Government had meanwhile issued instructions to Sir Percy Loraine to remain neutral in the quarrel between the King and his premier. Loraine, who believed that diplomacy "is not a policy maker but an agency which takes its orders and its guidance from the

56. Ibid., 14:83.
57. Ibid.
58. Ibid., 16:29.
59. Sir P. Loraine to Sir J. Simon, June 27, 1932, F.O. 371/16109.

government that it serves,"[60] followed his instructions closely. Loraine was relieved to see Nahhas go, regretting only that Nahhas had not remained in office long enough for his popularity to wane.

When the King accepted Nahhas's resignation so promptly, the Wafd announced to the public that their "ouster" was a British plot. Not only was that a convenient face-saving device with which to justify a senseless resignation, but also the result of a certain convoluted process of thought. Wafd reasoning went something along these lines: the King had accepted Nahhas's resignation; therefore he must have been assured in advance of British support, which meant that King and British authorities had a plot up their sleeves. None of them believed in the absolute neutrality of the British government, and so Nuqrashi assured Campbell.[61] If the British government was not pro-Wafdist, then they must obviously be anti-Wafdist; there was no other alternative.

In this instance the King proved a fit match for the Wafd and for Mustafa al-Nahhas, for he had authority on his side. Fuad therefore called on the one man he knew who would give the Wafd a very rough time — Ismail Sidqi — who agreed to lead the new cabinet.

---

60. Waterfield, *Professional Diplomat,* p. 149.

61. Memorandum by Cecil Campbell, July 19, 1930, F.O. 371/14616; also an earlier memorandum, June 30, 1930, F.O. 371/14614.

V

"Allah Created the English Mad"

SIDQI was a member of the Ahrar, but upon agreeing to form a cabinet he divested himself of party membership. He announced that his cabinet was entirely neutral, and to mark the point that it was not connected with any political party, two Ahrar members, Hafiz Afifi and Abd al-Fattah Yahia, also resigned from the party before joining the cabinet.

In the minds of many Egyptians Sidqi was identified with palace-dominated, repressive government, since in the past he had been the éminence grise of the Ziwar cabinet. He was the strong man who could be relied upon to quell opposition, hence Fuad's choice. The King planned to use Sidqi to crush the Wafd, and then to crush Sidqi who had no popular backing, in fact no backing of any kind save what the King allowed him. Because of his absolutist tendencies Sidqi's good friends Adli and Tharwat had not included him in any of their cabinets albeit he had many talents, especially financial. Egyptian historians like al-Rafii have interpreted this reluctance on the part of the two premiers as an example of their respect for constitutional rule and of their desire to rule accordingly.[1] It might also have been based on their knowledge that it was difficult for any premier to control Sidqi.

Sidqi was an opportunist and a pragmatist, and for the moment he was ready to carry out Palace demands, which represented a third attempt on the part of the King against constitutional government and parliamentary rule. Once again, political conflict took on the

1. al-Rafii, *Fi a^cqab*, I, 209 ff.

textbook characteristics of a life-and-death struggle wherein each of the contending groups sought to destroy the other politically, socially, and intellectually in a struggle for mastery. For the next three years Egyptian politicians were to strive in vain to overthrow Sidqi and were to learn from him the bitter consequences of remaining out of power for so long a time.

Sidqi's first act on taking power in June 1930 was to order the postponement of the parliamentary session for one month from June 21. Before the fall of the cabinet a parliamentary session had been scheduled for June 23 and the President of the Lower House, Wisa Wasif, said that the session should convene in order that parliament be legally apprised of its prorogation. Sidqi agreed on condition that the President give him a firm undertaking that no business beyond reading the act of prorogation be conducted. Wasif indignantly refused and accused Sidqi of interference with the legislature.[2] Sidqi's response was brief and graphic. He ordered the gates of parliament locked and chained and the building surrounded by a police cordon.

The members of parliament, the overwhelming majority of whom were Wafdists, once more chose to defy the government, and on the day appointed for the session the deputies appeared en masse outside the gates and demanded entry. Wisa Wasif ordered that the chains around the gates be smashed. The deputies streamed in, despite feeble police attempts to restrain them.[3] Both Houses sat in session. The order of prorogation was read out amid tremendous agitation on the part of the deputies. Their spirits, which had flagged during the events of the past six months under Nahhas's uninspired leadership, were now aroused by Sidqi's arbitrary behavior, and they girded themselves for battle against the forces of reaction. Together the deputies swore a solemn oath to respect and support the constitution and to defend it against those who would seek to jeopardize or destroy it.[4]

A few days later the deputies met at the Saadist Club under the presidency of Nahhas and repeated their oath to uphold the constitution against its enemies and to register a formal protest at the recent actions of the government.

Sidqi continued his policy of coercion undaunted by the agitation of the other parties and by the inevitable bloody clashes that broke out between the populace and the students who were demonstrating in

2. Barakat Memoirs (1930), 14:111; also al-Rafii, Fi aᶜqab, II, 131 ff.
3. Ibid., p. 134; Barakat Memoirs (1930), 14:118.
4. Ibid., p. 119; al-Rafii, Fi aᶜqab, II, 136-138.

protest against the government, the police, and the army, which had been called out to help quell the riots.

The Wafdist deputies scattered all over the Egyptian countryside in a concerted effort to reach every village and rouse the populace against the government. Every tour undertaken by the Wafd members ended in bloody battle between them and their supporters and the forces of law and order. During one incident in Mansura, one of the largest towns of the Delta, and a seat for the Mixed Courts, Sinut Hanna was stabbed through the arm with a bayonet and some 145 people were wounded by the police.[5] Similar incidents occurred in Port Said, Suez, Ismailiyya, Tanta, Bilbais and in Cairo and Alexandria where eighteen people were killed and four hundred wounded in incidents that revived memories of early Wafd activities, except that in the present case the opposition was not an alien government in occupation but an Egyptian government led by a man who during the earlier period had also battled on the side of the nationalists.

All these clashes served to pinpoint the fact that the Wafd was in fact a popular party, the only one in the country. The magnitude of the manifestations would lead one to suspect that they were genuine responses and not entirely paid for by the party, although no doubt the ringleaders and organizers were paid party members. Later experiences have shown that when the manifestation was composed entirely of paid members it usually disappeared at the first sign of gunfire, although it might hold firm in the face of fisticuffs or nabuts (staves). Yet the crowds continued to battle the police and the toll was high in dead and wounded.

The British government became sorely alarmed over the internal situation and feared for the lives and the property of foreign residents, especially in Alexandria, Mansura, Port Said, Suez, and Ismailiyya where there were large concentrations of foreign communities. British Premier Ramsay MacDonald issued a stern warning to the Egyptian government and the opposition alike, holding them jointly responsible for any further incidents. With monotonous predictability two gunboats once more were sighted in Alexandria harbor. Sidqi dissolved parliament forthwith, but the deputies met ex-camera at the Saadist Club on July 26 to register their protest against the government. Some provincial councils had been organized by the Wafd to lodge formal protest against the procedures used by the government, and in retaliation Sidqi issued an order to disband all provincial councils.

5. Barakat Memoirs (1930), 15:27 ff.

If the government thought that these methods would end popular agitation they were mistaken for they only exacerbated the hostile feelings. Numerous strikes were announced. Tramways came to a halt, shops were closed, and community life ground to a virtual standstill. Demonstrators paraded daily in the streets shouting slogans like *"Yasqut al-Malik"* "Down with the King," and "Fuad ʿadu al-dustur,"[6] "Fuad is the enemy of the constitution." Even the populace seemed to realize that the true villain in the land was the monarch and not the premier who was only his willing instrument.

The much criticized iron grip of the Liberals by now resembled child's play compared with the steely vise of Sidqi and the Palace. Desperate means were considered by the Wafd. During one session some members of the Wafd Central Committee suggested that all their members refrain from paying taxes to the government. Fathallah Barakat reasoned that banks would then foreclose on loans and mortgages and financial ruin would face all property owners. More important, he believed that there could be no unanimity in such a policy and the Wafd would lose face. Nuqrashi who had made this suggestion countered these arguments with a terse, "So what! Suppose a hundred rich landowners should suffer!" Barakat (who was himself a rich landowner and who knew Nuqrashi's penury) thought bitterly to himself, "Of couse, why should you care, you won't be the one to suffer."[7] By that time the members of the Wafd Committee seemed to be divided into moderates and extremists, with moderates like Fathallah or Shamsi belonging to the affluent segment of the Wafd and extremists like Nuqrashi and Makram belonging to the nonaffluent groups. The gaps between the haves and the have-nots was one of ideology and of approach, but with material undertones, and it was soon to widen into a break.

Clashes between people and government reached a climax in August when someone attempted to assassinate Sidqi during a train journey from Cairo to Alexandria. The assassin was foiled but Nahhas and the members of the Wafd were forbidden to travel around the country or even to leave the Cairo city limits. That rule was frequently infringed by the Wafd members who plotted devious means of evading police supervision and of rousing the population, but the government just as frequently and as deviously managed to prevent them from reaching their destination.

6. Ibid., 16:21.
7. Ibid., 15:40.

In one notorious incident in 1931 the members of the Wafd secretly
planned to travel to the Delta region on a campaign. When the
authorities learned that the Wafd members had managed to evade
police supervision and board the train, they emptied the other carriages of passengers and diverted the railway carriage holding the
Wafdists to another line. The train was shunted back and forth
between two remote areas of the desert in the Tura region without
stopping at either end. The discomfitted Wafdists found themselves
trapped on a train in the heat of May without food or water and with
no means of getting off. Many of them were elderly gentlemen with
the usual assortment of ailments found among the elderly and they
suffered intensely. They were only released after eight hours of the
brutal, humiliating treatment.[8] On another occasion, after they had
successfully completed their speaking assignment, they were arrested
on the way back to Cairo and held for several hours in a police station
for interrogation.[9]

Newspapers were censored, and *al-Siyasa* and *al-Balagh* were closed
down for a while. Adversity seemed to bring the parties together, and
it brought them closer to Adli Pasha. Adli had always been highly
respected by all the politicians who recognized him as an honest and
upright man, and he had achieved the position of doyen of Egyptian
politicians, the Grand Old Man of his country. In times of crisis all
thoughts turned to him, not only because he was leader of the Senate
but also, as Barakat confided to his memoirs, because of his respectable standing in the eyes of the nation and "because the experiences
of the past had shown how precious Adli's talents were in interceding
at the right time in order to spare the nation much evil,"[10] which was
indeed high praise for a Wafdist to give to a Liberal Constitutionalist.
In spite of their past cavalier treatment of him, Adli joined with the
Wafd in a concerted effort against the Sidqi government. As a consequence all the other political personalities who were not committed to
the Palace followed Adli's example to protest to the King and to the
public at large the actions of Sidqi's government. For while they all
knew that Sidqi was sustained by the King, they thought they could
force the King, or shame him, into a change of government by showing
their adamant opposition to Sidqi.

8. Ibid., (1931), 19:31.
9. Ibid., 18:29, passim.
10. Ibid., (1930), 16:29, passim; Loraine to Henderson, Feb. 21, 1931, F.O.
371/15403.

In reality, what had galvanized the opposition against Sidqi was his announced plan to draw up a new constitution. Faced with the prospect of an inevitable Wafd majority in any forthcoming election, Sidqi, who was determined to rule as a strong man and destroy the power of the Wafd, definitely planned to create a new constitution that would disenfranchise a large number of Wafd supporters, and he announced a new electoral law on October 22, 1930.

The most important projected changes in the constitution were as follows: Since the constitution of 1924 had been abolished by royal decree, in spite of the fact that the King had taken an oath to respect the constitution, the new constitution was couched in terms of an octroi from the King to the people, and not, as in the past document, in terms of a popular right. The new constitution was not subject to change or to amendment for the next ten years. It shackled parliament's right to issue a vote of no confidence against the government by making it mandatory that any such vote be preceded by a written exposition of the issues to be discussed, signed by at least thirty deputies, and presented to the parliament a week ahead of time. The vote would then take place two days after a discussion of the issues. While that clause had its importance one must keep in mind that no government had yet fallen from a vote of no confidence. The constitution forbade both houses from initiating legislation dealing with financial questions and reserved that right to the King. It permitted the King to veto any law enacted by parliament by the simple expedient of refusing to ratify it for a period of two months. Other clauses, such as the King's right to nominate the majority of senators, strengthened the monarch's powers and hamstrung the legislature by shaving it of most of its powers of legal protest and check over the executive.[11]

The new electoral law abandoned direct elections in favor of election by two degrees and raised the proportion of voters to electors from the previous 30 to 1 to 50 to 1. It raised the voting age from 21 to 25 years and specified property qualifications. The law prohibited any member of the liberal professions who resided outside Cairo from advancing his candidacy for election, which precluded doctors, lawyers, engineers, merchants, and journalists residing in the provinces from becoming members of parliament. At the same time the electoral law permitted umdas and village shaikhs to advance their candidacies. That clause was the most outrageous one in the law, for it was obvious to anyone cognizant of the internal politics of the country that any premier could

11. al-Rafii *(Fi a'qab,* II, 153-158) gives a detailed critique of the project.

dominate umdas and village shaikhs, who were government appointees, but not the members of the liberal professions who were not
subject to direct government pressure.[12]

A wave of resignations by umdas and shaikhs al-balad followed in
protest at the electoral law and 275 out of an estimated 4,000 resigned.[13] The government refused to accept the resignations, brought
the officials to court on charges of dereliction of duty, and fined them.
Orders were issued to the mudirs to arrest the umdas and collect the
fines from them, by force if necessary.[14] Many umdas did not have
funds available, so a few Wafd members suggested that they be
supplied with funds from the Wafd war chest. Nahhas refused to
consider the suggestion, which had met the approval of the majority of
the party's Central Committee, asserting that Wafd moneys were all
tied up in stock. He suggested that the ayan notables be canvassed for
donations.[15] Many of the members, who were notables themselves and
who had contributed the funds, were roused to anger and suspicion.
They said that the funds were there for an emergency and not for
investment capital, and they asked Nahhas for an accounting. Nahhas
assured them that he had all the accounts but refused to give them any
details, which roused suspicions of his probity, but no one wished to
make an issue at so critical a time and they let the matter rest. It was
estimated that the government collected over £E18,000 in fines. Not
until 1936 were the moneys refunded to the umdas and shaikhs
al-balad by parliament.[16]

In preparation for the forthcoming elections Sidqi formed his own
political party, Hizb al-Shaab, the People's party. Like the Ittihad
party with which it eventually merged, the Shaab was created as a
front. Its sole function was to bolster the government in power. It had
no real following—only the fictitious backing of paid members and
people with vested interests in the Sidqi regime or links with the
Palace. Notwithstanding the motives for founding the party, it had a
platform which was based on internal reforms and especially on
economic reforms but which seemed determined above all to liberate
Egypt from a political caucus.

In later days when Sidqi was writing his memoirs, he claimed in
justification of his actions that parliament had been handicapped by

12. Ibid., p. 158.
13. Ibid., p. 164; Loraine to Henderson, Feb. 21, 1931, F.O. 371/15403.
14. Ibid.
15. Barakat Memoirs (1931), 17:35.
16. al-Rafii, *Fi a'qab*, II, 165.

a Wafd majority intent on opposing any measures that did not originate with their party, regardless of their value to the nation. To his mind, the only way out of the impasse so that Egypt could get on with parliamentary government was to set aside egotistical partisan politics and deal with the issues in a neutral fashion by judging them on the basis of their intrinsic merit. His "reform of the constitution" and the changes in the electoral laws were designed, he said, to allow the executive leeway to function in the face of an inexperienced and hence obstructionist and inept parliament.[17]

Sidqi was not the only politician in Egypt to think along these lines. Muhammad Mahmud and his party had followed identical thought processes when they had dissolved parliament and ruled by decree, except that Mahmud had not tampered with the constitution, although he fully intended to change the electoral laws and for the same reasons.

Had the majority of Egyptian politicians — Ahrar, Wafd, or any other party — been polled at that time they would undoubtedly have considered the constitution as their prime safeguard against the tyranny of the King rather than a document that spelled out the rights of the people. Each party reasoned that the rights of the people were safe in their hands, for "the Wafd is the people" or the "Ahrar represent reason and good government," as their slogans said. The rights of the people were only jeopardized when the opposition took power. In brief, they could only think in terms of party interest which they confused with national interest, whence sprang the nefarious partisan spirit of the times. Sidqi was no different from the rest, just more ruthless and more thorough, and in his case the Shaab party was a feeble camouflage for his own person.

The origins of party intransigence had their roots first in Anglo-Egyptian relations and in the glory that would accrue to any group that succeeded in negotiating a settlement with Britain. Every other consideration remained of secondary importance to that one major objective. That was the Holy Grail or the cancer of Egyptian political life. Anglo-Egyptian relations were also a most convenient scapegoat on which to blame unwise or ineffectual leadership. Thus Nahhas, who had resigned on the spur of offended pride when the King turned down his projects, soon began to claim that he had resigned over the Anglo-Egyptian negotiations.[18] He announced to the public that the Wafd was engaged in a deadly duel for the survival of constitutional life with

17. Ismail Sidqi, *Mudhakkirati* (Cairo, 1950), pp. 43 ff.
18. Memorandum by Cecil Campbell, July 19, 1930, F.O. 371/14616.

Sidqi who was just a British front, so that in fact they were engaged in conflict with England. Second, party intransigence resulted over the inability of parties to rise above partisan politics.

The fact that the Wafd under Zaghlul had arrogated to itself the task of arbiter of the national weal only exacerbated the issues under Nahhas who continued to espouse the same principles, which in fact meant that no government was entitled to rule in Egypt except the Wafd.

Although a succession of British officials in Egypt laid claim to understanding the mind of the Egyptian, when very few of them really did, not many Egyptians laid claim with any conviction to understanding the mind of British officialdom. They were convinced, however, of three constants in British policy toward Egypt. The first was British support for the King of Egypt; having brought him to power the British government would never allow him to be ousted by a popular movement, especially if Wafd inspired. The second was that whatever British policy was being followed at the time it was primarily favorable to their own interests and only incidentally to Egyptian ones, hence all offers and suggestions from England were to be greeted with suspicion and the question posed, "What's in it for Britain?" The third constant, a sine qua non, was that an Egyptian cabinet survived for as long as the Resident permitted. Government survived by the grace of His Majesty's representative in Egypt, and once it was withdrawn the cabinet fell through British machinations. The conclusions drawn by the politicians from such a picture was that a majority or a minority cabinet was irrelevant, for in the final analysis the only really decisive factor was the support of the Residency, which was not only stronger than that of the Palace but also less tyrannical and less vindictive.

The British Foreign Office, which for once had counseled its representative in Egypt to remain neutral in any quarrel between Nahhas and the King, was taken aback at Nahhas's allegations that he was battling Britain behind Sidqi's government. They were unable to realize that the pattern of continued interference which they had set in the past, and had over the last few years sustained by calling out the gunboats with deadly regularity to meet any contingency, would hardly instill in the Egyptians a belief in neutrality. In spite of all British protest to the contrary, everyone believed that Sidqi remained in office only because he had British support and that once that support was withdrawn he would inevitably fall like so many others before him. And they were right, for Sidqi, despite the resident's protestations of neutrality did have the support of Sir Percy Loraine, hence that of the

British Foreign Office, so that he was able to survive even when the King had tired of him; he finally fell when Sir Percy was transferred, and the British government saw a need for change, as we shall see later.

With that logic, Egyptian politicians of all parties multiplied their efforts with the British Resident to get him to maneuver Sidqi's downfall. They were all ready to promise the immediate signature of a treaty if only Sidqi fell and they were brought to power, but to no avail; Sidqi remaned in power and unshaken, enjoying the support of both Residency and Palace.

Much of the odium ostensibly directed against Sidqi was directed more against the King than against the person of his premier. The antipathy that the Egyptians had for their King and the suspicion with which they favored every one of his moves were justified by the King's own behavior in the country. Fuad seemed to be motivated by a basic distrust of parliamentary government and a contempt for Egyptian politicans. Some assumed the contempt was the result of his having been educated abroad, and he could therefore in no way identify with the Egyptians, whose language he at first could not even speak correctly. Others less generous assumed that he simply behaved in character like any son of Ismail would. But Fuad's tyranny was not the sole reason for the general dislike of the King. His father Ismail had been an absolute monarch but some of his subjects had liked and respected him where they did not his son. Many Egyptians high and low despised Fuad's vindictiveness toward people who had displeased him. A monarch was expected to show magnanimity, an old Arab virtue, and noblesse oblige which the King lacked. All people resented his palace camarilla, where one henchman followed another and was rewarded by odium not only from the population—who cynically expected their rulers to behave reprehensibly—but by the politicians as well. If Nashat had been detested, Zaki al-Ibrashi, his replacement, was even more so, not because both men had made large fortunes through peddling their influence but because of their open interference in the government of the country. This was obviously done at the King's instigation, for, although a few assumed that the Palace men acted without the King's knowledge, and muttered that if he but knew what his men were doing, heads would roll, they were in the minority. Many more had heard Fuad describe his men as *des fantoches*[19] and therefore knew where to place the blame: squarely on the monarch where it belonged. Within the span

19. Bahi Eddine Barakat (Pasha), Cairo, personal communication, October 1971.

of seven years of parliamentary life, three palace attempts against the constitution had been crowned with success and resulted in rule by decree. This was possible only because men of some political standing like Ziwar, Mahmud, and Sidqi agreed to collaborate with the Palace in spite of their suspicions of the King's motives. There was much to blame in their conduct and in that of many Egyptian politicians. They were cowed by the Palace and the Residency and too inclined to run to either for succor when the slightest difficulty loomed. Many were simply not accustomed to self-rule and sought to lean against a higher authority, expecting it to shoulder a responsibility with which they had not learned to cope. (The British believed that that was a character failing in all Egyptians). It was far more convenient to shrug off failure with the excuse that it was a by-product of British intervention or of royal tyranny, especially when both had frequently been guilty of interfering.

The Palace and the Residency had conveniently short memories and were indignant, and on occasion genuinely surprised, when the parties accused them of wrongdoing. The King firmly believed that whatever he did was for the good of Egypt since parliament was merely a pack of fools and he the only competent man in the land. He failed to realize that every politician held the same opinion of himself, and much of party opposition is explained not so much by opposing principles as by rival personalities. Zaghlul, for example, believed that only he could lead Egypt and negotiate a settlement. Yet he did not realize that he was a poor negotiator because he was too blunt and his actions too precipitous. Nahhas was equally convinced that he was a great statesman. Most of his colleagues did not share that opinion, and though he turned out to be a canny political animal and to have the necessary appeal that made the people like him, he was distinctly lacking in the finesse that makes for a statesman.

Throughout the entire period of Sidqi's rule the Wafd was in the throes of the most severe crisis of leadership since Paris in 1920. The more moderate group among the Wafd would have been very pleased to be rid of Nahhas and to replace him with a more rational leader. The extremist faction supported Nahhas, in the first place because they could and did manipulate him, and in the second place because he had popular appeal and a certain charisma. Nahhas was not entirely the irresponsible buffoon that some of the opposition claimed he was. He was an astute politician despite his lack of finesse and subtlety. His approach was one based on vested interest, and it served him well in garnering votes in the rural areas, since he was not averse to promising much that he had no intention of delivering—a trait he shared with many politicians of diverse nationalities and in varying epochs. His speeches were geared to the man in the street, who appreciated Nahhas's style. Whenever he was due to make a public speech large sums of money were paid to a claque who continually interrupted the speech with cries of *"yahia al-Nahhas Basha."* Contact with the public gave Nahhas a charge of excitement, which the more mundane attributed to a touch of hysteria. Sometimes he got so carried away by his own demagoguery that the hurrahs for which he had paid got in his way and he would yell at the crowd *"Ikhras ya ibn al-kalb inta wi huwa,"* "Be silent you son of a dog," at which the crowd in appreciation yelled even louder, drowning him out completely, but obviously enjoying every minute of the performance, and liking the performer for the circus he was staging.[20] Some members of the party who despised Nahhas chose to remain within the Wafd because of its past associations. Wasif Ghali was one. The Wafd had represented the spirit of nationalism in Egypt and therefore much was forgiven its leader in deference to the party and its principles. The strong spirit of cohesion and of party loyalty was unique to the Wafd. It was forged during the nationalist struggle and through Zaghlul's personality which had demanded absolute loyalty. Those who could not tender such loyalty left the party, but those who remained were consistent in their loyalty even when the leadership proved inadequate, for they were able to distinguish between the party and its members.

Unlike the members of the Wafd the Liberal Constitutionalists had little party spirit and little cohesion. They were all men with leadership qualities which they wanted to exercise. As one wit put it, they were an officer corps without any rank and file. No one led the group; they were all equals, but all considered themselves part of the elite and did not appreciate contact with the people. At a later date, when the Ahrar joined with the Wafd in touring the country to speak against Sidqi's rule, they were welcomed by the exhilarated crowds. The police, who had orders to suppress such Wafd exuberance, used extremely brutal methods, thereby immeasurably shocking the Ahrar. More than ever were they convinced of the futility of going to the masses.[21] Mahmud believed that the people should choose their delegates and leave them to get on with the business of governing without

20. Witness by me.

21. Barakat Memoirs (1931), 18:2, 31, passim; (1931), 20:69 and 25:112. Fathallah wrote, *"al-Ahrar ghurabaʾ ʿan al-maʿrik al-wataniyya, la yaʿrafun laha taʿman, wa la yafhamun laha faʾida,"* "the Ahrar are strangers to nationalist battles; they neither

interference. But he and the Ahrar had thereby argued themselves
into an impasse, for if they believed in the value of government by
the peoples' choice they would never reach power, so they insisted that
before people were allowed to choose their delegates they needed to be
taught how to make a wise choice so that they could avoid falling under
the spell of demagoguery. The argument savored of Cromer's excuse
that Egypt was not ready for self-government and was a typical elitist
reaction.

Nahhas was exasperating an increasing number of Wafd members
by his stubbornness in refusing to make a deal with the Ahrar for a
coalition cabinet and by the court of sycophants with which he was
constantly surrounded, the men Barakat called the "intriguers,
climbers and would-be-ministers"[22] meaning Makram, Nuqrashi, and
Mahir, who acted like his puppets but were in fact the puppeteers.
The moderates were convinced that only a coalition cabinet would
make the British consider ousting Sidqi. Nahhas also was convinced of
the need for British intervention, but he put a different interpretation
on British reasons for interfering with the cabinet. Blandly overlooking
his past errors and the realities of the present situation, he informed
the Wafd committee that Britain would inevitably be forced to support
the Wafd and the constitution against the King, for only the Wafd
could negotiate a treaty. Nahhas believed that the British would help
him oust the King from his throne and he closed his eyes to the futility
of the illusion that Wafd influence would increase in the country with
that help when it was diametrically opposed to British interests.[23]

Moderate Wafdists therefore continued to wonder at the irresponsi-
bility of their leader.[24] A move among the moderates for a working
alliance with the Ahrar was begun without Nahhas' knowledge. Atta
Afifi approached Muhammad Mahmud, and Mahmud agreed to a
rapprochement and eventual cooperation.[25] When Nahhas got wind of
it he was furious and in a stormy meeting of the Central Committee
which Barakat described in his memoirs he ranted against such a

---

appreciate their value nor see its use." In the second passage Fathallah claims that the
Ahrar objected to popular measures for it laid them open to insult *(taʿrid al-zuʿama
li-l ihana)*.

22. Barakat Memoirs (1930), 16:80.

23. Ibid., 16b:20, 28; (1931), 22:1.

24. Ibid., (1930), 16:86, *"at-takhabut waʿadam al-ittizan,"* "hasty and lacks equilibrium," was his description of Nahhas. In another passage (1930), 17:28, he wrote
"al-Nahhas asbah majnun," "Nahhas has become mad."

25. Ibid., 16b:100.

rapprochement. The wind was taken out of his sails when Ilwi al-Jazzar bluntly asked whether he had any pretensions of leading another cabinet, implying that his last effort ruled out any such intention. This quieted Nahhas long enough for the Committee to nominate two of its members to act in liaison with the Ahrar. Nahhas immediately chose Nuqrashi; the other members overruled him and chose Barakat and al-Gharabli. Nahhas banged the table with his fist, and shouted, "I have decided, and anything else is out of the question."[26] But Nahhas was no Zaghlul and was not allowed to get away with bluster. Wisa Wasif said, "We cannot accept such commands," and Nahhas stalked out of the meeting in high dudgeon, followed by his men. Atta Afifi at once suggested that the Wafd Committee announce the deposition of Nahhas as the party leader on the ground of his "unsuitability." There were many who were willing to go along with Afifi's suggestion, but others were afraid of a rift in the Wafd at so critical a juncture. Eventually Nahhas apologized to the members and accepted their choice of liaison officers. The irony of it was that Nahhas wanted Nuqrashi in the belief that Nuqrashi would scuttle any rapprochement, whereas Nuqrashi, on his own initiative, had been in touch with the Ahrar, notably with Mahmud Abd al-Raziq, but had not mentioned a word of it to his fellow Wafdists until Barakat embarrassed him into admitting it. He was also secretly meeting with the Residency and with the Palace. Such one-sided efforts by party members served to accentuate the divisions in Wafd leadership and to deepen their suspicions of one another so that a break was in the offing.

Some of the younger Wafd members like Ibrahim Abd al-Hadi were troubled by Nahhas's bizarre behavior and his love of secrecy which bred suspicion. Wisa Wasif believed Nahhas unable to function and told Barakat that he was ready to form a ministry, if he were ever called upon, because tradition had decreed that any leader whose policy had failed should cede his place and allow others to take over, "for the rights of the nation must not be made a pawn to personal ambitions."[27] Barakat himself was distressed at Nahhas's behavior.

As the Wafd and al-Ahrar go-between Barakat consulted closely with Adli, whom he admired, and Shaikh al-Maraghi, who had been the most progressive rector of al-Azhar and a man of integrity and sound judgment. The various groups were agreed on manifesting their

26. Ibid., pp. 111 ff.
27. Ibid., 17:18, 45.

disapproval of Sidqi's unconstitutional behavior by boycotting the forthcoming elections. The Ahrar, however, needed to be reassured that the Wafd would not play them false as they had done in the past with Adli and Tharwat, and once they received these assurances they agreed on a concerted plan of action.

For over a year from June 1930 Sir Percy Loraine, in keeping with his so-called neutral policy, maintained a maddeningly aloof position and invited the members of all parties to the Residency indiscriminately to avoid any charge of bias. When the Egyptians asked him for his advice, as they all inevitably did, he was content to opine that the opposition parties had better unite ranks before they could hope to get anywhere. Henderson was anxious that Loraine arrange some kind of coalition government supported by the Wafd in order to negotiate a treaty which he hoped to get signed in 1930, but Loraine reported that no Egyptian wanted a coalition. Loraine did not wish to undermine Sidqi's position in the country as the British government had undermined Mahmud's; least of all did he want a return to power of Nahhas, "the cross-eyed albatross."[28] The Wafd and the Ahrar, however, read into Loraine's vague words a hint that a coalition cabinet would move the British authorities against Sidqi. They were confirmed in that belief when Walter Smart, the oriental councillor, reiterated to Barakat Loraine's advice to unite.[29] Wild rumors made the rounds of Cairo as they did in any critical situation, rumors that Adli was to lead a coalition cabinet, that one was in the offing. While there was no foundation to the rumor, since the two parties had not yet ironed out their differences, it agitated everybody, including Sidqi. Barakat faithfully reported these rumors in his memoirs, but, contrary to Loraine's statement that no Egyptian wanted a coalition, his memoirs testify to the feverish activities of Wafd members and Ahrar to form a coalition.[30] Those who did not want a coalition were Nahhas and his court. The memoirs also show how rapidly Egyptian politicians took British embassy officials into their confidence and treated them as partners in the game of getting rid of Sidqi.

In talks he had with Shaikh al-Maraghi, Barakat noted that al-Maraghi had met with Loraine and had suggested that the 1924 constitution be restored, that a coalition cabinet headed by the Wafd

28. Waterfield, *Professional Diplomat*, p. 187.

29. Barakat Memoirs (1931), 17:42 ff; also p. 92. See Loraine's despatch, Jan. 30, 1932, F.O. 371/15407.

30. The whole of Barakat Memoirs (1931) vol. 17 testifies to that, as does Loraine's despatch, Dec. 3, 1930, F.O. 371/14623.

be returned to power, that a treaty be negotiated and the Sudan
question held in abeyance for future negotiations, and that the opposition, the Ahrar, be granted sixty seats in government. There is no
mention, however, of Loraine's reaction to those proposals, although
one suspects that he greeted them with his usual cold stare. Barakat
agreed to al-Maraghi's suggestions, but Mahmud demurred that sixty
seats were not enough — when his party had never won even half that
number in any election — and refused to consider any cabinet that was
headed by Nahhas, the man he blamed for the downfall of his own
cabinet.

Barakat then approached Smart once more, Nuqrashi talked to
Cecil Campbell, Ali al-Shamsi talked to Loraine, all with the same
offer of a prompt signature of a treaty once they were returned to
power. The Liberal Constitutionalists on their part carried out the
same demarches. To all these offers the British authorities in Cairo
returned the same advice: to settle their internal dissensions and offer
a united front.[31] After nearly ten months of dillydallying the parties
finally came to an agreement on April 31, 1931, to boycott the
elections that were due to take place in June. The following month
they issued a joint declaration to the King giving in detail their
objections to Sidqi's government. The declaration, which was viewed
as a national charter, was signed by nine hundred leading figures
headed by Adli, Ziwar (who had traveled down from Alexandria by
train just to sign the declaration), Shaikh al-Maraghi, and all the Wafd
and Ahrar leaders, with Fathallah taking it from door to door before
the government got wind of it.[32] When the King saw Maraghi's name
on the manifest his anger burst and he wanted to remove him from
his post in al-Azhar and to expunge his name from the roster of
ulama. Only Loraine's intervention saved Maraghi from the King's
vengeance.[33]

That summer Muhammad Mahmud went to England to see what he
could do, but he returned emptyhanded to inform them only that the
British government would never agree to negotiate with Nahhas
again.[34] Loraine had by then convinced the Foreign Office that the
country would become pro-Sidqi after the elections and that they
could negotiate with him.[35] Nahhas, on the other hand, was busy

31. Barakat Memoirs (1931), 17:85, 92, passim; Dec. 14, 1931, F.O. 371/15407.
32. Barakat Memoirs (1931), 19:32.
33. Ibid., 20:9.
34. Ibid., 21:35.
35. Waterfield, *Professional Diplomat*, p. 188.

informing all and sundry that the British Labour government was getting ready to oust Sidqi.[36] Adli on his part was attempting to reason with the King. After a meeting with Loraine, Adli tried to talk some sense into Nahhas and suggested that new elections be declared, that the ten-year clause in the new constitution be canceled, and that they could decide after the elections what to do with the constitution.[37] Nahhas refused all the suggestions and irritated the unflappable Adli so that he made the gesture of tearing his clothes, the ultimate act of exasperation in an Egyptian.[38] Nahhas then proceeded to give Barakat and Muhammad Mahmud a totally erroneous version of his talk with Adli, much to Barakat's disgust, for he had already been given an account of the talks by Adli.[39]

Barakat had been meeting regularly with Haikal, his Ahrar counterpart, and both men were agreed that the leaders of both parties were ineffectual. Both men were also agreed that it would be a very good idea if the leaders resigned; the British authorities might then view their successors as more capable of forming an acceptable cabinet.[40] No doubt both men had hopes that they would be elected the successors.

By then the cleavage in the Wafd ranks was marked, and a newspaper article referred to a minority and a majority faction in the Wafd. Makram published an article in answer to that allegation in which he wrote that there was no room for minority or majority in the Wafd, for those who disagreed with Nahhas should simply resign from the party.[41] Barakat and his supporters Najib al-Gharabli, Hamad al-Basil, Ilwi al-Jazzar, Murad al-Shirai, Ali al-Shamsi, George Khayyat, Fakhri Abd al-Nur, and Atta Afifi, who correctly believed that they formed the majority group in the Wafd, decided to have a showdown and requested a meeting of the Wafd Committee in order to put before them their project for a coalition cabinet. Barakat ominously commented in his memoirs that he had used a certain pen in drawing up the request, the same pen that had drawn up three letters for the resignation of three cabinets, that of Zaghlul in 1924, that of Adli in 1927, and that of Tharwat in 1928.[42] After much heated discussion Nahhas finally agreed not to push for the premiership of a cabinet on condition that he lead the delegation that would

36. Barakat Memoirs (1931), 22:1.
37. Ibid., p. 65; Haikal, *Mudhakkirat*, I, 337-342; al-Rafii, *Fi aᶜqab*, II, 171-173.
38. Barakat Memoirs (1931), 22:65.
39. Ibid.
40. Ibid., p. 1.
41. Ibid. (1931-1932), 24:5.
42. Ibid., p. 11.

start treaty negotiations with Britain. A vote was taken and it showed twelve members in favor of the project and six members against it. The six were Nahhas, Makram, Mahir, Nuqrashi, Sinut Hanna, and Hasan Hasib. Nahhas, who had hoped to carry the opposing motion to a vote, then withdrew his terms, once again illustrating his instability. He said he would not accept such a project and flounced out, followed by his cohorts.[43]

Adli, who doubted that the British authorities would take any action against Sidqi so long as the Wafd was embroiled in factional disputes, offered to mediate between both parties and patch up a break that threatened to become final.[44] By the time all the contenders had agreed on a common formula summed up in the restoration of the 1924 constitution, to be followed by new elections after which the majority party would form a cabinet but with the spirit of coalition reflected in the membership of the delegation negotiating the treaty, Adli threw a bombshell. He informed them that Loraine no longer entertained the notion of a change of government and implied that the opportune moment had long passed—a position that Adli described as fickle, considering what they had been led to believe, and as proof of British perfidy.[45] The rest thought it simply one more example of British madness, for, like Kipling, they believed that "Allah created the English mad, as mad as they can be," but for different reasons than those expressed in the rest of the poem. None of them suggested that the fault might have rested with them in their delay in coming to an agreement for over a year.

His Majesty's Government, on the other hand, knew where it stood and what it wanted from Egypt in terms of a future alliance that would be accepted by all Egyptians and not subject to repudiation by the next cabinet that succeeded the negotiating government. The key element in the picture was how much the British government was willing to concede to Egypt in return for such a treaty. These concessions shifted slightly with every attempt at negotiations, leading the Egyptians to believe that if they just pushed hard enough they would manage to negotiate a good treaty. Like the British the Egyptian politicians wanted a treaty that would be binding and could not understand how anyone would want to negotiate with Sidqi when a coalition cabinet was ready to offer such assurances. Loraine's policy of neutrality was construed as support for Sidqi, and there was some

43. Ibid., p. 39.
44. Ibid., p. 53.
45. Ibid., p. 58.

truth in that belief. The Egyptian politicians wondered why the British government should choose to be neutral with Sidqi in power, and not when anyone else had been in power. The obvious conclusion they drew was that "neutrality" was a sham to cloak support for Sidqi.

The elections took place in June 1931 in the wake of more outbursts of violence and a greater flow of blood. When the Syndicate of Lawyers called a strike in protest at the new electoral laws and constitution the police forcibly prevented the lawyers from entering Abdin Square.[46] The government halted all telephone and telegraph communications between the urban centers and the rural areas. Clashes with the police were so violent that the head of the Red Crescent reported to Muhamad Mahmud that on May 14, 262 were wounded and 40 killed.[47] Sidqi told Loraine that he was convinced of the necessity of parliament because he did not believe in the "viability of Egyptian dictatorship."[48] In view of the King's past pattern of behavior toward cabinets that were dependent on palace support, Sidqi knew he had little to expect from that direction in the long run. He therefore was convinced that a parliament that would lend support to his cabinet and give it some semblance of legitimacy was more likely to lead to a stable form of government and was therefore the most pragmatic solution.[49]

The elections were completely crooked, in spite of the fact that the major parties had boycotted them. No doubt Loraine knew that, for Grafftey-Smith wrote in his memoirs: "Groups of unhappy men were led from polling booth to polling booth to make their mark" while Sir Robert Greg was told by his gardener that he had voted ten or eleven different times under various names. The provincial results of the elections were ludicrous: Qina had 97 percent, Jirja 98 percent, and Aswan 105 percent.[50] In whose favor were these elections condoned, the politicians wondered, if not in Sidqi's?

Loraine's support of Sidqi stemmed from his belief that Nahhas had thrown away his chance for negotiating a treaty in 1930, and therefore deserved to find himself and his party in political limbo for being irresponsible. He knew that the Wafd would abort any attempts at a treaty that was not concluded through them, for that would lead to

46. Ibid., (1931), 18:60.
47. Ibid., 20:51.
48. Percy Loraine to Arthur Henderson, Feb. 21, 1931, F.O. 371/15403.
49. Ibid.
50. Grafftey-Smith, *Bright Levant*, p. 125; While in London Mahmud had denounced the election returns as faked.

their extinction as a party that allegedly had a "mandate" from the people to that end, whereas a treaty negotiated through them would guarantee their survival. The King, on the other hand, believed that Egypt's future depended on its links with Britain and that the Wafd would "compromise" Egypt's independence unless they were eliminated from the political scene. Loraine believed that if a choice rested between a treaty supported by the King and one supported by the Wafd, the former offered a safer guarantee. "The guarantee of the King plus Sidqi is an even better one,"[51] he wrote to London in a more optimistic vein than the events warranted.

The policy of neutrality that he was following would, he felt, end in a clash between the Wafd and the rest in which "one or the other will be submerged in the absence of residency intervention," and while the anti-Wafd were an admitted minority, they nevertheless represented the "administrative and intellectual aristocracy" of the country and, unlike the Wafd, had the sympathy of the King.

Loraine, who always got on well with the top person in the government, liked Sidqi and admired his administrative talent and tactics.[52] He believed that "Sidqi was strong enough to conclude a treaty and to proceed with its implementation," but since he also rightly believed that implementation of a treaty was more difficult than its ratification, then "the best guarantee for successful implementation in Egypt is harmony and coordination between King, Government and Parliament," and while there was always the possibility that at some future date the Wafd would denounce and reject the treaty, but then, added Loraine optimistically, the Wafd is torn by dissent and discontent with its leadership and is not as vigorous and confident as it once was.[53]

As for the Liberal Constitutionalists, Loraine believed that their reputation for striving for independence by peaceful and persuasive means had been blemished when they joined the Wafd, that the "party's personality was lost and its existence threatened," and that many of its former supporters had left the party,[54] for example, the three Doss brothers and Hafiz Afifi, who had become a minister in Sidqi's cabinet.

Quite conveniently, then, but not in keeping with the realities of the situation, Loraine chose to believe that the opposition to Sidqi was weakening, when it was in fact growing stronger, and that Sidqi's hold

51. Loraine to Simon, June 27, 1932, F.O. 371/16109.
52. Grafftey-Smith, *Bright Levant*, p. 120.
53. Loraine to Simon, June 27, 1932, F.O. 371/16109.
54. Ibid.

on the government was strengthening. He refused to recognize that Sidqi's hold was entirely based on strong-arm tactics and the use of the police and the army to check opposition, that it was, in brief, a dictatorship and a form of government that was in direct contradiction to all prior British protestations of a desire to see constitutional government established in Egypt. The only interpretation the Egyptians could put on British attitudes was to call them perfidious and to believe that Britain's talk of desiring a constitutional government in Egypt was as untrustworthy as their previous 120 declarations of the intention to evacuate Egypt from 1882 onward had been.

Loraine discussed the policy of intervention with his superiors and concluded that a policy of physical intervention was unavoidable in certain circumstances, but, he added, each time we intervene politically in order to avert physical intervention, we stultify our declared policy of nonintervention in internal affairs and shake Egypt's credibility, hence he believed in the need to pursue the present policy of neutrality.[55] Once again we have an example of the gap that lay between the minds of British and Egyptian politicians. The Wafd believed that British sympathy for parliamentary institutions would compel cooperation with the majority party, while Sidqi believed that British sympathy for good administration and stability, hatred for demagoguery, and exhaustion with the Wafd would allow him to retain power. The British authorities on the other hand were basically interested in (a) prospects for a treaty, (b) anxiety not to have to use physical intervention, and (c) a desire for gradual disengagement from a responsibility for internal affairs in Egypt, and would therefore be more likely to opt for that government that would supply all three requirements,[56] even if it were a dictatorial one.

That the British government changed its policy toward Egypt with the change of Resident was quite normal in hindsight for it was at that time occupied with other internal and international matters. That Britain should resort to intervention in Egyptian affairs only when British interests were at stake was also perfectly understandable, but the irony of the situation was that while loudly crying out against British intervention Egyptians sued desperately for it as a tool against the opposition when it suited their purposes. Every party resorted to British aid against its enemies and the Wafd was no exception. While Nahhas and the Wafd were heaping odium on the British officials in

55. July 1, 1930, F.O. 371/14616.
56. Ibid.

public, in private they were desperately trying to make a deal in order
to return to power. And just as they resorted to England for help
they turned to the King and begged his intervention to topple a
cabinet. And when England and/or the King responded they resented
it. It was little wonder that both Resident and King had little respect
for the politicians and little patience with them.

By early 1932 Nahhas was at the end of his rope and dreamed up
an appeal, *nida*, to the public, in which the Wafd would declare open
enmity toward the British and call upon the population to do likewise.
Once again the moderates were appalled at his suggestion as were the
Ahrar; the latter preferred another alternative: an appeal addressed
to the King cautioning him of the dangers that lay ahead if Sidqi were
permitted to continue in government. Mahmud had just had dinner
with Cecil Campbell who told him that Sidqi had fallen out with the
King and that the fall of his cabinet was imminent, but if Nahhas's
appeal were made public just then it would play into Loraine's hand
and bolster Sidqi's position as the man necessary to keep law and order.
Mahmud therefore strongly advised against an appeal such as Nahhas
proposed and refused to be remotely connected with it, or with those
who would issue it.[57] The vaunted union of Ahrar and Wafd thus
teetered on the brink of divorce. After all, it had been nothing more
than a marriage of convenience which Mahmud was ready to dissolve
at the slightest hint that he might be called on to bigger things.
Another meeting took place and there was an almost total opposition
to Nahhas's idea of an appeal. Nahhas predictably lost his temper
and defied his colleagues in language that was highly reminiscent of
another meeting, in Paris, announcing that he did not care for his
colleagues' opinion and that he would issue the appeal in his own
name. He said that the people were sneering at him for doing nothing,
al-nas akalit wajhi, and he would not commit political suicide,[58] and
walked out of the meeting this time· leaving behind a roomful of
people who wondered out loud at his sanity. There was even some talk
of the need to dissolve the party.[59] Atta Afifi and Wasif Ghali stopped
attending party meetings. The chasm in the Wafd elite had widened.

Nahhas then made a public speech, which was his appeal in a new
guise, in which he announced that the real enemy of Egypt was
England. The speech met with little success and served only to annoy

57. Barakat Memoirs (1932), 25:70.

58. Ibid., p. 112.

59. Ibid., p. 6.

the Ahrar. Mahmud addressed his petition to the King. He requested
in the name of his party that the King order a national cabinet that
could handle the economic crisis, which the present cabinet, because it
was corrupt and oppressive, seemed unable to do. The new cabinet
would restore the constitution, carry out new elections, and embark on
immediate negotiations with England. The only answer the King and
his government gave was to resurrect an old charge of slander, *qadhf*,
against Mahmud, Haikal, and al-Mazni, the editors of the two party
organs, and take them to court.

Meanwhile, thoughts of a coalition cabinet were revived once more
when Prince Saif Allah Yusri assured the Wafd that he came as an
emissary from Loraine who, Yusri claimed, was beginning to be
dissatisfied with Sidqi's government and wished to see the old constitution restored and new elections instituted, in order to begin negotiations.[60] News of these talks leaked out, and *al-Ahram* on April 19,
1932, announced that talks had begun between Yusri and Loraine.
Both men promptly denied the allegation and denied any intention to
begin talks. It appeared that Yusri's son-in-law, Ahmad Hasanain
Pasha, a Palace official, had heard of Yusri's talks with Loraine and
had informed the King. The King confronted Loraine who denied any
knowledge of it.[61] In his history of the period Abd al-Rahman al-Rafii
claimed that the notion then of a coalition cabinet was a British
invention and the cause for the schisms in the Wafd, for some of the
members of the Wafd insisted on a coalition cabinet when it was
contrary to the terms of the agreement made between Ahrar and Wafd
in 1931 which settled that the cabinet would be a majority one.[62] Yet
it is clear from Barakat's memoirs and from Loraine's correspondence
with London that thoughts of a coalition cabinet had been put forward
from the day Sidqi's government was formed and that the differences
between the members of the Wafd were deeper and more critical than
over a matter of coalition cabinet: they were differences of principle
and of approach to problems and were of long duration, not the
creation of the moment.

By June 1932 Sidqi felt sufficiently confident in the stability of his
government to request the resumption of negotiations with Great
Britain. He explained to Sir Percy Loraine that he had the "real
Egyptian peasant behind him" and that he had preserved law and
order, had handled the economic difficulties satisfactorily, and also

60. Barakat Memoirs (1932), 25:93 ff.
61. Ibid., 26:53.
62. al-Rafii, *Fi a‘qab*, II, 195.

had a large majority in parliament; for all these reasons he claimed that the time to negotiate had arrived.[63] Sidqi needed to prove that his government was acceptable to the British government and that he was considered just as worthy a premier as Mahmud, Zaghlul, and Nahhas had been, and as capable a negotiator. He too aspired to become the man who brought the treaty back to Egypt. He therefore met with the British Foreign Secretary Sir John Simon, who assured him that while His Majesty's Government looked with favor upon the regime, negotiations could begin some time in the winter of 1933.

Matters between the majority and minority factions were soon to come to a head consequent to a trial involving a Wafdist, Najib Iskandar, who was accused of having thrown a bomb. Iskandar was being defended by Makram and al-Gharabli, but Makram withdrew from the trial and was fined by the court for contempt. Gharabli stayed on to defend the accused and was insulted by Makram for his pains. He tendered his resignation from the Wafd, but withdrew it later on. Nahhas, however, insisted on accepting the resignation. Barakat and his friends, who regarded Makram's behavior in withdrawing from a case reprehensible, objected to Nahhas's insistence on accepting the resignation and announced their support for Gharabli. Makram accused Barakat and Shamsi of trying to set up the rest of the Wafd against Nahhas and himself, and on November 20, 1932, Nahhas divested Fathallah Barakat, Hamad al-Basil, al-Shirai, al-Jazzar, Fakhri Abd al-Nur, and Atta Afifi from membership in the Wafd.[64]

Although the situation seemed to be critical for the Wafd, and its very survival was at stake, it was saved from further calamity in the nick of time by a crisis in Sidqi's cabinet.

A great many rumors had been spreading around Egypt charging Sidqi and the members of his family with financial irregularities, and even with peculation, mostly in connection with a project involving the Corniche at Alexandria. Some members of the cabinet had decided to resign, in part because of the mounting feeling of opposition to Sidqi in the rest of the country and in part because of these accusations. The King, however, urged them not to resign, and since they were his men, they obeyed.[65] Matters became critical over a case that came to be known as the Budairi affair. The affair had very little direct connection with political events, but was certainly a by-product

63. Waterfield, *Professional Diplomat*, p. 189; April 4, 1931, F.O. 371/15403.
64. Ibid. (1932), 37:73 ff.
65. Loraine to Simon, Dec. 10, 1932, F.O. 371/16110.

of the policy of repression which the government had encouraged. The mamur of Budairi had been murdered by two men whom he had once arrested on a minor charge and then tortured in the most vile and demeaning fashion. The two men were tried for murder and sentenced, one to hang and one to life imprisonment. The sentences were appealed and duly came before the Cour de Cassation when the facts of the case concerning torture were made public. Abd al-Aziz Fahmi, the president of the Cour, described the mamur's methods as criminal, asserted that the torture provided extenuating circumstances, and drew the government's attention to the gross miscarriage of justice. In strong terms he requested that it investigate instances of alleged torture.[66]

Sidqi may have felt that an inquiry would open a floodgate of similar cases, for he knew the methods his men used to coerce people, and when two ministers in his cabinet insisted on the necessity for such an investigation he offered his resignation on January 4, 1933. He had previously come to an understanding with King Fuad that the cabinet would be reconstituted but without these two ministers, who were also the ones who wished to resign over the rumors of his peculation, and he therefore wanted to be rid of them. The men were Ali Mahir, Minister of Justice, and Abd al-Fattah Yahia, Minister of Foreign Affairs. Tawfiq Doss, Minister of Communications, was also dropped from the cabinet.[67]

Nonetheless in the new cabinet there were inevitable symptoms of tension between the King and Sidqi. In the interim Sidqi had suffered a severe stroke; while he was incapacitated the King ruled the cabinet through his man, Zaki al-Ibrashi, and may have come to believe that Sidqi was expendable. A direct clash occurred between King and Premier over the appointment of the Minister of Finance. Sidqi wished to appoint Hafiz Afifi, who was Ambassador at the Court of St. James, and the King wished to appoint Hasan Sabri, his brother-in-law.[68] Loraine, however, believed that the break had taken place because Sidqi had come to regard his position as impregnable and to wish to decide all matters himself, without consulting the King, a course that the King could not condone. Sidqi's resignation was therefore inevitable. He also resigned the presidency of the Shaab Party, and Abd al-Fattah Yahia became the new prime minister and was duly elected president of the Shaab party as well.

66. al-Rafii, Fi aʿqab, II, 201.
67. Loraine to Simon, Jan. 1933, F.O. 371/17007.
68. Memorandum by Sir Percy Loraine, Aug. 1933, F.O. 371/17007.

The Sidqi regime, which was the longest period of rule by decree since 1922, set further rules for future political behavior. The riots and strikes which the Wafd had incited against the government and which were reminiscent of early Wafd fervor were now used as an instrument against all opposition cabinets. From then on the pattern of government coercion to which the population responded by violence, whether spontaneous or fabricated, became the norm, to be used by all the parties. The students were the first group to be incited by the parties, not only because they were the most concerned elements in a population that was largely illiterate, or because they were the most volatile, but also because many of the student leaders were on Ahrar, Wafd, and Shaab payrolls and received regular monthly salaries from these groups. But although the students were bought by the parties, (or at least some among them were), the rest were soon to take the bit in their teeth, to develop an autonomy of action, and to use strikes as a weapon at their own discretion, so that the Wafd was to have trouble with them. In later days quite a number of cabinets were to fall through student strikes and demonstrations, which to this day have continued to exert pressure on the government. Once the element of violent protest had become an established factor of political life, the next step was to organize groups who would initiate protest actions in imitation of Fascist organizations that were then being created in Italy and Germany. The Wafd therefore created the Green Shirts, while Ahmad Husain created their counterpart, the Blue Shirts. Both of them were to develop into highly dangerous and disruptive elements in society.

The most important lesson that the Wafd party learned during their period in outer darkness was never to willingly cede government again and to treat the opposition as ruthlessly as Sidqi's government was treating them. A greater element of unscrupulousness therefore entered Egyptian political life, so that any means justified the need for seizing and retaining power. The King, who had been instrumental in bringing about such a sorry state of affairs, was henceforth regarded as an archenemy. That enmity between the monarch and the major political party was to extend to Faruq's regime. The public, in the form of that sorely put upon "man in the street," regarded these goings on with its habitual cynicism. Whatever respect the earlier governments had gained in public eyes in their struggle for the nationalist cause had been effaced by the present behavior of the parties. The gap between the rulers and the ruled, which had existed since time immemorial and had only closed under the impetus of special conditions such as the Urabi revolt of 1881 or the nationalist revolution under Zaghlul, once again widened to a chasm, and the constant suspicion of government motives revived in Egyptian hearts. That period of political instability gave birth to the Muslim Brethren a society founded on Muslim principles of the more rigid Hanbali school. In the beginning, in 1928, the society aimed at social reform, and was a form of operation bootstrap, hence constructive and socially valuable. But its founder Hasan al-Banna eventually turned his attention to political affairs, and, when he was frustrated in his designs by the Wafd, resorted to violence, as a result of which a spate of assassinations followed, that of the prime minister and, in retaliation, his own.[69]

Sidqi did not have an easy time governing the land. Bloodshed had become commonplace, throughout his rule, not only through clashes between demonstrators and police, but also through a rash of bombs which were thrown at Egyptians and Englishmen alike. The press, which attacked Sidqi's regime, was soon muzzled by a censorship that was stricter than any Egypt had ever known and which made it virtually a crime to write anything that was derogatory or critical of the government. Thus newspapers were forbidden to report on any affair in litigation or on criminal inquiries since they might prejudice judges or witnesses (law no. 28), and the government imposed a £E 500 fine or a five-year prison sentence on newspaper people infringing the law (no. 97).[70]

The Sidqi regime might not have become as violently hated as it was had it not coincided with the nadir of the worst economic depression that modern Egypt and the world had known. The price of cotton plummeted in 1930 to half its 1929 price, followed by a fall in price of all other agricultural products, so that farmers and landowners could not cover their costs or meet their commitments (pay loans, rents, or even buy seed and fertilizer). The people looked to the government to help them out of the economic depression, and certain measures were indeed taken, but they were not sufficient, and great hardship ensued until 1934. Sidqi, who was the cleverest financier in Egypt, saw one way out of the morass by creating the Crédit Agricole Bank in 1931 and its subsidiary the Crédit Hypothéquaire Bank in 1932 which were to lend money at a lower rate of interest. (Detractors of Sidqi take pleasure in pointing out that the idea for the Crédit Agricole had been formulated during the previous govern-

69. The prime minister was Nuqrashi Pasha.
70. al-Rafii, Fi aᶜqab, II, 178 ff.

اقتراح لمقاومة ازمة الجوع

(رئيس الوزراء) : فضيلتك دلوقت بقيت بطل زينا ا... مش عندك يأء اقتراح لتفريج الازمه ؟

.(شيخ الازهر) : ابوه امله ا.... مادامت الناس جعانه ومش لاقيه تاكل ، تصدر الوزارة مرسوما بجعل رمضان ثلاثة شهور .. يبق مع صيام واقتصاد وثواب ا

من كاريكاتير روز اليوسف

Suggestion for Combating the Hunger Crisis

Prime Minister [Sidqi Pasha]. Your Eminence is now a hero like us. . . . Have you no suggestions to offer on the crisis?

Shaikh al-Azhar. Hm . . . let me see. . . . Since people are hungry and can't find food, let the cabinet issue a decree making Ramadan three months long . . . that way we combine fasting, economy, and merit.

SOURCE: Ibrahim Abduh, *Ruz al-Yusif* (Cairo, 1961), p. 172.

ments and the plan only put into effect by Sidqi.)[71] Land rents for 1929-30 were decreased by one-fifth the agreed sum, and the following year they were decreased to three-tenths. Loans totaling £E850 thousand to small farmers were deferred, as was the cost of fertilizers bought from the government. In November 1930 a sum of £E3 million was offered in loans to small farmers against their new cotton crop. The Crédit Agricole Bank was entrusted with repayment of part of the loans against small farmers in order to arrest foreclosures for debt or mortgage. The Crédit Hypothéquaire Bank was charged with the purchase of land that had been foreclosed with a view to restoring it to its previous owners, and a further sum of £E3 million was added to its funds. All these measures were helpful, especially to medium- and large-scale landlords, but a mere drop in the economic bucket. Notwithstanding the depression, the government collected its taxes with extreme rigidity and it was alleged that the kurbaj was used in some villages.[72] Peasants were forced to sell livestock and personal goods in order to pay the taxes, so that while the government was helping out the small farmers in some slight measure, it was dealing most harshly with the large majority of taxpayers.

The government did nothing to decrease the rate of interest on bank loans. In 1933 it passed a law that extended loans for a number of years in order to lessen foreclosures, but it also added the interest to the principle and divided it into two portions: the first was to be repaid over thirty installments beginning January 1933, and the second, which comprised interest and back payments, was to be divided into two unequal parts of one-third and two-thirds, the first third to be repaid by yearly installments and the other two-thirds by the government. Thus the banks were not to lose any money, and indebtedness continued. In 1936 mortgaged land was still 18 percent of the cultivated area and the aggregate of debts totaled 5 percent of the estimated value of the cultivated land. Only in 1942 were some definite attempts made at solving the problem of indebtedness.[73]

Labor fared no better under Sidqi's regime in 1930. The repressive measures undertaken by the government served to bring about a merger of all the labor forces in opposition. Thus Prince Halim's Al-Ittihad al-ʿAm li Niqabat ʿUmmal al-Qutr al-Misri merged in 1931 with the Wafdist union IttihadʿAm al-Niqabat under Halim's leadership. The merging unions drew up a project based on European labor

71. Ibid., p. 186.
72. Ibid., p. 188.
73. Ibid., p. 191.

programs which demanded labor legislation and better working conditions, workers' representation in political activities through local municipal government, compulsory education for all Egypt, and the establishment of relations with the International Federation of Trade Unions and other labor associations.[74] The Sidqi government met these requests with its customary heavy hand and closed down the headquarters, which were immediately transferred to Halim's house. The Union voiced its protest to the International Federation of Trade Unions Congress then meeting in Madrid and the IFTU secretary was sent to Cairo to meet with labor leaders. In spite of Sidqi's attempts to stop the meeting the secretary managed to meet with representatives of thirty-three trade unions, after which W. Scavenlis put pressure on the government to carry out labor legislation.[75] The Sidqi government set up a Labor Bureau to implement labor legislation. The Bureau, which was housed in the police station, was understandably not effective and soon disappeared. The provisions of the child labor law of 1919, however, were extended to more than twenty industries listed as "dangerous," but enforcement was lax and conditions remained unsanitary and dangerous.

The Wafd then prodded labor into demonstrating against the Sidqi government and strikes became rampant. The following year, 1932, the government was forced to turn its attention to labor conditions. H. B. Butler was invited to come on a fact-finding mission, and his recommendations were implemented—over a decade later. Since there was no one in power representing labor, very little clout lay behind any legislative project that was presented, and very few were presented, whether by this or any other cabinet.

In 1933 a law was passed which prohibited the employment of children under twelve save in agricultural or domestic work, and while that stopped some of the worst industrial horrors, it still allowed children to be hired as domestics and be virtually bonded to their employers. Another law was passed that year limiting working hours for women to a maximum of nine hours, but the nine-hour-day became a general rule only in 1935. In 1936 a bill was passed making an employer liable for any on-the-job accident.

The trade unions in Egypt had very little dynamism because the leaders were themselves not workers but intellectuals or dilettantes like Halim, who knew theory but not practice. The workers themselves

74. Rauf Abbas Hamid Muhammad, *al-Haraka al-ʿummaliyya fi Misr: 1899-1952* (Cairo, 1968), pp. 72 ff.

75. Ibid., p. 95.

had little in common with their leaders, who in a crunch were likely to withdraw from the battle. Thus the labor movement in Egypt during that period was ineffectual and, in general, manipulated by the Wafd in their own interests, with promises of forthcoming changes once the Wafd returned to power. But when the Wafd returned to power the changes never came forth.

Throughout that difficult financial period from 1930 to 1933 Sidqi in his early campaign speeches had the temerity to say that Egypt's economic condition was healthy. The fallahin to whom he made these statements, and who were feeling the brunt of the depression, nonetheless accepted the bribes they were paid by the regime and voted Sidqi's government to power. They were confirmed in their opinion about the injustice of government, *zulm al-hukuma,* and thought that at least they would get something concrete out of it, by accepting 5 piasters for the price of a vote, adding the standard Egyptian cynical saying, *"ahsan min*c*aynihum,"* "better than their eyes."

Squabbles among politicians are commonplace. Conflict between politicians and the monarch are an equally prosaic factor in political history. The obviously crucial variable in the Egyptian experience was the British presence which imposed British imperial interests, and the personalities of the varying British residents, on the palimpsest that was Egypt. Egypt has had the reputation of being the easiest country to govern when an absolute authority is in charge, and the most difficult country to rule when that authority is diffused. The reasons lie in the Egyptian makeup and in historical factors. The Egyptian has not learned to obey the law because he has never identified with the lawmakers. The government, hukuma, has from time immemorial represented oppression and exploitation, and its laws were created to that end. The British occupation had introduced a fairer and more just system of government, but one that was alien, therefore suspect, and one that was motivated by British interests first and Egyptian ones second. Native Egyptian governments had as yet done little to prove their worth and to invite trust, so the government continued to remain suspect, and its laws were obeyed only when absolutely necessary, and if no loopholes could be found. The political parties in their internecine warfare had showed the man in the street that the vote was not a civic duty, but a commodity to be bartered since they were ready to buy it from him. The next step was for the average man to vote only if someone was willing to pay him. In the same sense the law was obeyed only if it was convenient, and not because it was the law. The bureaucracy functioned only if it feared dismissal, and not out of an esprit de corps. Their loyalty also was at a premium. An old Turkish proverb says, *"Balik bashtan Kokar,"* "A fish rots from the head," that is, the head sets the tone for an administration. Zaghlul had set the tone for an honest administration, but one that rewarded loyalty and penalized opposition. Nahhas had the reputation for being an honest man who had been ruined by a corrupt wife, and yet the first thing he did on reaching power was to raise his own pension, when it was still under discussion by the legal authorities.

Sidqi's government garnered the greatest number of financial scandals for Sidqi himself had few financial scruples. His greed was second only to that of the Palace camarilla who all rapidly enriched themselves and the King at the expense of the country, by selling titles and decorations and by peddling influence. The King, who was well aware of their game, did little to stop them; he may even have encouraged them as a means of rewarding their loyalty toward him. Corruption was therefore condoned just as it had been during the previous centuries, except now it was better organized. And yet there were more bureaucrats and politicians who were honest and had integrity than in the past and they were dismayed and disgusted to see their ideals trampled by the politicians who had promised them total reforms, along with independence, and who had managed to achieve neither. The intellectual climate of the thirties was therefore one of despondency and frustration which led to a feeling that ideas of Western liberalism were a failure and a sham, to the rise of various extremist factions (as we shall see later), and to various movements all seeking a way out of the moral and political stagnation of the country.

Although relations with England were the main preoccupation of Egyptian politicians, there were secondary problems closely tied to the first. Egypt was still subject to the Capitulations and was to remain so until the Montreux Convention was signed in 1938 which phased them out over a period of ten years. The Egyptian government was not entirely free to make laws or to implement them until the Capitulations had ended, and a whole generation of Egyptians bred on nationalist ideals of independence and national dignity had to accept the fact that they were second-class citizens in their own country. The richest communities in Egypt were exempted from taxation and from the law and yet they screamed the loudest when their interests were threatened, even when the threat was imaginary. The Egyptians knew that when gunboats were sent to Alexandria during the riots it was not to protect the local citizens but to protect the lives and property of the foreigners;

it was no wonder that a sense of bitterness welled in the young and a revulsion at what they considered the pious sham of Western principles.

At a time of economic recession, the screws were tightened on the population by the banks, which were in foreign hands, and by the mercantile and commercial concerns, which were also in foreign hands. Foreigners thus came in for a large share of popular opprobrium, and they and the government were jointly held responsible for the economic calamities of the day.

The British had loomed larger than life in Egyptian eyes since 1882, but the thirties were to diminish their stature. Mussolini's rise to power and his eventual occupation of Ethiopia in 1936 were soon to force both Egypt and Britain to rethink their positions, and lead to a successful negotiation of an Anglo-Egyptian treaty. Palestine and the increasing disturbances between Jews and Arabs was another factor that tarnished the British image of invincibility and roused Muslim feeling against her. The time had come when Egyptian intellectuals were no longer divided into those inspired by the Western ideas of the enlightenment and those inspired by Islamic ideals; they were now shattered into a multitude of sympathies and of different sources of inspiration. Pro-Fascist sympathies, mostly Italian inspired because Mussolini made the trains run on time and seemed to give his country back its dignity, arose in emulation. Muslim revivalist plans surfaced in reaction to the teaching of the materialist and therefore Godless West, communist movements started to appear, and socialist movements gathered strength. All these contradictory movements had one factor in common, the search for a moral revival, for the need to find a way out of the political morass into which Egypt and her squabbling politicians had fallen. Where the twenties were years of political anticipation and hope in Egypt, the thirties were years of intellectual ferment and soul searching and therefore intellectually much more fascinating to study, for the seeds they sowed were to lie dormant during the war years but to sprout afterward into the revolution of 1952.

VI

Détente and Return to Constitutional Government

AUGUST and September 1933 were months of rejoicing for the Wafd. August saw Sir Percy Loraine's exit after an Irish promotion as ambassador to Ankara, some said because he had offended the British community in Cairo and a visiting member of parliament.[1] Others claimed it was over an affair with a woman. September brought Sidqi's downfall and a new government under Abd al-Fattah Yahia, another palace-oriented cabinet. The new resident, Sir Miles Lampson, came from a post in Peking and was to be the last high commissioner and the first British ambassador in Egypt. He was a giant of a man, with a bluff, genial manner which contrasted favorably in Egyptian eyes with Loraine's cold mien. Although his name was to become anathema to all Egyptians in 1942, he was to enjoy a brief spell of popularity when a treaty between Britain and Egypt was finally signed in 1936.

On first arriving in Egypt, Lampson reported back to his government on the need for a reversal of his predecessor's policy of neutrality as a means to check excesses of palace rule, more blatant now than ever with the strong arm of Sidqi replaced by a compliant premier. The King had ruled with and through Sidqi, who could and did put some check on Fuad. Now Fuad ruled through the ministers and through Zaki al-Ibrashi, the director of the royal waqfs, a capable administrator of the domains, but also obedient in carrying out the King's wishes, which were not always in the best interests of the

1. Grafftey-Smith, *Bright Levant,* p. 125.

171

country. For instance, it was alleged that the royal estates were provided with all the irrigation water, roads, and bridges they requested, as a matter of priority over any reclamation schemes that the government may have planned.[2]

The British cabinet, a coalition under Ramsay MacDonald, was happier with a policy of neutrality but they quite saw the need for a change of policy if and when such an event became necessary, that is, if it concerned any of the four reserved points. A new factor, however, changed the situation, and that was the King's state of health in August 1934. Fuad had become seriously ill, and several specialists gave a very gloomy prognosis so that his demise was expected within a matter of weeks. According to the provisions of the Egyptian constitution, in the event of a minority the King's office is discharged by a regency council. The procedure was for the King to place three names in a sealed envelope to be opened after his death in the presence of Parliament. Miles Lampson was on holiday at the time, and Acting High Commissioner Maurice Peterson became quite worried over the regency council. Since Crown Prince Faruq would be a minor for another three years, a council known only to himself had been chosen by the King. Peterson was afraid that the council would consist entirely of the King's men, specifically Zaki al-Ibrashi, an appointment that would undoubtedly bring about "serious disturbances" for which British neutrality, termed support of the government by the Egyptians, would be blamed.[3] He therefore approached the prime minister and requested Ibrashi's ouster. Abd al-Fattah Yahia hesitated for a week before obtaining Ibrashi's dismissal, and then resigned himself, which did not make much sense for if the ouster of Ibrashi had been the true issue he would have resigned rather than effect the ouster. Abd al-Rahman al-Rafii claims the real reason was that Peterson had hinted that he would like to know the contents of the sealed envelope, which even Yahia found altogether unacceptable. Moreover Yahia realized that Fuad had decided on a change of government.[4] Presumably, Fuad felt that the end was near and that his son would have a better chance of success with a more popular government than with a palace cabinet. He therefore named Tawfiq Nasim as premier, and the latter accepted on condition that the present parliament be dissolved and new elections carried out. The King issued a rescript

2. Acting Oriental Secretary Peterson to London, Oct., 1934, F.O. 371/17977.
3. Memorandum from Peterson, Oct., 1934, F.O. 371/17980.
4. al-Rafii, *Fi aᶜqab*, II, 216.

abolishing the constitution of 1930, dissolving both houses of parliament, but with no mention of either a new constitution or a return to the 1924 one.

Some Egyptian historians, like Rafii, have chosen to believe that the 1924 constitution had been abolished in 1930 as the outcome of a deal between the British government and Fuad as a form of revenge on the Wafd for not accepting the negotiation terms offered. In the preceding chapter I have shown that the case was quite different. Rafii, however, was right in believing that Fuad did not mention a return to the 1924 constitution for two reasons: first, because the King was not happy with the prospect of an immediate return to constitutional life and, second, because the British government was not happy with the 1924 constitution. In fact, when the King mentioned to Lampson that he should return to the 1924 constitution, Lampson wondered if that were not suggested by the King out of spite.[5]

Meanwhile, there was a growing malaise inspired by a belief among some Englishmen that Italy, which was becoming very martial in Ethiopia, was ready to step into British shoes in Egypt. The Palace circles in Egypt were sure that in an Anglo-Italian conflict the Italians would win. Egypt, however, seemed less worried about Italian aggression and more worried about the impact of the Italian war in Ethiopia on their own relations with Britain.[6] With the external situation so ambivalent, Lampson felt it would be wise not to arouse the active opposition of the Wafd, who for the moment were behind Nasim. Thus Lampson urged British support of Nasim who "was so pliant and willing a collaborator"[7] unless the Wafd forced him to resign. The Wafd itself was facing internal difficulties once more and seemed to be splitting into two different factions than those of 1933. This time Nahhas and Makram were pitted against Mahir and Nuqrashi. The last two were in favor of exploiting the international situation and using more militant methods to force Britain's hand by bringing down the Nasim government.[8] Nahhas and Makram this time counseled moderation and support of Nasim.[9]

In October 1935 Nasim informed the oriental secretary that the

5. Sir Miles Lampson to Sir Robert Vansittart, Jan. 1, 1935, F.O. 371/19068.

6. Ibid.; also Haikal, *Mudhakkirat*, I, 377-378.

7. Oct. 1, 1935, F.O. 371/19076.

8. Zayid, *Struggle for Independence*, p. 150; *The Times*, Sept. 1, Oct. 1, 1925.

9. Ibid., Oct. 24, 1935; Lord Killearn, *The Killearn Diaries: 1934-1946*, ed. Trefor Evans (London, 1972), p. 71.

Wafd had demanded a return to the 1924 constitution and negotiations for an Anglo-Egyptian treaty, Nasim therefore proposed that he resign. Lampson was outraged and described the Wafd demands as "the crudest blackmail."[10] He did not think that the time was opportune for constitutional or treaty considerations when Britain was occupied with the international situation and was pouring troops into Egypt and transferring the fleet from its naval base in Malta to Alexandria.[11] Nasim agreed with him but said that the Wafd was adamant. Lampson promised him British support if he would hold out.

Egyptian politicians, who knew that the continued suspension of parliamentary life was the work of the British government, were afraid that the Italian situation would cause Britain to relegate Egypt to a protectorate status once more, and they were not far wrong. In his memoirs Lampson recounted, on June 5, 1936, a meeting with British Secretary of State for Foreign Affairs Anthony Eden concerning the Anglo-Egyptian problem. Eden asked him whether he did not believe that ultimately the "only fundamental solution of the problem was the inclusion of Egypt in the British Empire?" Lampson answered that the same question had been in his mind from the first moment he had reached Egypt in the summer of 1934, and he had recorded his belief in a report that he sent to London six months later; he went on to say, "Neither Egyptian nor I imagined British opinion was ripe for it. Consequently I had at that time advised that we should proceed slowly but systematically in an endeavor to tighten the material interests of the two countries in one another."[12] It would seem that British officials had learned little in over half a century with regard to Egyptian feelings of nationalism, and could still think in terms of bringing Egypt within the fold of the Empire; yet when Egyptians accused their British friends of these intentions they were pooh-poohed as being paranoid.

Lampson had to consider a list of likely successors should Nasim's cabinet fall, and the leading choice was Ali Mahir, who was regarded as likely to concur with British suggestions, so long as he did not demand assurances regarding the constitution or a treaty.[13]

Muhammad Mahmud criticized Nasim in a speech for governing without a constitution, as did many Egyptians, and for accepting British interference in Egyptian affairs, thereby diminishing Egypt's

10. Oct. 21, 1935, F.O. 371/19076.
11. Arnold Toynbee, *Survey of International Affairs* (London, 1937), p. 672.
12. Killearn, *Diaries*, p. 71.
13. Sir Miles Lampson to London, Nov. 4, 1935, F.O. 371/19076.

independence. He said that the only basis for a possible agreement between England and Egypt lay in a clear understanding founded on respect for Egypt's rights and sovereignty. He added that Egypt was ready to support England as an ally and to give the English all the facilities, in the event of a war, envisaged in the proposed Anglo-Egyptian treaty. If England did not respond soon, then Egyptians would feel that they were not getting a fair deal and the result would be regrettable.[14]

Mahmud and the Ahrar were still informally cooperating with the Wafd, for in spite of their mutual antagonisms they had been forced to remain together by circumstances. The students had been mainly responsible in bringing that forced coalition about. They had appealed to the Wafd and to the Ahrar to set aside their differences and to show some real patriotism by uniting at so critical a juncture in their country's history. Apparently Hafiz Afifi, who believed that unity was the only sound policy to follow, had acted as an intermediary between both groups who were shamed by the students into cooperating.[15] The students demonstrated repeatedly, shouting for a return to parliamentary life. Severe clashes between them and the police had occurred and during one clash four of the students were killed. The parties in consequence came closer together. Mahmud also improved his relations with the Palace,[16] and it seemed as though all the Egyptian elements were once more united and agreed on urging the British government to show a favorable attitude at such a critical time.

On November 9 Sir Samuel Hoare, the secretary of state, made a speech at the Guildhall, London, in which he discussed Egypt. The British government, he said, was not against a constitutional government in that country, but they had advised the Egyptian government, when it had consulted Britain, against a return to the constitution of 1924 because it had proved "unworkable" and against that of 1930 because it had proved "unpopular."[17] The Egyptians greeted that statement with rage, viewing it as an admission of guilt on the part of the British government of interfering in Egyptian internal affairs. It roused a furore among all levels of thinking Egyptians, especially among those who were most aware of the full extent of British intervention. At a Wafd meeting on November 11, Nahhas called upon

14. "Egitto: La lotta per la Costituzione in Egitto veduta da fonte francese," *Oriente Moderno,* 15, 7 (1935), 335; *al-Musawwar,* Nov. 15, 1935, p. 12.

15. Haikal, *Mudhakkirat,* I, 385.

16. Sir Miles Lampson to Sir Samuel Hoare, Oct. 28, 1935, F.O. 371/19077.

17. *The Times,* Nov. 11, 1935.

the nation not to cooperate with England as long as they encroached upon the constitution and upon Egypt's independence.[18] He also demanded that Nasim's cabinet resign to mark its disapproval of the British government, adding that if it did not resign the Wafd would no longer support it and would continue to oppose any cabinet that agreed to cooperate with England and that acted in opposition to the will of the nation. That same day Makram spoke to the students assembled at the Saadist Club and reiterated the same point of view.

Massive demonstrations, which included labor as well as students, once more broke out on November 13, the anniversary of the Wafd's historic meeting with Wingate. The following day, a number of students were killed by police fire. On November 28 a strike was called in mourning over the students who had been killed in the incidents, and shops were closed in the capital. The students continued to demonstrate throughout the month of December and their slogan was *"Al-Istiqlal, al-hurriya, al-dustur,"* "Independence, freedom, and the constitution." The events of 1919 seemed to be repeating themselves sixteen years later. All the political parties then declared themselves a United Front, and their representatives drew up a declaration which they addressed to the King on December 12, 1935, in which they requested a return to the constitution of 1924 and a settlement with Britain on the basis of the Nahhas-Henderson talks of 1930.[19]

Together with the war in Abyssinia the situation had imposed a "new set of circumstances," and Lampson saw that "closer Imperial Connections" with Egypt at that time were not practical but should nevertheless be kept "in reserve."[20]

Muhammad Mahmud told Cecil Campbell that the recent events could only be blamed on the British government, whose inflexible attitude had left the Egyptian moderates no recourse but to join with the majority party. If the constitution was restored, Mahmud believed that he could get Nahhas committed to signing a treaty and so "destroy the Wafd's raison d'etre," but if the constitution was not restored and prospects of a treaty settlement remained remote, then continued violence was inevitable. Nasim would be sure to resign and would most likely be replaced by a strong-arm premier, notably Mahmud himself.[21] By then Mahmud had become convinced that he was persona grata with the King because his party organ, *al-Siyasa,* had not criticized the palace during al-Ibrashi's ouster.

18. Haikal, *Mudhakkirat,* I, 382 ff.; *The Times,* Dec. 13, 14, 1935.
19. al-Rafii, *Fi aʿqab,* II, 232 ff.; al-Rafii was the representative of Hizb al-Watani.
20. Killearn, *Diaries,* p. 71.
21. Cecil Campbell to Robert Vansittart, Dec. 18, 1935, F.O. 371/19077.

On the day that the Declaration made by the United Front was delivered to the King, Nasim resigned and the King agreed to restore the constitution, for by then Lampson also had agreed on the need for restoring the constitution.[22]

There was great rejoicing among the Wafd and the other parties. Makram jubilantly called Nasim "the cleverest old man in Egypt with the supreme advantage of looking to be the most stupid."[23] He gave credence to the story that the students had played a conciliatory role between the two major parties precisely by denying that the students had played any part and claimed that the rapprochement was his own inspiration. In the same mouthful he praised Hafiz Afifi for his mediatory activities.[24]

With the restoration of the constitution elections were expected to follow within a few months, and they would no doubt return a Wafd government to power with a larger majority. The students who by the 1930s had become disillusioned with their leaders, started acting on their own, often in opposition to Wafd directives, and they were beginning to pose a problem now that their agitation was of no further use to the Wafd. In an effort to bring them under stricter Wafd discipline, a plan evolved to create the Rabitat al-Shubban al-Wafdiy-ya, League of Wafdist Youth, known as the Blue Shirts, which was expected to turn the students who joined into a disciplined and obedient organization. Thus, on coming to power after the election, the Wafd government would have an organization to support their policies.

On December 14, 1935, the United Front presented the high commissioner with a request for a statement by the British government regarding their willingness to conclude a treaty with the Egyptian government on the basis of the Nahhas-Henderson 1930 negotiations. Miles Lampson forwarded the request to London.

The British government was now faced with three alternatives: (1) to offer a two-clause treaty of alliance between the two countries which contained a recognition on the part of the Egyptian government of England's right to maintain troups in Egypt in order to secure Imperial communications; the reserved points would be resolved at a later time, although the capitulations could be ironed out, but a military alliance might not be acceptable to Egypt; (2) to present a complete draft treaty; (3) to temporize that no negotiations could be

22. Haikal, *Mudhakkirat,* I, 388.
23. Campbell to Vansittart, Dec. 18, 1935, F.O. 371/19077.
24. Ibid.

considered for the time being owing to the crisis created by the Italo-Abyssinian war, but that as soon as the international situation permitted such a treaty could be considered as long as Egypt kept peace and order within her territory.[25] The second alternative was eventually chosen.

After the resignation of Nasim's cabinet it was expected that a coalition cabinet would replace it and supervise the elections, but a rift had already appeared in the United Front. Muhammad Mahmud had been receiving student leaders at his house and was offering them large sums of money in return for their support on the side of the Ahrar and against the Wafd. The Wafd got wind of these events and screamed betrayal by Mahmud and his party.[26] Nahhas refused to join a coalition cabinet and insisted on a Wafd cabinet. Negotiations were hurriedly carried out among all the parties and eventually a modus vivendi was worked out in which a neutral cabinet was to be appointed by the King and immediate negotiations with the British government started. The negotiators were to be Ismail Sidqi, Muhammad Mahmud, Hilmi Issa, Ali al-Shamsi, Hafiz Afifi, Abd al-Fattah Yahia, Ahmad Hamdi Saif al-Nasr, and Mahir, Makram, Nuqrashi, Wasif Ghali, and Uthman Muharram were to join with Nahhas to form the Wafd contingent, all of whom were under the presidency of Nahhas. Elections were scheduled to take place in May 1936, and Ali Mahir, the Chief Royal Chamberlain, was chosen to lead an interim neutral cabinet.

King Fuad, who had been ailing since the end of January, died on April 28, 1936, at the age of sixty-eight, and was succeeded to the throne by his son King Faruq who was still a minor. Fuad had reigned over Egypt as Sultan and King for nearly nineteen years.

Fuad was a despot at heart, even though early in his reign he had mentioned to Sir Reginald Wingate his desire for a national assembly and a constitutional monarchy.[27] That was early in the nationalist movement when Fuad thought he could control Zaghlul and the budding Wafd; he had posed as a patriot in an effort to end British influence in Egypt. In so doing he seems to have taken a page out of his nephew Abbas's book when the latter had supported the nationalist movement and Mustafa Kamil in his bid to be rid of England in Egypt. But Fuad's support of the Wafd and of constitutionalism was ephemeral, and his real proclivities became obvious during the

25. Memorandum by Sir Anthony Eden, April 1, 1936, F.O. 371/19077.
26. Jan., 1936, F.O. 371/20097.
27. Wingate to Hardinge, Nov. 6, 1918, Wingate Papers, Durham University.

gestation period of the constitutional council. His pride suffered in his inevitable clashes with Zaghlul, when he found that he was outwitted and outmaneuvered by his former poker-playing partner, who even threatened his very throne. The history of Fuad's reign in Egypt can be briefly summed up by nationalists as a constant attempt on his part to undermine the constitution and undercut the government, often with great success. Like a modern-day Faust he offered ambitious men the position of premier in return for their obedience, and when the time came he cast them aside. His ruthlessness knew no bounds save those imposed on him by the Residency and the temporary ones that Zaghlul was able to erect. For all his defects Fuad had stature and a keen intelligence, which made his acts all the more heinous to his people, a people whom he despised and whose leaders he scorned, and who therefore returned these feelings doubly by detesting him wholeheartedly. Withal Fuad was a king who worked hard at his job and knew the ins and outs of government, unlike his son who would never be anything more than a playboy masquerading as a monarch. The one thing that father and son had in common was the love of amassing riches. Fuad, the poor prince, had become an excessively wealthy king, as his man of business informed the British resident.[28]

In the rubric of credits one must cite Fuad's efforts in founding the state university in 1908 and in inducing his sister, Princess Fatima, to donate over £E100,000 in real estate, waqf funds, and jewelry to erect the university buildings. He also founded other institutions of scholarly value, among them the Société Royale de Géographie, the Agricultural Museum, and the Entomological Society; and not least, he commissioned eminent French scholars like Hanotaux to set up an archival system and to write the history of modern Egypt. And while some of these works belong to the realm of panegyrics more than to that of history, many more works were valuable additions to our knowledge of Egyptian history and were based on the rich material of its archives. For the anomaly of Fuad was that with one foot in the nineteenth century and the other in the twentieth century he was intellectually able to recognize the urgent need for scholarly research in the history of his country and family, yet he turned a blind eye to his country's need for social and political advancement. In this he was a true son of his father who while wanting Egypt to become independent had driven her headlong into a foreign occupation.

The elections that followed the death of Fuad brought a large

28. Killearn, *Diaries,* p. 60.

Wafd majority and a new Wafd cabinet, headed for the third time
by Nahhas Pasha. The King's status as a minor had caused the
creation of a Royal Regency Council.

A new King and new elections elated the country. Faruq, who was
young and remarkably handsome, became invested with an aura of
glamor as a fairy tale prince, which brought him the adulation of his
countrymen who were ready to see in him every virtue that they had
missed in his father. His advent was regarded as a good omen to a
people who guide their lives by omens and signs. Hopes therefore ran
high that a favorable conclusion to Anglo-Egyptian relations was in the
offing. The parties, tired of their squabbles over the past years and
shuddering at the memory of collectively being cast into outer political
darkness as they had once been under Sidqi, buried their differences
long enough to agree to a committee that would represent all the
different parties negotiating the treaty. The Wafd were sure that this
time they would achieve the goal they had set for themselves since
1919, that of negotiating a treaty with Britain which would give
Egypt real independence. The Liberal Constitutionalists hoped that a
treaty settlement would thoroughly defuse the Wafd and thus mitigate
the need for their demagoguery and public disturbances. Each party
suffered from battle fatigue and assumed that it would emerge from
a treaty settlement that would also squelch the opposition. The despondency of the early thirties gave way to a brief euphoric spell, which even
the fears of a world war did not dispel.

Parliament passed new legislation which decreased agricultural loans
by 20 percent of their value and declared amnesty for all political
crimes since 1930. The more repressive of Sidqi's laws were repealed.
The period of political stagnation was now making way for a period
of constructive activity, the end of which was the Anglo-Egyptian
settlement of August 1936.

Only the exigencies of the international situation could have brought
the Egyptians to accept a treaty that gave them little more than
the terms that had been offered a decade ago. Now, however, the
Egyptians were willing to make concessions, as were the British. During the Sidqi regime both Wafd and Ahrar parties had assured the
British government that they would be willing to accept the previous
terms negotiated and set aside the Sudan question for future negotiations. (That was exactly the way Nasir was able to effect the evacuation of British forces from Egypt, by agreeing to separate the Sudan
question from the rest of the issues.) Britain's rising preoccupation

with the Axis, and especially with the Italian presence in Libya and
Abyssinia, had made her conciliatory. Both sides were willing to
compromise.

The 1921 Curzon-Adli talks failed because Egypt insisted that British
troops withdraw from Egyptian cities to the Canal Zone area. The
1924 Zaghlul-MacDonald talks failed because they had disagreed on
all points. (Nevertheless Egyptians were less angered at the failure
of the talks than at what they considered MacDonald's shabby treatment of Zaghlul.) The 1927-28 Tharwat-Chamberlain talks failed
because the Wafd had refused to accept the presence of British troops
in Egypt. The 1929 Henderson-Mahmud talks failed because Mahmud
could not secure popular support in Egypt. The 1930 Nahhas-Henderson talks failed over the Sudan.

The 1936 talks opened with the military terms. The Egyptians assumed that these terms had been settled in 1930 and were surprised to
find the British delegates discussing terms other than the ones they had
previously settled. The weakness of the United Front may have been
one reason for reopening the military question. The change in the
international strategic situation and Britain's growing fear of a global
confrontation and her need for a secure military base and backing in
Egypt were definitely other reasons. Even when an agreement over
the military terms was finally reached by the delegates, however,
they continued to be a principal source of objection to the treaty on
the part of many Egyptians.

The main features common to the abortive talks of 1929, 1930,
and 1936 were: (1) termination of the occupation; (2) establishment of
a treaty of alliance between the two countries; (3) support by Britain
of Egypt's admission into the League of Nations; (4) mutual consultation between the two parties; (5) neither party to complete with a
third power any agreement prejudicial to the other; (6) responsibility
for the protection of foreigners resident in Egypt and of minorities
to pass to the Egyptian government; (7) the United Kingdom to
assist Egypt in the abolition of the capitulations; (8) both parties
to offer mutual assistance in the event either party became engaged
in a war; (9) an interchange of ambassadors to take place; (10) nothing
in the treaty to prejudice the rights and obligations of either party
under the Covenant of the League of Nations or the Kellogg Pact;
(11) any differences arising in regard to the application or the interpretation of the treaty which the parties are unable to settle by direct
negotiations to be dealt with according to the terms of the Covenant

of the League; (12) the Suez Canal Zone off limits for aircraft other than British.[29]

Muhammad Mahmud objected to the stipulation that required the Egyptian government to build roads in Egypt to facilitate British troop movements in case of an emergency. He also feared the clause that required Egypt to render assistance to Britain in the threat of war or of "an apprehended international emergency," a clause he felt could embroil Egypt in any number of situations in the wake of British policy. Muhammad Mahmud explained his reservations to Mahmud Abd al-Raziq, Husain Haikal, and Abd al-Aziz Fahmi, and asked their advice. Fahmi agreed that an "international emergency" could cover an infinite number of situations, but suggested that since the rest of the delegates were in favor of continuing the negotiations Mahmud accept the military terms on condition that in return the capitulations be completely revoked.[30] The British government agreed to that stipulation and on August 26, 1936 the Treaty of Alliance between Britain and Egypt was signed.

According to the terms of the treaty (see appendix) British forces were to be stationed in the Canal Zone although units were to be allowed to remain in Alexandria for not more than eight years until barracks had been constructed for them by the Egyptian government. These barracks were to become inviolable to Egyptians and under the exclusive authority of the British officers. The British Air Force was to be allowed the freedom of the Egyptian skies while the air space over the Canal Zone, except for an air corridor for passage from west to east, was to be prohibited to all airplanes excluding the Egyptian (art. 8, sec. 11).

While the Suez Canal was recognized as an integral part of Egyptian territory, it was to be defended by British forces until the High Contracting Parties agreed that the Egyptian army was in a position to take over its defense. After twenty years had elapsed, the matter would be reopened and if no agreement was reached by the High Contracting Parties then it would be submitted to the Council of the League of Nations or to any other mediator that the Parties agreed to. (The actual terms of article 8 said that British forces "in

29. Peterson memorandum summarizing the situation, Jan. 6, 1936, F.O. 371/19077; see also Zayid, *Struggle for Independence*, pp. 136 ff. For a full discussion of the negotiations see Shafiq Ghorbal, *Tarikh al-mufawadat al-Misriyya al-Biritaniyya*, Vol. I (Cairo, 1952).

30. Haikal, *Mudhakkirat*, I, 414; also Zayid, *Struggle for Independence*, p. 169.

cooperation with Egyptian forces" were to ensure the defence of the Canal, but no Egyptian forces were in fact used for that purpose.)

Article 13 stipulated the desire of the High Contracting Parties for bringing about the speedy abolition of the capitulations and the application of Egyptian legislation to all foreigners residing in Egypt. After a transitional period Egypt would also be free to abolish the Mixed Courts. (On April 12, 1937, the capitulatory powers met at Montreux and signed the convention by which the capitulations were abolished and the Mixed Courts were to continue until October 14, 1949, when they too were abolished.)

The High Contracting Parties agreed to negotiate a revision of the treaty after twenty years, although the alliance between both countries, which was of a permanent nature, was to continue. Egypt was to be admitted to the League of Nations on May 27, 1937, and it was to be responsible for the lives and property of foreigners (art. 12), which had been one of the reserved points. Both countries were to be represented by ambassadors but the British ambassador in Egypt was always to be senior to all other ambassadors (contrary to international usage which decrees that the ambassador who had been longest at his post, i.e., the first comer to the host country, be the senior ambassador, so that the seniority ranking changes continually). British personnel were to be withdrawn from the Egyptian army and so were the British judicial and financial advisors (oral declaration made by Nahhas on August 10, 1936). Egypt nevertheless accepted the services of a British military mission, and agreed that the armament and the equipment of its army should be furnished entirely by Great Britain. The command of the police was to continue under a British officer for a further five years when it was to pass into Egyptian hands.

Both High Contracting Parties undertook not to adopt toward foreign countries an attitude that was inconsistent with the alliance nor to conclude treaties inconsistent with the terms of the present treaty. In 1942 this clause was to give Sir Miles Lampson, who had become Lord Killearn, the opportunity to surround Abdin with a tank division and threaten Faruq with instant deposition if he did not change his pro-Axis premier and replace him by Nahhas, who had pro-Allies sympathies. Yet when Egyptians interpreted pro-Zionist British policy in Palestine as an infringement of the terms of the treaty their objections were swept aside as impertinent and irrelevant.

The Sudan, which could have developed into a major barrier to any agreement as it had done so often in the past, and was to do in the future, was deliberately shrouded in ambiguity, although in 1934 the King of England had assured Sir Miles Lampson that England intended to abide by the promises given to the "Shaikhs of the Sudan and hold it."[31] The British governor-general in the Sudan was to continue to exercise his powers as in the past, and the Egyptian inspector-general of irrigation was to attend the governor-general's council. An Egyptian officer was to join the governor-general's military staff, and the Egyptian army was to be allowed to participate in the defense of the Sudan. The High Contracting Parties agreed that the primary aim of the administration of the Sudan was to be the welfare of the Sudanese peoples.

The Treaty of Alliance purported to regard both High Contracting Parties as equals, yet no English official expected His Britannic Majesty's Government to design foreign relations in accordance with Egyptian interests, although the converse was very firmly required of Egypt. No one expected the Egyptian forces to help the British forces defend the Canal—although lip service was paid to the idea—but the Egyptian forces were not even allowed to enter the Canal Zone without prior British authorization, let alone defend it.

The terms of the treaty were touted by Nahhas as the best that could be had at the time. On his return from England he announced that the treaty negotiated was one of "honor and independence." Many thought quite differently and believed the terms to be not much better than terms that had been negotiated in the past by other premiers and turned down by the Wafd as not good enough. The Liberal Constitutionalists were dissatisfied the most with the treaty, which they did not believe gave Egypt complete independence, and they insisted on reserving the right to continue the "struggle for complete independence without restrictions" after the treaty had been ratified.[32] That was entirely consistent with the line they had adopted from the very early days of the nationalist movement, when they had assumed that any agreement negotiated was a preliminary to further negotiations for better terms at a later date. The Wafd, on the other hand, had always held out for the optimum terms in any treaty before they would agree to ratify it, yet here they were two decades later accepting terms that were not even satisfactory to the Ahrar.

Before the treaty was ratified it was presented to parliament for

31. Killearn, *Diaries*, p. 22.

32. Zayid, *Struggle for Independence*, p. 185; Ghorbal, *Tarikh*, p. 304; Haikal, *Mudhakkirat*, I, 417.

المصرى افندى

تقى دى المعـاهده اللى حتحقق أمانينـا

يا وقتى السـوده يا خسـارة تهـانينـا

والله غرقنـا خـلاص وعملتها فينـا

جون بول ينول الورود وجايب لى حزمة شوك

فيها حنش قرصته ع القـبر رمينـا

_____

النحاس باشا

حنش فى عينك ازاي تخاف من التعبان

أمسك بلاش الدلـع أما حقيقى جبـان

نعم نعم قرصته صعبة وسم كمان

لكن دا أصغر حنش نقيته بأيديه

امسك بقى يا أخى يمكن ما لوهش سنان

دأى روز اليوسف فى المعاهدة

Ruz al-Yusif's Opinion of the Treaty of Alliance
(In rhyme in Arabic)

Misri Effendi. What calamity has befallen us! John Bull gets the flowers and we get thorns with an asp in them.

Nahhas Pasha. Don't be a coward and fear an asp. I know it is lethal but I chose the smallest I could find, and perhaps it has no teeth.

SOURCE: Ibrahim Abduh, *Ruz al-Yusif* (Cairo, 1961), p. 172.

discussion. Muhammad Mahmud discussed the terms with his colleagues in the Ahrar party and publicly in parliament. He considered
the treaty only a step toward complete independence, for though it
had definite advantages it had equally definite disadvantages. It
placed Egypt in the awkward position of having to commit itself to
helping Britain in times of international crisis, as well as committing
it to build roads for military purposes which would place a tremendous
economic burden on the country which had only barely recovered
from the economic crisis. Moreover the clause that allowed Britain the
freedom of the Egyptian skies may be all very well in terms of defense,
but he saw that it could easily become a form of domination and of
supervision of the country. He added that had the international
situation not been so volatile he would not have accepted the treaty,
but since so much effort in the past had been expended over a treaty
with England which should have been spent for internal reforms he
tended to favor endorsement of the treaty, although that would not
stop him from continuing to strive for the removal of all restrictions
on Egyptian independence. Ismail Sidqi agreed with Mahmud that
the treaty did not give Egypt complete independence but, he added,
one should face matters realistically. The Egyptian army would be in
no condition to undertake the defense of Egypt for a long time to
come, so the alternative was to allow the British army to do so.[33]

Haikal said that he did not know whether he was for or against the
treaty, and then proceeded to analyze the terms in great detail. He
said that the terms of the treaty granted Egypt the right to build up
her army, but were England to stop supplying the army with arma-
ments for one reason or another, the army would simply degenerate
into a collection of athletes, without weapons (these were almost
prophetic words). On the other hand the defense of the Canal implied
a permanent British presence in Egypt for it was made part of the
unchangeable nature of the alliance. According to the terms, the
Sudan might be interpreted as coming eventually under complete
British or complete Sudanese domination, but in no way as coming
under Egyptian domination. After all, had not so many negotiations
floundered on these same terms? Egypt, he said, was forced by the
terms of the treaty to abandon henceforth a stance of neutrality and
become actively involved in any British adventure. Do we want a
country that is free to strive according to the dictates of the times? he
asked. Do we wish to think in terms of an Eastern, Arabic, Islamic

33. Ghorbal, *Tarikh*, p. 305.

policy which would join us in common with our neighbors? Or are we willing to settle for internal reforms leaving our foreign policy to be conducted by the British government? If you, he said, addressing his colleagues, want complete independence for Egypt, then the treaty does not give it and you will have to reject it. If you want Egypt to enjoy the rights and privileges of the British dominions, then the treaty does not give them and you must also reject it on these grounds. But if you wish to change the present tedious conditions without worrying about the consequences, and there may be good in such a stand, then accept the treaty, but on condition that whatever terms and limitations it placed which hinder Egyptian independence be modified as soon as possible.[34]

The general feeling among educated Egyptians, students, intellectuals, bureaucrats, politicians, even moderates was one of limited satisfaction with the treaty, for it was plain that its terms allowed the British occupation to continue, albeit in a less obtrusive manner than in the past, since the British forces would be out of sight in the Canal Zone. But they were still very much there in the country as the events of 1942 and 1951 and following were to prove, for while no one could foretell with any degree of certainty the events of later years, most Egyptians were quite sure that the British government would have no compunction at bringing their forces out of their corner in the Canal the minute events in Egypt required it. Their very presence on Egyptian territory could hardly be construed to spell independence for Egypt, but they also knew that British forces were not about to evacuate Egypt at that critical time of world history.

More important in immediate terms was the fact that Egypt had undertaken to shoulder a heavy financial burden in terms of building barracks in the Canal Zone, roads—like the road from Cairo to Alexandria across the desert, which was called Tariq al-Muᶜahada, the Treaty Route, and the roads from Cairo to Ismailiya and Port Said, from Cairo to Suez, and from Suez to Port Said—and bridges, all for the use of the British army. There were some who feared that the roads might be used against Egypt at some time in the future.

Those who were equally dissatisfied with the terms of the treaty, but for entirely different reasons from those which exercised the Egyptians, were the foreign communities resident in the country. For nearly a century these communities had dominated the economic and commercial life of the country without abiding by its laws, and without

34. Ibid., pp. 310 ff.

paying its taxes; now they were faced with a situation by which they were to lose their preferential position and to be forced to abide by the rules and regulations of the land; they would have to depend on the local courts of law for litigation instead of on the Mixed Courts where some of the judges were foreign, or on the consular courts in criminal cases. The outcome looked bleak to them, and the immediate reaction was a rapid transfer of capital out of Egypt.

The British government, on the other hand, was satisfied with the treaty which gave it the necessary military guarantees that it needed, and which dealt with only one of the reserved points, the protection of foreigners and minorities (who had never really asked Britain to protect them) while shelving the other three points for a long time to come. The treaty paid lip service to Egyptian independence while allowing Britain to continue in the role she relished as guide, mentor, and big brother. England could interfere in Egyptian internal affairs when the occasion called for it, in the name of protecting British interests as spelled out in the treaty. For the first time since the occupation of 1882, Britain's presence in Egypt had been rendered legal, and by virtue of an agreement with the Egyptian government.

The Egyptian politicians knew full well that in accepting the treaty they were paying the price for getting rid of the capitulations and for entering the League of Nations. The price was high but it was worth it to acquire internal legal and economic control, and it was the best deal that could be had at the time, for it left open the way for a better deal in the future. But if that were the case, replied the intellectuals, why were the earlier terms not accepted with the same proviso? Why could they not have accepted equally imperfect treaties instead of prolonging the agony for so many years? The question was, of course, rhetorical. Autres temps, autres moeurs, and certainly international considerations, like an imminent world war, had been one of the prime motives in accepting the treaty by the Egyptians. But if any one were innocent enough to labor under the delusion that British influence in Egyptian affairs internal or external was to lessen, he was soon to lose these delusions and face the fact that as long as Britain maintained a large army on Egyptian soil, it was in control of Egypt. That was a lesson that all colonized countries were to learn through bitter experience.

The immediate gains to Egypt of the Anglo-Egyptian Treaty of Alliance seemed to be positive, for in addition to a certain measure of administrative freedom, Egypt entered into an agreement with the Suez Canal Company by which two Egyptians were appointed to the board of directors. The annual payment by the company to Egypt was raised to £E300,000 and the company agreed to hire Egyptians up to 35 percent of her work force. These were gains for Egypt which had financed over half the total costs of the canal, which had literally dug it with the blood, sweat, and tears of the population working under corvee-like conditions and consequently dying like flies, which had incurred a monumental debt much of it in order to finance the canal, and which had resulted in a foreign occupation. It is no wonder that Egyptians to this day regard the history of the Suez Canal with bitterness; it may be a major waterway but in local terms it was also a gigantic stone of Sisyphus.

King Faruq assumed his full powers of majority in July 1937 and was to continue the duel between palace and Wafd which his father had begun. The Wafd was even more weakened by serious internal dissension which culminated at the end of the year in the expulsion from the party of Ahmad Mahir and Mahmud al-Nuqrashi. Nahhas, by now, completely under the thumb of Makram Ubaid, who had egged him on, assumed after having negotiated a treaty successfully that he was sufficiently in command of the Wafd party and of the country to be able to dismiss his two ablest, although extremist, advisors, an act that left Makram as the sole éminence grise. In turn Nuqrashi and Mahir founded a new party, the Saadist party, in which they adopted the name Saad as an indication that they were the true followers of Saad Zaghlul, unlike the Wafd which had become deca-dent in the hands of Nahhas and Makram and had deviated from the true nationalist principles. It is notable that Makram too was soon to become displaced and to be cast out of the party. In 1942 he too founded another political party, al-Kutla al-Wafdiyya, the Wafdist Bloc, which also claimed to follow the true Wafdist principles. Makram, however, went a step further than Mahir and Nuqrashi and published al-Kitab al-Aswad, The Black Book, in which he exposed Nahhas's misdeeds and financial irregularities of a mini-Watergate nature which left Egypt for months buzzing with tales of political high jinks and for which Makram was arrested and tried. The Black Book was banned, but, as usual in Egypt as elsewhere, it managed to circulate clandestinely and to reach a larger audience than it might have done had it been available in a normal fashion.

By that time Nahhas had lost his reputation of pristine purity (which some had always doubted anyway, but which the majority had credited him with having) and of financial integrity, having married a woman who was determined to get rich quickly.

King Faruq, sustained by his mentor Ahmad Hasanain, an Oxford blue in fencing and a charmer, was determined from the very beginning to show the Wafd that notwithstanding his youth he was not to be bullied or dominated by anybody, least of all the Wafd. Faruq's tragedy was that he had lost the firm guidance of his father at too early an age and had been allowed to do as he willed from the outset. His mentors spoiled him and indulged his every caprice so that he grew up without developing a sense of responsibility. And since he had considerable charm he managed to fill the court with those who would cater to his whims. They all assumed that he would acquire wisdom with age, little knowing that wisdom cannot be picked up along the way like a commodity, and that in the words of Lord Acton, nothing corrupts more than power, especially absolute power. Like his father, Faruq had obtained the support of the religious institution, al-Azhar, which was once more directed by that extremely able and enlightened alim, Shaikh al-Maraghi. Shaikh Mustafa al-Maraghi was an honest man, truthful, and much respected by the Residency and by all the Egyptian politicians, a rare tribute. He had done much to assist in forming the coalition between the dissident parties during Sidqi's regime and was a patriot. He had been won over by Faruq from the start and had given him his unswerving loyalty, as most Egyptians had done, for Faruq was the first ruler in the long history of Egypt to come to the throne on a wave of rising expectation and was rewarded with the undivided love and loyalty of his people. Faruq could have done anything in Egypt, and he did, repaying the love and trust of his people with treachery, which brought about his deposition and exile in 1952. The adulation with which Faruq was surrounded because of his winning personality, in contrast with the feelings of hatred his father had roused, was reflected in the political arena. The only ones not to be taken in by Faruq's charm were the British authorities. Lord Killearn's diaries are filled with entries where he considers the need for removing Faruq from the throne.[35] History seemed to repeat itself, except this time the principals were Faruq and Killearn rather than Abbas and Cromer.

The first conflict between the young king and the Wafd involved Shaikh al-Maraghi. The issue revolved around the oath of allegiance that Shaikh al-Maraghi wanted the King to take in al-Azhar as a form of coronation ceremony which was to have the overtones of a Muslim *bayʿa*. The King was then toying with the concept of becoming caliph

---

35. Killearn, *Diaries*, pp. 121, 131; "AE [Anthony Eden] The only thing to do is to kick the boy out," p. 134 passim.

of the Muslims as his father had done, and to that end the ulama of the Azhar were to trace his genealogy back to the Prophet, causing not a few eyebrows to rise at the idea that a man known to be of French and Albanian ancestry could have pretensions at descent from Quraysh. Nahhas objected to the ceremony and rightly insisted that the King need only swear an oath to uphold the constitution, for as head of a secular state that was the only ceremony necessary. Another source of friction was over the appointment of Ali Mahir Pasha as chief of the royal cabinet. Unlike his brother Ahmad, Ali Mahir had been one of King Fuad's supporters, and was therefore strictly opposed by the Wafd who were suspicious of any influence he might have over the young king.

By then the Wafd party had seen the need for bringing the students in line and had set up Rabitat al-Shubban al-Wafdiyya, League of Wafdist Youth, under the leadership of a lawyer, Zuhair Sabri. Later on this was to develop into the paramilitary, fascistic organization, al-Qumsan al-Zarqa, the Blue Shirts. Other similar organizations were founded by the opposition, one of which, Misr al-Fatat, Young Egypt, also called al-Qumsan al-Khadra, the Green Shirts, had been founded in 1933 by Ahmad Husain representing the extreme right wing, with the slogan "Country, Islam and King." In 1940 Ahmad Husain was to turn socialist, but in 1938-39 he was used by the King (and had links with palace men like Ali Mahir) as a lever against the Wafd.

The program of Misr al-Fatat was designed to attract youth, for it posited the revival of former glories at the hands of the young. It aimed to unite Egypt with the Sudan when as allies of the Arab states Egypt would lead them all. That was a fairly novel idea at the time, and one that was not popular with many nationalists who saw no connection between the problems facing Egypt and those facing the other Arab lands. It was a period in which Sati al-Husri carried out a debate with Taha Husain and Lutfi al-Sayyid in the vain attempt to draw them to the side of the pan-Arab movement. The movement did however win the favor of King Faruq, much as a similar movement headed by Kawakibi at the turn of the century had met favor with the Khedive Abbas, and for the same reason, since it called for the creation of an Arab caliphate.

The Misr al-Fatat preached an end to foreign economic domination by nationalizing all such interests and by curtailing foreign privilege. That was bound to be a popular move especially when we keep in mind the fact that the issue of the capitulations was only to be discussed in 1937 at Montreux and to come to an end twelve years later.

On the local level the organization planned to set up cooperatives, to use mechanized farming (thus doubling arable land), and to give encouragement to local industries by the use of protective tariffs including the creation of an adequate infrastructure. The first protective tariff had been set up in 1930 with tariff reforms that allowed Egypt fiscal autonomy and the liberty to impose protective tariffs on imports instead of the former practice of adhering rigidly to an 8 percent duty imposed ad valorem on all imports. It was this measure that allowed large-scale industrialization to proceed in the country.

Lastly, the organization spread the concept of an "Egyptian mentality" which was to be exported to the Arab world and which was to bring all the Arabic-speaking countries closer together. The budding Misr Company for Cinema production which was founded in 1925 and the Egyptian State Broadcasting Corporation had done much to spread Egyptian culture throughout the Arab world, to enhance Cairo's position as the cultural capital, and to turn the Egyptian dialect into the equivalent of BBC English. But in order to spread and awaken civic awareness in the remote rural areas of Egypt and the Arab world, the organization preached the need for the expansion of mass media facilities.

The members of the group were enjoined to lead a clean, spartan life, to eschew the loose morals associated with the westernized elite, and to develop martial virtues. They attacked corruption in its outer forms of alcoholism and prostitution and campaigned for clean living.

The palace men who sympathized with Misr al-Fatat's ideals were Ali Mahir and Aziz Ali al-Misri. Al-Misri was a born revolutionary from his early days when as an officer in the Ottoman army he had been sentenced to death for his activities in founding secret societies among the officer corps. Later on he was to become known as the mentor of the young officers who had organized the 1952 coup d'etat. It was alleged that the social program that the Free Officers carried out as soon as they seized power was in effect derived from Misr al-Fatat especially in the fields of spreading a new mentality through mass media, nationalization, limitation of landownership, closer links with the Arab world, and many others.[36] It can also be pointed out, however, that the program posited by Misr al-Fatat was to an extent similar to the program spread by another organization, that of the

36. P. J. Vatikiotis, "Nasser: A Political Portrait," lecture, University of California, Los Angeles, Feb. 26, 1974.

Muslim Brethren, which was to rival and overwhelm Misr al-Fatat. Their programs in terms of industrial and social reforms were similar, with slight variations where in one the Islamic content was stressed above all others whereas in the other it was updated in the forties by socialist principles. Both, however, preached a martial spirit of sacrifice for the homeland, and preached by example.

The Blue Shirts and Green Shirts were manned by the toughest elements among the youth and both used strong-arm tactics to terrorize the opposition. Many of Egypt's leaders were said to have paid off the Green Shirts to avoid being harassed by them. In time the control of the Wafd party over the Blue Shirts weakened, and the Central Committee disbanded it once it recognized their potential danger, but that was not until all the moderate elements had banded round the King in fear of the Wafd's use of such organizations. The moderates and the King anticipated a Wafd dictatorship for, after all, the Western precedents were there. The King cleverly marshaled all the forces of opposition against the Wafd: the moderate politicians, the dissident Wafdists, the palace old guard, the religious hierarchy, Misr al-Fatat, and the university students who adored him and looked upon him as one of themselves, as the hope of youth in the future, and last, but most important, the army. One of the recent developments consequent to the 1936 treaty was the expansion of the military academy which in the past had been a strictly limited aristocratic bastion for the less intelligent sons of the rich. It now opened its doors to all ranks of society and became a means for vertical mobility in Egyptian society. One of those who was to benefit from this change was Gamal Abd al-Nasir. The move to open up the military academy could have earned the Wafd the loyalty of the officer corps and spelled victory for the party, had not the King stolen a march on them by giving the army his patronage and offering it special favors, clearly indicating that he was their main protector. The army, in consequence, became his tool and stood aloof from party politics. Allegiance to the King became its cornerstone, an allegiance that was not shaken until 1948 when the King shoved his army into a war for which it was ill prepared and supplied it with defective arms on which he had made a financial profit.

By its insensitivity the Wafd had allowed the King to outmaneuver them and to isolate them from the rest of the power groups in the country. Even the fallahin, who formed the backbone of Wafd supporters, were also won over by the young king. The Wafd's position for the time being seemed bleak indeed. By using the powers that the constitution gave him over the budget and the appointment of senators, the King was able to precipitate a crisis by the end of 1937. During a mass rally of students, the Wafd, for the first time heard people yelling for its downfall and shouting their support for the King. Faruq seized the opportunity to dismiss the Wafd cabinet in somewhat discourteous terms. Parliament was dissolved a month later and new elections followed. In the interim a government under Muhammad Mahmud was formed.

The 1938 elections brought victory to the newly formed Saadist party and to the Liberal Constitutionalists who together won 193 of the redistricted 294 seats; the Wafd won only 12 seats. Muhammad Mahmud had a difficult time running a cabinet composed of Saadists, Ahrar, and Royalists, all with diverging interests, and his ministry lasted for only one year, but during that period a number of important bills were passed: a civil service act, a capital gains tax, and an inheritance tax.

The Mahmud government was dismissed in August 1939 and succeeded by a cabinet headed by Ali Mahir and formed of a majority of Saadists.

The same political pattern that had been established under Fuad continued under Faruq. Cabinets did not fall through a vote of no confidence nor did they finish a term of office; they were dismissed at royal will. Parliaments never lasted their term of four years but were invariably dissolved by decree. The average life of a cabinet was eighteen months and during the ten-year period from 1926 to 1936 parliament sat a total of thirty-two months. The constitutional life of Egypt therefore had little stability and even less continuity, buffeted as it was by the waves of internecine conflict and at the mercy of royal prerogatives.

When World War II broke out in Europe, repercussions were felt in Egypt. British wartime preoccupation with imperial security and with survival was to bring back a Wafdist government on the heels of a military incident. The wheel had turned full circle and the party that had started its existence locked in a battle for national integrity against the British forces of occupation ended the cycle by joining the British forces in coercing the King to accept a change of government, for Faruq and Mahir had laid plans to open Egypt up to the German advance in North Africa. One often wonders what would have happened had Nahhas, who succeeded Mahir on British orders, refused to serve under British dictates, and had the Egyptian politicians showed a united front by refusing to buckle under Lord Killearn's threat of deposition and by rejecting the King's plot to deliver Egypt to the Germans. No doubt the King would have been deposed in 1942 for Killearn and Sir Anthony Eden, the secretary of state, had been indulging in such talk.

Egyptian political life was to continue in a more stilted and shackled fashion during the war years, and to deteriorate to the point where only a revolution could effect any change. In July 1952 a military coup d'etat overthrew the regime; on July 26 Faruq was sent into exile and his infant son was made King of Egypt under the aegis of a regency council formed of a member of the royal family, the Prince Abd al-Munim (son of the deposed Khedive Abbas II), Dr. Bahi Eddine Barakat (Pasha) (son of Fathallah Pasha Barakat and the former *rais diwan al-muhasaba,* chief state auditor), and an army officer, Rashad Muhanna. The following year Egypt was declared a republic.

VII

The Second Dimension: Socioeconomic Factors

Egypt's liberal experiment could not hope to be entirely successful because of certain basic political and socioeconomic factors. Assuming that political events comprise the first dimension in any description of a society, then socioeconomic factors comprise the second dimension and cultural and psychological factors the third.[1]

Certain changes occurred in Egyptian society in the wake of that brief attempt at instilling a constitutional way of life in the country which brought it closer to becoming a modern society. A comprehensive picture of the economic developments that occurred is beyond the scope of this volume but the more salient features are underlined in so far as they affected Egyptian society. Irrespective of whether the changes were positive or negative in nature, they were vital to the growth of the nation and may be described as inevitable growing pains, no different than those undergone by industrialized societies, except that they were concentrated in time and took place later than in Western countries. The overall picture of the exploitation of the poor

1. This chapter is based on the works of Charles Issawi: *Egypt at Mid-Century* (London, 1954); *Egypt in Revolution* (London, 1963); "Economic and Social Foundations of Democracy in the Middle East," *International Affairs*, 32, 1 (Jan. 1956), 27-42; A. E. Crouchley, *The Economic Development of Modern Egypt* (London, 1938); W. Cleland, *The Population Problem in Egypt* (New York, 1936); F. Harbison and I. A. Ibrahim, *Human Resources for Egyptian Enterprise* (London, 1958); Ali M. M. Barakat, "Tatawwur al-milkiyya al-ziraᶜiyya fi Misr wa atharuh ᶜala-l haraka al-siyasiyya." Unpub. Ph.D. dis. Cairo University, 1972.

by the rich is commonplace, as is the fact that a society sharply divided into educated rich and ignorant poor is one in which government represents only the rich and their interests, until some of the poor become richer and more educated and develop into a middle group which demands a share in government. No land can go from misery to affluence in one generation, or from autocracy to democracy—by which I mean from the rule of the few to the rule of a popularly elected assembly that represents the many—without shredding its social fabric and creating a new one tailored to the new society. The liberal period was an interim period in which certain economic, social, and intellectual trends arose. These trends manifested the link with the traditions of the past and the link with the future—the continuity and change so dear to the heart of social scientists.

The Egyptian nationalists had accused the British occupation in Egypt of two major, concrete shortcomings and a variety of lesser defects: keeping the country uneducated in order to justify a continued occupation and killing off Egyptian industry in favor of a lopsided agricultural policy geared at supplying cotton to the mills of Lancashire. There was much truth and, of course, some exaggeration in these accusations. The need for education thus ranked high in the nationalist mind, and, while industrialization was paid lip service, it ranked lower in the agenda of priorities because of the system of capitulations and the fact that industry and commerce were tied up in the hands of the foreigners. Both education and industrialization were begun in the twenties and thirties and started an invaluable process of change within Egyptian society.

Education had been the cry of all social reformers from the time of Shaikh Muhammad Abduh onward. The education of men and of women had become the cry of young reformers like Qasim Amin and Ahmad Lutfi al-Sayyid. Thus the emancipation of women came to rank as the first positive result and the foremost contribution of the nationalist movement to the social history of women in Egypt, for no country can progress when half its population remains intellectually stagnant.

Under the impetus of the nationalist cause, the rich, upper class Egyptian woman, who had led a cloistered life of leisure and indolence, burst from her cocoon and joined in the strikes and demonstrations that swept the land. When the men were imprisoned the women agitated, made speeches, and organized boycotts, and while none of it had much impact save that it added to the ferment of the times it had the advantage of bringing the women out into the world. The veil, that symbol of the subjection and the alienation of the privileged woman, was discarded.

The movement for the emancipation of women began with the privileged classes because they were the ones who were veiled and secluded in a harem. The fallaha had never been veiled nor secluded but had spent her life working side by side with her husband. The nonworking-class urban woman, who imitated her more affluent sisters, was veiled and secluded. When the social leaders came out of seclusion the rest of society followed suit after a time lag that characterized the middle class clutch at respectability until change had become respectable. It is necessary to remember that women had to face the prejudices of their own sex as well as those of the male sex, so that their emancipation might have necessitated a longer period of gestation had not the 1919 revolution showed the need for their talents and allowed them the occasion to prove themselves in action, and so prove to themselves that they were capable of action. One must also remember that the emancipation of women was limited to the social sphere and did not confer the right to vote, or even the right of equal pay for equal work. Besides, that would have been anachronistic, for women did not perform the same work as men, and, indeed, women had to fight in order to go to work. It was not until 1956 during the Nasir regime that women were granted the vote.

According to Muslim law, women had the right to own property. Even Muslim women hidden in the harem have managed estates and transacted business, as Jabarti clearly recounts. Even though the woman's share of inheritance was legally half that of the male, it was in some way mitigated by the institution of the dowry, by the fact that no woman remained unmarried, and by the fact that the husband was entirely responsible for the support of his wife, regardless of the degree of her personal wealth. He could therefore not touch or dispose of her property without her prior consent. Discriminatory practices in the field of divorce, alimony, and child custody do exist, and the woman's movement began agitating against the worst abuses of the social system, like *bait al ta{^c}a,* a practice that forced a wife to return to the conjugal home by police force if necessary, arbitrary repudiation, and child marriage. It is not my intention to go into the history of the woman's movement in Egypt, but simply to point out that today *bait al-ta{^c}a* no longer exists, that the legal age of marriage for girls has been set at sixteen, and that women can more easily sue for divorce than in the past and can appeal against the abuses of the system.

The difference in the rate of literacy between males and females has also showed an appreciable change. Whereas in 1913 females formed 10 percent of the school population, in 1924 they came to 19 percent, with 122,114 girls out of a total school population of 634,618; in 1930 the figure went up to 24 percent with 218,165 girls out of 891,682 schoolchildren.[2] In the twenties the university opened its doors to women, and the first girl students met resistance, not from the rector, Ahmad Lutfi al-Sayyid, who was an advocate of women's education, but from their male classmates, whose sense of propriety was offended at having to associate and compete with women. That first breach, with the passage of time, caused the walls to collapse, and within the past decades women have invaded that last stronghold of male monopoly, the Faculty of Engineering, with gratifying results. It was not an easy victory but a long uphill struggle for women to prove themselves academically and in the business world. They had to break down traditional social disapproval which was clothed in a spurious religious garb, family objections, and the whole gamut of customs and mores which for centuries had shoved women into a harem. Once women had become educated they had to face a second battle in order to get a job, and there even the most progressive families, which had approved of educating them, disapproved of their attempting to go out into the world, so to speak. Tradition had decreed that only poor women needed to work; the rich must not. It was one of the reasons so many women engaged in volunteer social work which did not bear the stigma of "earning a living." In time that barrier also went down and today we see Egyptian women in every field of activity from cabinet minister to dean of faculty to head of a hospital. They belong to the upper cadres of the government bureaucracy, where they receive equal pay for equal work, and equal promotion. Discriminatory practices still continue although in much diluted form, but professionally and legally women have certainly come a long way—from the harem to the cabinet in fifty years.

The one field of social life which bears the unmistakable stamp of Egyptian women is social welfare, and in the twenties and the thirties that was the field where they concentrated their efforts and where they were most successful. When Egyptian politicians were busy with matters of independence, their wives took over the domain of social

2. *Annuaire Statistique: 1932-33* (Cairo, 1934), Table V, pp. 58-59.

welfare. Organizations such as al-Mar³a al-Jadida, Mubarat Muhammad Ali, and Tahsin al-Sihha set up a network of clinics, hospitals, schools, and orphanages all over the country. They pioneered every aspect of social welfare that exists in Egypt today, from homes for the aged and Braille institutions for the blind to rehabilitation centers for war casualties. All their activities were financed privately through donations and their volunteer labor. Whenever an epidemic struck the land, such as the dreaded malaria outbreak in 1944, the members of the women's organizations were the first to volunteer their services. Through their organizational network they galvanized sanitation units, set up mobile vaccination clinics (when they were needed), toured the land nursing the sick, and gathered funds for the needy, with the cooperation and the blessings of the ministries of Hygiene and Social Welfare, who had neither the funds nor the personnel necessary to cope with such emergencies, and who needed all the help they could get. These privileged women were able to raise enormous funds by taxing their friends and relatives and by never taking no for an answer. Their clinics took root in the villages because they represented the class of landowners and knew the local power structure. They would embarrass the local landlord into donating a plot of land, set up a dispensary, use the umda to entice the population into visiting it, charge a minimal fee, and within a few years the clinic would be self-supporting. The managerial and executive talents of these women produced remarkable results. One of the most outstanding among them was Mme. Hidiya Barakat, who was decerned the highest decoration in the land by a grateful government just a few days before she died in 1969 for having organized a clinic, dispensary, and hospital in nearly every major town in Egypt.

The picture was of course not entirely rosy, and for every Mme. Barakat there are three to ten Mme. Xs who could not care less about social problems, but Egypt is no different in that respect from any other country. The majority of women in Egypt are still in a secondary position, just as they are in countries the world over, but without the impetus of the nationalist women's activism their progress would certainly have taken a much longer time to reach today's level.

The second positive result of the nationalist movement and of the liberal experiment was better general education. The Egyptians had accused the British of restricting education to the production of government clerks and the inhibition of an intelligentsia. Education was therefore viewed as a panacea for all ills, and the rush toward education continues unabated to the present day.

In the nineteenth century education of a Western secular nature had been introduced under Muhammad Ali and his successors, but up to this century elementary education was largely carried out in the kuttab where a faqih taught the three R's, reading, writing, and religion, and perhaps the rudiments of arithmetic. Memory, the Quran, and the teacher's rod were the main tools of learning and teaching. The few primary and secondary schools that existed turned out government employees, while the growing number of foreign schools, many of which were confessional schools, catered to the minorities and to an exiguous number of Egyptians from the privileged families who could afford to pay the fees. The budget for education under Cromer was about 1 percent for he believed that if the Egyptians wanted education they should be made to pay for it, or do without and rely on British talent. In 1910 out of a total state budget of £E 15,130,000, the expenditure for education was £E 515,063, that is, 3.4 percent; in 1920-21, the budget went up th £E 40,271,000 and the expenditure for education rose slightly to £E 1,584,161, that is, 3.93 percent. By 1930-31 the budget had become £E 44,915,999, of which the sum expended on education reached £E 4,894,614, that is, 10.90 percent.[3] In 1925 a law was passed making elementary education compulsory in an effort to wipe out illiteracy, *mahw al-ummiyya,* which was recognized by the rulers as a barrier to the establishment of truly representative government. The intention was laudable, but compulsory education meant the building of schools on a large scale, the massive training of teachers, and the availability of government funds. Since the funds were not available, the program could not be adequately carried out, and primary education became compulsory only in the areas where schools and teachers were available. Nonetheless, the level of illiteracy began to drop, and even though to this day illiteracy has not been eradicated it was estimated in 1960 that 70 percent of the children of school age were enrolled in the primary schools.

Whereas primary education was aimed at stamping out illiteracy, secondary education was regarded as a step toward a career or a profession, either through the university or through the higher schools of learning, that is, it was a passport into the professions or into what was then socially more prestigious, government service. Thus, schools of secondary and higher education were a means to a better job, and the students who attended such institutions acquired social

3. Ibid., Table I, p. 148.

standing as future "effendis." Students therefore became a corps
d'elite in the country, and their importance in social and political
life far outmatched their real' contributions. The use of students in
political agitation, first against the British then against the monarch
and the opposition, caused the years 1935 and 1936 to be dubbed
the "years of youth." But these were years of youthful disenchantment
with the politicians, in part as a consequence of the political situation
and in part as a consequence of their own professional future which
seemed to be in jeopardy. For if the number of students had grown,
the absorptive capacity of the country had not, and by 1937 we see
the sorry spectacle of the unemployment of the intellectuals in a land
where the majority of the population was still illiterate. In that year
there were 7,500 baccalaureate holders who were unemployed, and
3,500 graduates of the university and of the higher schools who were
jobless. The total number of students who had graduated from a
higher institution of learning over the prior five-year span was as
follows:[4]

1928-29	1,061
1929-30	1,640, a growth of 54 percent
1930-31	1,269, a decrease of 8 percent
1931-32	1,544, a growth of 12 percent
1932-33	2,017, a growth of 30 percent

The general average growth was 21 percent. The government could
not cope with such rapid growth and was altogether unprepared for it.
In 1928 it had passed a measure that obliged all foreign firms to
recruit at least 25 percent of their personnel from Egyptian university
graduates, but that was a mere drop in the bucket. The *shahada,* or
degree, was no longer sufficient to guarantee its holder a job unless
it was accompanied by a *wasta,* a recommendation, so that employment accordingly went to those who had pull and connections rather
than to those who had only merit. Foreign firms preferred to appoint
graduates of the foreign schools who had a better knowledge of
Western languages than graduates of Egyptian institutions; and since
the foreign schools catered to the minorities, it added to the bitterness
of the Egyptians against the foreign firms, foreign schools, and minorities, and caused them to turn to those groups which urged that
Egyptians take over the economy and nationalize the foreign firms.

In time secondary education was rendered compulsory, and in the
fifties Taha Husain, who was minister of education, instituted free

4. Ibid., Table VII, pp. 175-179, see also Issawi, *Mid-Century,* p. 67.

university education. The outcome was that every classroom in Egypt bulged with students, facilities were overstrained, and the standards of instruction perforce fell. The problem still exists, and in worse form since the number of universities has tripled. Some bureaucrat assumed that the pressure could be eased by doubling the number of the bureaucracy, since the government was held responsible for finding jobs for its graduates, so several men were set to performing the job previously entrusted to one man, with consequent decline in bureaucratic standards and a heightening of general discontent.

Nothing is more threatening to the stability of a society than a mass of educated but unemployed people, the more so when in the past that mass had been encouraged to agitate for political reasons. The politicians had played at sorcerer's apprentice with the students and were overwhelmed by the activism they had roused. The unemployment of the white-collar worker and of the intelligentsia was another symptom of the changing face of Egyptian society, and another tear in the old social fabric. New ideas arose, and some of these were to burgeon into the revolution of 1952.

Among the projects which one can place in the rubric of education and which was a by-product of the 1936 Treaty of Alliance was the change in the military academy. Before the treaty the academy had been restricted to the sons of the wealthy who simply formed a guard for the palace, and a tiny officer group for the country's equally tiny army. The British army of occupation was the real army of Egypt. After the treaty had been signed Egypt was free to create an army of its own, and the academy opened its doors to let in the sons of the middle class and some of the sons of the lower class, for 10 percent of the students were allowed to enter free of charge. The most famous officer to come from the poorest milieu was Gamal Abd al-Nasir, the son of a postman. Whereas in 1928 only 21 men graduated from the academy, in 1948 the number had gone up to 229, a rise of over 1,000 percent.[5] The majority of the new army officer and new police officer corps came from the middle-income brackets, urban and rural, and formed the growing middle class of professionals, bureaucrats, and intellectuals. While it was then not customary to rank army or police officers among the intellectuals (and it is certainly not customary now to rank them among intellectuals in the highly developed countries) it has become more than obvious that today they should be ranked among

5. *Annuaire Statistique: 1932-33*, Table VII, p. 178, and *Annuaire Statistique: 1949-51* (Cairo, 1953), Table XV, p. 286.

that social group in developing countries, even though their contribution to the development of their countries is still the subject of acrimony among scholars. Whether or not we consider at least some of them to rank among the intellectuals, all certainly belonged to the educated milieu. Socially army and police officers were solid middle class, and their support of the regime, and especially of King Faruq, was the basic reason for its continuity. The regime did not collapse until the army withdrew its support from the King.

The third positive result of the nationalist movement was industrialization, which received its impetus with the founding of Bank Misr and its affiliates by Talaat Harb and his associates. The tariff reforms of 1930 gave it a boost, and the advent of World War II and the needs it created accelerated its rate, although Egypt's major industrial push came in the fifties. In theory the consequences of industrialization are the rise of a new urban bourgeoisie and the creation of a new working class, both of which in time challenge the hegemony of the landowning elite and replace it by a representative form of government. In practice the case is often different.

In Egypt the new infant industries did indeed develop a small, native bourgeoisie, but it was still dominated by the larger financial bourgeoisie which was made up of foreigners (Greeks and Italians, among others) and members of the minorities (especially Jews) who dominated economic life until the revolution of 1952 and the subsequent nationalization-cum-Egyptianization of the economy. Many of those who were registered as foreigners were members of Syro-Lebanese and Jewish communities, long-time residents in Egypt, who preferred to benefit from the advantages conferred upon aliens by the capitulations. Some of those registered as Egyptians were of other origins including Greek, Italian, and Armenian and had become naturalized subjects. The new native bourgeoisie, which in the past had mostly comprised the bureaucracy and ulama (although before Muhammad Ali there had been a flourishing native merchant and artisanal class, a protobourgeoisie or middle layer between the poor and the mamluks), and which now comprised entrepreneurs and "industrialists," was still small enough to feel insecure when measured against the foreign "giants." Rather than challenge the landowning class they joined forces with them, a common enough pattern. In turn the landowners invested in industry, so that many of the new "industrialists" were members of the landowning gentry. To give but one such example, Talaat Harb's associates were Fuad Sultan, Muhammad Shaarawi, and Ahmad Midhat Yakan, all large landowners. Capital for native Egyptian industry came from the large landowners and was basically financed by profits from cotton, although it was managed and organized by the new entrepreneurial, professional, and managerial class.

Once the beginning link was forged between landowners and industry, landowner/industrialists and landowner/merchants became the rule. Ahmad Abbud, who started as a young engineer and parlayed his entrepreneurial talents into one of the largest industrial empires in the land, became the owner of 5,000 faddans in Armant which supplied the sugar-cane for his sugar factory. Ali Amin Yahia owned the largest Egyptian cotton-exporting house and was also a landowner, as were the members of such families as Badrawi Ashur, Siraj al-Din, Sultan, Shaarawi, Shawarbi, and others. All these families invested in industry, commerce, real estate, and diversified their holdings. It was in a sense a return to the pattern prevalent among the affluent in the mamluk era as well as a definite capitalist trend. The links among political activity, economic enterprise, and landowners were positive and strong, and explain why there was no challenge to the power of the landowners from the new industrial elite, for they were to a large extent one and the same, or wanting to be. A relatively small number of the new bourgeoisie were not landowners, but they threw their lot in with the rest. From that period we note a definite trend in the educational pattern among the sons of the affluent. Whereas in the past they had gone into law and letters as an entrée into government service, there was now a push into engineering, medicine, and commerce, that is, into the professions, as an alternative to government service which was becoming more and more overcrowded. The younger generation was therefore a professional one, and with few exceptions only dropouts among the sons of the rich remained full-time landowners with no other occupation. The trend intensified during the war years, and in the forties and fifties mothers of marriageable daughters turned up their noses at rich landowners who did not have an occupation other than land. Even when land was their main source of income, mothers preferred suitors who also had a profession, because by then the professions had become more prestigious.

The landowning class and the new bourgeoisie fused even closer with the war years. The war caused inflation and a dislocation of food supply so that in 1942 there were famine riots, labor disputes, and strikes for higher wages. Prime Minister Nahhas is alleged to have said in another connection earlier that strikes were only permissible for political reasons,[6] and the workers were severely repressed by force

6. Berque, *L'Egypte*, p. 578.

and imprisonment. It had not occurred to Nahhas and his group that unemployment was one of the foremost political reasons for disturbance in the land. These socioeconomic problems, however, roused fears of a class war among the newly affluent bourgeoisie, who immediately saw their interests threatened and their profits cut by the rising discontent of the working classes, so they sought for a greater degree of cooperation with the landowning elite and followed a policy of subservience rather than of opposition to the government, again not an unusual political pattern. The government did force some salary raises on the employers, but they also saw that the workers remained quiescent.

The war years and the malaria epidemic of 1944, which devastated the countryside, shocked some social consciousness into the rulers. Whole villages in Upper Egypt had been wiped out by a new strain of malaria which weakened the undernourished peasantry, made them susceptible to pneumonia, and killed them. The euphoria of postwar philosophy, the Atlantic Charter and its ideals, all together served to develop ideas of social justice in the forties. It is then that we note the beginning of an awareness of the need for agrarian reform, of the plight of the fallah, of the gulf between the rich and the poor. And while the project for agrarian reform fell flat in a parliament dominated by landowners, it was to surface with greater success the following decade. The need for social and economic reforms became obvious to any but the most obtuse. To recognize a need is not necessarily to do something about it; it is, however, a step in the right direction, which led to the events of the fifties and the sixties.

It is notable that Egypt's *Annuaire Statistique* of 1932-33 mentions industry in one table, page 39, among a listing of occupations, but has a chapter headed "Agriculture" and another headed "Cotton," pointing out the importance of these occupations. The *Annuaire Statistique: 1949-51* has a chapter on "Syndicates and Cooperatives" and one on "Industry." In 1932, 555,969 men and women were listed as employed in industry out of a total population of 14,177,864. If we add those employed in services, commerce, and transport, the number of workers rises to 1,401,170,[7] that is, 10 percent of the population. The picture was to change in later decades but that does not enter the scope of this work, and one need only refer to the massive amount of books written on Egyptian economy for further enlightenment; what does fall within our scope is that during these two decades a labor move-

7. *Annuaire Statistique: 1932-33*, Table XII, p. 36.

ment was in the making and some form of labor legislation did come into existence.

In their book entitled *Egypte en Mouvement*, Jean and Simone Lacouture called one chapter "Les Guerres Accoucheuses de Révolution," for whereas World War I gave birth to the 1919 revolution, World War II and the Palestine campaign of 1948 gave birth to the 1952 revolution. World War I had caused a severe economic dysfunction in Egypt, and that was one reason why the workers and fallahin joined in the Wafd movement as an expression of general discontent which became focused into nationalist activity. Nationalist movements do not spring from ideals only; they are bred on real grievances. The workers in Cairo and in the other urban centers joined the strikes on the second day of the revolution, on March 10, 1919. The strike of tram workers succeeded in paralyzing public transport. When the authorities arrested the Italian labor leader who had founded a Bourse de Travail on the charge of being a "Bolshevik," the union of printers to which he belonged staged a strike which closed down the nation's newspapers, except for three which managed to hire nonunion workers. Although the efforts of the workers were useful to the Wafd and emphasized the total nature of their popular support, their number was small compared with the number of students and fallahin, and the Wafd members were concerned over left-wing elements among the workers, who were attempting to organize labor unions. They were particularly susceptible to the charge of Bolshevism which the London *Times* of August 20, 1919, had leveled against labor leaders. In 1920, when a Russian Jew, Joseph Rosenthal, organized a labor association and a socialist party with definite communist sympathies, people were convinced that labor associations were Bolshevik groupings. In 1921 a law was passed prohibiting the "transference of salaries" to trade unions, thereby impugning the legality of the organization.[8] The large-scale strikes of workers throughout 1924 made the Wafd see the need for taking over the workers' associations. When Abd al-Rahman Fahmi, who had set up the secret Wafd organization, was released from jail, he set about creating a Wafdist labor organization, later renamed Ittihad al-ʿam li-niqabat ʿummal al-qutr al-Misri, General Association of Labor Unions in Egypt.[9] Anis claimed that the group embraced 120 unions and comprised 150,000 workers, a somewhat inflated figure for the time.

8. Harbison and Ibrahim, *Human Resources*, p. 175.
9. Rauf Abbas Hamid Muhammad, *al-Haraka al-ʿummaliyya fi Misr:* 1899-1952 (Cairo, 1968), p. 85.

The program of the association included demands for labor legislation and better worker-employer relations. The following year Fahmi
quarreled with Zaghlul and resigned from the association; a more
experienced labor organizer, Mahjub Thabit, took his place. Little
could be done in the following years, which covered the Ziwar era and
its repressive measures, and Wafdist attempts to create a united labor
front failed. The Liberal Constitutionalists tried to woo labor organizations and won some of the unions over by the fact that they were the
first party to do something concrete for labor, but most of the unions
were chary of a party that so clearly represented employers. Inter-
party strife was therefore mirrored in the labor unions who were pitted
against each other by the political parties or enlisted by them in the
service of the nationalist cause, all of which may explain in part the
unions' lack of solidarity. The number of labor organizations was
slowly growing and by 1930 there were 55 unions. The total number
of urban workers was then over 1.4 million. Nearly half the workers
resided in Cairo and Alexandria so that a strike carried out by labor
in either city was most effective, as the Wafd tried in vain to prove to
Sidqi, who retaliated by the customary brutal measures when they
organized labor strikes.

Labor legislation was enacted subsequent to the Butler mission in
1932, but only four laws were passed over the next nine years: a
regulation on the employment of children in industry; minimum hour
regulations for women employed in industry and commerce; regulation
of work for males in specific industries regarded as hazardous or
unhealthy; compensation for accidents during work.[10] Labor conditions continued to be poor; the employers disregarded the laws and
looked upon workers as expendable and replaceable in a rapidly
populating society. A wave of strikes broke out in 1936 influenced
perhaps by worker agitation in France after the Front Populaire had
come to power in May, but that was severely repressed by the
authorities.

World War II gave an impetus to industry and labor legislation,
especially when continued labor strikes occurred. In 1942 the Trade
Union Act was passed recognizing the unions of industrial workers but
prohibiting the establishment of such unions among agricultural
workers. In 1948 the Labor Act established the framework for compulsory arbitration and government intervention in labor disputes. To
the workers the most important measure that was passed was the
Individual Contract of Employment Act in 1944 which outlined the

10. Harbison and Ibrahim, *Human Resources,* pp. 154-155.

relationship between employer and worker, the conditions of employment, the manner of payment, responsibility of the employer for the worker's health and safety, and the conditions governing discharge. That was the first instance of legislation limiting the authority of the employer. Since then labor legislation has grown to cover more contingencies and to protect the worker more effectively, but the trade unions, although growing in strength, are dominated by the government who became the largest employer after 1952, so that collective bargaining is replaced by government legislation — not unusual in developing countries. The condition of urban workers has therefore shown a distinct improvement. A recognizable working class is emerging conscious of its rights, although somewhat hazy as to its obligations, and backed by trade unions who can and do exert pressure on the government.

None of Egypt's industrial ventures could have survived without a high tariff law and import restrictions, both of which were a direct result of Egypt's changing political condition. Thus the 1937 census lists 54,989 industrial establishments founded between 1928 and 1937, 17,011 founded between 1918 and 1927, 9,862, founded before 1918, and 10,159 with no date of founding.[11] While problems of industrialization do not fall within the scope of this work which leaves Egypt on the threshold of the industrial period, one must keep in mind that the unrest that occurred in the thirties and subsequently was a by-product of the change from an agricultural society to one that was in the process of industrialization. Industrialization is a disruptive force that breaks down traditional patterns and family relationships and generates ferment among the masses until new ways of life have arisen and had time to settle. Industrialization breeds social unrest, it fires aspirations, and produces protest among the workers in the early and the transitional stages.[12] The masses, uneasy in their new roles, are subject to the seduction of agitators and demagogues, which aptly describes much of the appeal of organizations such as al-Ikhwan and Misr al-Fatat which fed on popular discontent. Ferment is necessary for the social development of a country and is preferable to apathy; in time the masses will, one hopes, come to see through the demagogue and the agitator.

The basic barrier to the development of representative government in Egypt was the unequal distribution of wealth, which placed the many at the mercy of the few. A study of national income undertaken

11. *Annuaire Statistique: 1949-51,* Table VIII, p. 475.
12. Harbison and Ibrahim, *Human Resources,* p. 144.

in the forties showed that where the annual income of an agricultural laborer was £E 30, that of an industrial worker was £E 75, that of a cabinet minister was £E 2,000, and that of a bank president £E 5,000. The value of national capital was estimated at £E 1,200 million which was broken down as follows: (in £E million) 660 from land, 170 from residential houses, 130 from industry and commerce, 140 from state property, and 100 from Egyptian securities held abroad and from property owned by foreigners in Egypt.[13] About half the land was owned by 21,000 persons (see table 3). About 10,000 persons owned the bulk of bank deposits, and 18,000 persons owned 58 percent of the total value of taxed property in buildings. In brief, about 10,000 persons owned the larger part of the national capital. That small, affluent oligarchy controlled the political life of the country as well, and government was representative of their interests and not of those of the rest of the population, who were manipulated by the few. The monopoly of the wealth by the few is the hindrance to the development of representative government, not whether a country is industrial or agricultural. But the rule of an oligarchy can also be regarded as a normal step away from autocracy and toward the development of representative government. In time even an oligarchy can be over-whelmed by a democracy.

Among those who controlled the financial destinies of Egypt were the aliens, a large percentage of whom until the twenties completely controlled Egyptian economy and until the fifties retained the lion's share. Compared with them the Egyptian oligarchy was new and insecure. True, there were some families who could trace their wealth back several generations, like the Yakan (whose wealth could be explained by their relationship to the royal family), the Sultans, and the Shaarawis. Others came from the rural gentry, were sons of small landowners and umdas like Zaghlul. A few like Nuqrashi, never accumulated wealth, nor indeed even tried to do so. Still others made their fortunes through their professional skill as lawyers, doctors, or engineers. In brief it is necessary to emphasize that many of the members of the oligarchy had only recently acquired wealth and were therefore strongly affected by the economic fluctuations of their times.

The twenties and thirties were thus not only decades of political change but also decades of extreme economic stress. Three waves of depression characterized these years and greatly contributed to the feelings of insecurity and instability which swept rich as well as poor. Economic fluctuations were especially devastating to the rural gentry

13. Issawi, *Mid-Century*, p. 84.

and to the new rich, who had increased their land ownership through the practice of buying new land on credit, through bank loans, and by mortgaging property. Basically they were economically insecure even though large landowners. The diaries of Barakat, for instance, abound in entries that express his increasing financial worries and his lack of ready capital. For this reason the new rich were in favor of law and order, which would protect their interests, and frowned on agitation, which might threaten them. At the same time the confraternity of wealth brought together people of conflicting political goals but similar economic ones. Sidqi was closely allied to industrial capital, hence his opposition to labor. Landowners in parliament refused to adopt measures favoring the fallahin, for that would cut down their margin of profit, but they strongly supported irrigation projects, for that would increase their profits. Whenever an economic crisis loomed they all turned instinctively to the government on the assumption that it would manipulate matters in their favor. Insecurity and instability of an economic nature found an echo in the political malaise of the time. Prosperity never lasted long enough to give the fallah some breathing space before depression decked him once more, or to allow the landowner enough sense of security to invest large sums in new industrial ventures, hence their limited growth.

The desire of the Egyptian elite for political independence was echoed in their need for economic independence: independence from relying on foreign banks for loans, from foreign trade for products, from foreign manipulation of the whole economy in favor of foreign interests, which threatened the Egyptian landowner with ruin. The government was therefore the buffer between the Egyptian moneyed class and the outside world. But even while the affluent Egyptians wanted independence, economic and political, they also realized that they needed the British market for their cotton, hence the ambivalent attitude toward Britain, the love/hate relationship which characterized that period and which explained in some measure why Egyptian politicians were willing to ally themselves with the British against fellow Egyptians. I am not trying to minimize the fact that divergent ideologies or world views played an important role in alienating Egyptian politicians from one another, but the economic factor did play a part in determining political behavior and political alliances. The Wafdists became more moderate with increasing wealth, and developed a common outlook with the Ahrar than had previously been so. The bond that united all the parties against Sidqi was not only political adversity but also economic animosity at what they regarded as his inadequate handling of the situation. Especially were they incensed because Sidqi had more industrial and commercial interests than agricultural ones, which represented the interest of the majority of the politicians, and so rightly or wrongly they tended to believe that Sidqi did not have their interests at heart.

The waves of depression that hit Egypt came in 1921, 1926, and 1931. Between the waves came peaks of prosperity, all of them linked to cotton. World War I had produced a wartime demand for cotton for military purposes, so there was a boom. Cotton rose from an average price of $19.28 in 1915-16 to an average price of $38.52 in 1918-19. The price of land and the rents of agricultural land rose high, and the price of foodstuffs multiplied. Beans *(ful)* and maize, the two basic ingredients of the fallah diet, multiplied four times their price in 1914. The cost of living index went up to 237 from its prewar level of 100. The profits of these war years therefore went to the landowners and the merchants, but the mass of the population suffered from the high cost of living and from the shortage of cereals, with resulting stresses on society. Using 1913 as a base year, the index of agricultural production showed that where a faddan yielded 100 in 1913, the index went up to 166 in 1918, and to 294 in 1919.[14]

In 1921 depression set in and the index of land fell to 119.1. The price of cotton plummeted to $24, and the price of foodstuffs fell accordingly, which was a blessing for the poor. Landowners set up a clamor and demanded that the government provide some measure of relief. The government, in a mistaken belief that the size of the cotton crop had some effect on its price, restricted the acreage of cotton to one third of any holding.[15] That measure was a total failure as far as the international price of cotton was concerned, for the world price had little to do with the size of the Egyptian crop; all it did was rouse the animosity of the landowners, who would have lynched the minister of agriculture with deep pleasure. Oddly enough, that errone-ous notion continued to persist in government circles, and every wave of depression in Egypt was followed by a government measure re-stricting the cotton acreage. The next bad year came in 1926 when the price of cotton fell to $21 after a bumper crop in 1925; the index of land income fell to 114.6, even lower than in 1921.

The next two years were fairly profitable until the crash occurred in 1929 in New York and echoed round the world. Cotton prices fell from $20 in 1928 to $12 in 1930 to $10 in 1931, while the index of in-come per faddan fell from 110.5 in 1929 to 84 in 1930, to 72.2 in 1931

14. *Annuaire Statistique: 1949-51,* Table XXXI, p. 413.
15. For more details see Issawi, *Mid-Century,* p. 115.

and to 66.1 in 1932. Cotton and income from land were lower than they had been before the war. Landowners faced bankruptcy. They could not find buyers for their cotton and could not afford to pay off their loans or mortgages. General panic swept the land and once more everybody expected the government to take measures. The government bought up massive quantities of cotton, but that was only a slight help. The Crédit Agricole Bank in 1931 and the Crédit Hypothéquaire in 1932, which the government under Sidqi had founded, offered some measure of relief, as did a government measure decreasing rents by one-fifth, but Egypt took a long time to recover from the depression, so that the index of land income by 1939 had reached only 100.5, that is, 0.5 more than its prewar value.

The annual per capita income also showed a decrease, and where it had been estimated at £E 12.4 in 1913, the average was £E 12.2 for the years 1921-1928, £E 8.2 for the years 1930-1933, and £E 9.6 for the years 1935-1939. The consumption of cereals and pulses likewise declined from 3,588,000 tons in 1914-1916 to 3,915,000 tons in 1936-1938 for a population that had increased by 3 million people. To make matters worse, in 1930 a prohibitive tariff was put on cereals which stopped its import, but no government policy increased the acreage of cereals planted; to the contrary the acreage for wheat decreased from 20.4 percent in 1924 to 17.5 percent in 1930 and for maize from 20.2 percent to 20.1 percent in the same time span. The members of the urban working classes were therefore paying an annual subsidy of some £E 5 million to the agricultural population.[16] It comes as no surprise therefore that the thirties were years of unrest and violence, and that famine riots occurred in 1942. The economic and political dislocations of the country were but two sides of the same coin, and whether violence was stimulated by economic hardship or by political events is a moot point.

To make matters worse Egypt was rapidly becoming overpopulated. The first warning had been sounded in 1936 by an American, Wendell Cleland, in his book, *The Population Problem in Egypt,* but no one took that warning too seriously. Many were pleased at the growth in population, once again because of cotton, which demands a large population to service it. Few people worried that the increase in population had not been countered by an increase in agricultural land or in the founding of industries. The increase in population had shown a slight fragmentation in landholdings. Whereas in 1920, 90 percent of the landowning population having 5 faddans or less owned 27.9

16. Ibid., p. 123.

percent of the land with an average holding of 0.9 faddans, in 1933, 93 percent of the landowning population owned 30.4 percent of the land with an average holding of 0.8 faddan, a decrease of 11 percent in small landowners. On the other hand, landowners holding 50 faddans or more showed the contrary trend. Whereas in 1920, 0.007 percent of the landowning population owned 40 percent of the land with an average holding of 167 faddans, in 1933, 0.005 percent of the population owned 39 percent of the land with an average holding of 181 faddans, an increase of 9 percent (see table 3). The rich were becoming richer and the poor poorer.[17]

Social problems were practically shelved until the 1936 treaty had been signed, and economic problems were faced only when a crisis developed, never before. Such a situation is obviously not unique to Egypt, but the reasons for it were. Politicians were obsessed by the British presence and by the glory that would accrue to those who helped to end that presence, and they therefore shoved all other problems aside, including socioeconomic realities. The frustration of the population was augmented by the fact that no tangible rewards were forthcoming from the political situation. There was no vicarious national glory to wave before the populace and reward their misery. They had been told to wait until the nation was free from the foreign exploiter and then the golden age would come, but the end seemed to be as far away, if not farther, than when the struggle began. Both the economic and the political situations contributed their share to the feelings of pessimism and unrest, *tasha'um wa qalaq*, which characterized the early part of the thirties and which have been described by writers on the period. It is true that one cannot blame the world crisis on the Egyptian rulers, but the economic hardship in the country, which affected both rich and poor, and the inefficient measures taken by the government to control it could be blamed on Sidqi, who for a long time preached to the fallahin about the soundness of the economic policies his government had introduced, when they were in fact facing starvation and bankruptcy; and he used repression on the workers and the middle groups as well as on the political leaders, who were facing the same hazards.

Once the Treaty of Alliance with Britain had been signed there were no further excuses for the rulers to draw upon, and they were forced to face Egypt's twin problems of poverty and overpopulation. The definite

17. Comparison between *Annuaire Statistique: 1932-33*, Table I, p. 226, and *Annuaire Statistique: 1949-51*, Table II, p. 352.

TABLE 3
LAND DISTRIBUTION

Number of faddans	1920		1933	
	Number of proprietors	Area in faddans	Number of proprietors	Area in faddans
Total	1,886,761	5,535,352	2,299,979	5,818,390
Less than				
1 faddan	1,207,694	485,045	1,586,609	620,812
1-5 faddans	506,025	1,064,137	554,725	1,153,492
5-10 faddans	79,767	551,276	84,926	574,363
10-20 faddans	38,707	533,563	39,769	535,227
20-30 faddans	11,866	287,021	11,934	287,738
30-50 faddans	9,190	352,783	9,417	316,453
Over 50 faddans	13,512	2,261,527	12,599	2,285,305

SOURCE: Egypt. *Annuaire Statistique: 1932-33.* Chapt. x.

advances in education and in industry were handicapped by the unemployment of the educated and the rising expectations of the masses owing to the political promises they had heard. The advent of World War II allowed the rulers to assume that they would be granted a breathing spell from their internal problems. To the contrary, the dislocation of wartime exigencies in terms of food supply had caused violence to break out once more, this time directed at the government by a populace driven by hunger and not by a political element inciting for change.

The lack of social consciousness on the part of the rulers and a growing awareness for its necessity on the part of the intellectuals are not unique to Egypt. They are characteristic of governments the world over, democratic or otherwise. The first steps of industrialization in Europe had also been accompanied by a disregard for the welfare of the people and by rapacity on the part of the rich, but they had been checked by the growing power of labor and of the middle classes. That development had not been reached in Egypt during the two decades under discussion. The political system continued to function, unruffled by the country's growing problems, so long as the army and the police force remained loyal and kept order when the populace rioted. A few concessions were offered labor in the form of legislation, which kept it quiet. As for the rural areas, they were too isolated, lacking any sense of solidarity or agricultural unions to bring them together, so that any outbreak of violence among them was sporadic and easily dismissed by the authorities as unusual or uncharacteristic. In 1951 the fallahin erupted in violence on the estates of some large landowners and on government estates, but the administration concealed the reasons. But there were turbulent currents hidden under the apparently quiet surface of the country.

Egypt had had a political revolution, which had not changed the social conditions of the land radically for the majority; perhaps what was needed was a social revolution? So thought some intellectuals in the land.

VIII

The Third Dimension:
Intellectual Eddies
and Currents

CREDIT for the modernization of Egypt has been attributed by historians to the efforts of Muhammad Ali, to the efforts of Ismail, and to the British occupation of Egypt in 1882 — all three being nonindigenous agents. While Muhammad Ali, Ismail, and the British occupation were catalysts that prepared the terrain for the growth of Egyptian intellectuals along diffferent lines than they might have taken if left to their own devices, and their influence is not to be underestimated, in no way did they actively plan to formulate or even guide an internal intellectual life in the country; nor did they play any role other than a passive one in encouraging westernization, which they regarded as a synonym for modernization. Whatever intellectual life developed in Egypt in the nineteenth and twentieth centuries was peripheral to the interests of our three catalyzers. Muhammad Ali wanted an independent kingdom; therefore he needed a modernized army and bureaucracy, and, if as a by-product of such a policy an intellectual movement was born, it was one to which he paid little heed and which was dismissed as irrelevant to his interests. Ismail had pretensions of becoming a monarch in the European style, of joining the royal club, so to speak. Newspapers were necessary in order to project his image as an enlightened ruler. But when the newspapers sought to emulate their Western counterparts and criticized the ruler, he deemed them impertinent and subject to censure, if not to exile. In brief, the Egyptian ruling family used modernization as a means toward attaining a personal end—that of their greater glory—and never looked upon it as having an intrinsic value to the population. And why should they? Many European rulers in their day felt exactly the same about their own indigenous intellectuals as did the Egyptians, and abused the press in more extreme fashion than Ismail ever did, so that compared to the autocracy of the Romanovs or the Hapsburgs, Egyptian monarchs were positively enlightened.

The British authorities in Egypt from 1882 on did not appreciate these efforts at modernization at the hands of the Egyptians, which they labeled "trying to make a western purse out of an eastern sow's ear." They girded themselves to take up the White Man's Burden, which meant in practical terms that they would supply a *ventre plein* policy to the masses and would scotch the pretensions of the elite to self-rule by taking it upon themselves to act as absolute authority in the land—all in the name of teaching "subject races" the art of self-government by example of good government.[1] But the "subjects," some of whom had tasted the fruits of learning, were not content to perform within the narrow limits designed for them by their new rulers, and they yearned for a form of government which would allow them the free exercise of their talents.

Efforts at modernization, reformation, or westernization—which are not synonymous terms even though they have frequently been so used—however limited and circumscribed, obviously do not occur in an intellectual vacuum. Like jetsam in a river that is battered by eddies and currents to emerge in a different shape from the original, attempts at modernization in Egypt have roused intellectual movements and countermovements in the population. In general these currents can be described as ranging from one extreme, a pro-Western approach, to the other, an anti-Western, purely Islamic one, with gradations of mixture in between. This chapter sketches the three representative currents of sociopolitical import in the country which mirrored the trials and tribulations of political life and in turn influenced it.

Briefly, and perhaps in simplistic terms, the bureaucratic school that equated modernization with westernization—the late nineteenth-century philosophy of the British occupants—found favor with very few indigenous intellectuals, for it posited the introduction of entirely new cultural and religious values. Cromer firmly believed that Egypt could not remain Muslim if modernized, so, by the same logic, Egypt must become Christian in order to be modernized or westernized.

1. Cromer, *Modern Egypt*, Passim.

Many Western authors today, consciously or unconsciously, follow the same line of thought, and assume that Islam is the intrinsic cause for backwardness in underdeveloped countries that happen to be Muslim. To counter that philosophy an equally extremist school of Egyptian intellectuals posited the rejection of all westernization and clamored for the restoration of a purely Islamic society. At the turn of the century that group had the Azhar as its stronghold.

The twentieth century saw a shift in attitude: pro-Western supporters, who by the thirties were indigenous Egyptians, opted in favor of westernization with an areligious bent, one that eschewed all religion in favor of a scientific approach to problems, while a new, religiously oriented group developed outside the walls of al-Azhar among men who were not ulama by training and who acquired the trappings of a political organization preaching anti-Western slogans.

These two "schools" are best exemplified in the works of Salama Musa, Ismail Mazhar, and Husain Fawzi representing the pro-Western areligious line on the one hand, and in two organizations, the Muslim Brethren led by the Shaikh Hasan al-Banna, and the Misr al-Fatat led by Ahmad Husain, representing the religious on the other. In between these extremes lay another and earlier school of thought, whose advocates considered the possibility of reformulating religion in more modern terms, that is, men who believed in reformation as did Shaikh Muhammad Abduh and his followers, the main exponents of that line of thought. They believed in the compatibility of modernization within the native framework. They considered the necessity of adapting modern techniques to local needs, thereby creating a mutant that was neither Christian-Western nor Muslim-Eastern, but a judicious amalgam of the better elements in both. To my mind they were the true liberals, for though perhaps they could be considered dreamers, they projected a vision of the society of the future, seen within the framework of a secular government and within the framework of a reformed and updated Islam, which was most attractive. That liberal vision was the dominant one until the second decade of the twentieth century, and the extremist visions, whether of a wholly Muslim state or a totally areligious one, came to the forefront in the thirties.

The intellectual currents of the 1920s were tinged with enthusiasm and hope, in the belief that Egypt had come a long way since 1882 and that the end of its occupation was imminent. The intellectuals of that period, the heirs of Abduh, the French Enlightenment and British liberal thought, were best represented in the person of Ahmad Lutfi al-Sayyid. For although Lutfi invariably sang a more aloof and rational tune than the rest, his writings communicated explicitly the hopes and ideals of his generation and depicted their struggles and failures against the enemy—within and without. He was the political theorist and philosopher of that generation and the precursor of the liberal thought of the next generation.

Ahmad Lutfi al-Sayyid was born in 1872 in Barqain, a small village of Daqahliyya in the heart of the Delta about 20 kilometers south of Mansura.[2] His father, al-Sayyid Abu Ali was the umda, a self-made man who through shrewd business acumen had become a fairly affluent landowner and eventually a Pasha. Lutfi was the eldest son of thirteen children and the dearest to his father's heart. Al-Sayyid seemed to have been a progressive man. When Adham Pasha, the governor of Daqahliyya, impressed by Lutfi's intelligence, suggested that he be sent to a government school rather than to al-Azhar as the umda intended, al-Sayyid agreed; and he later sent all his unmarried daughters to school, much to the consternation of his relatives, some of whom thought he had gone mad. Progressiveness had nothing to do with his way of life, however, for throughout his long lifetime al-Sayyid remained steadfast in his life-style as a village umda, and acquired little of the trappings of modernity, so that his children were brought up in the traditional village fallah society until they went to school and encountered an urban way of life.

By his own account Lutfi's performance at school was average and he excelled only in the Arabic language, a subject that fascinated him and was to be his constant love to the end of his days. In time Lutfi entered the School of Law along with the men who became his closest friends, Abd al-Aziz Fahmi, Abd al-Khaliq Tharwat, and Ismail Sidqi. There he met Shaikh Muhammad Abduh who became his mentor and surrogate father, and who bore so striking a resemblance to Lutfi's own father that they were frequently mistaken for each other. While at the School of Law Lutfi's love of language led him into journalism. He translated telegrams for *al-Muayyad*, and became puffed with pride when Abdallah al-Nadim asked him to proofread *al-Ustadh*. He, Sidqi, and Tharwat founded *al-Tashri*ᶜ, a journal of jurisprudence, to explain the law to the people.

Once he graduated from the School of Law Lutfi entered government service as a deputy public prosecutor. In 1894 he and Abd al-Aziz Fahmi, who was stationed in the same town, founded a secret society aimed at liberating Egypt from the British presence. It seems

2. al-Sayyid, *Qissat Hayati*, includes early biographical details.

that the society was not very secret, for Mustafa Kamil, whom Lutfi knew from his law school days, told him that the Khedive Abbas had heard about the society and invited him to merge with a secret society headed by the Khedive that had the same aims. Lutfi agreed and joined the embryonic Hizb al-Watani. The Khedive had recruited Lutfi because of his pen and suggested that he spend a year in Switzerland, become a Swiss national, and then return to Egypt to found a newspaper that would serve the nationalist cause. The Swiss nationality would render Lutfi immune to government censorship under the system of capitulations, and he could therefore write as he pleased without fear of prosecution.

In Geneva Lutfi was joined in the summer of 1895 by Shaikh Muhammad Abduh, who enrolled in the university, Saad Zaghlul, and Qasim Amin. During that summer Lutfi wrote Kamil to say that they were nationalists working for their country, and were not in the service of the Khedive, and if the Khedive became an obstacle to national aims then it would be their duty to remove such an obstacle. Obviously Lutfi had become influenced by Abduh and Saad Zaghlul who had a low opinion of the Khedive. Kamil reported Lutfi's words to the Khedive whereupon Lutfi resigned from their secret society and returned to Egypt to resume his post in the government. But there he continued to chafe under British tutelage and the restrictions they imposed on native talent. In 1905 he resigned after a disagreement with the public prosecutor. He joined Fahmi in his law practice for a while, but that was not to his liking. The incident of Taba caused him to take up journalism once more.

The Taba incident involved Ottoman forces that had encroached on Egyptian territory and had set up an army post there. Cromer did not relish the presence of Ottoman forces on the shores of the Suez Canal and demanded their immediate withdrawal. When the British ambassador at the Porte gave the Sultan an ultimatum, couched in severe terms the Ottoman forces withdrew, but for a brief while matters looked exceedingly grave. The local press, headed by Mustafa Kamil in *al-Liwa,* came out vociferously in favor of the Ottomans, claiming that they were Egypt's suzerain and had full rights over Egyptian territory; Kamil's unedifying stand of cutting off Egyptian noses to spite Britain incensed Lutfi and many of his friends. They met to discuss the issues and decided to found an independent newspaper that would not be subsidized by Sultan, Khedive, or Residency, unlike *al-Liwa, al-Muayyad,* and *al-Muqattam,* edited respectively by Kamil Ali Yusif, and Nimr, but would be written by Egyptians, for Egyptians,

and with national interests in mind. On March 9, 1907, the first issue
of *al-Jarida*, with Lutfi as its editor, appeared, and gave a list of the
shareholders which read like a Who's Who of the landed gentry and
professionals of Egypt. Six months later the shareholders of *al-Jarida*
decided to form a political party, Hizb al-Umma, the first official
party in Egypt since 1882. A month later Mustafa Kamil, who regarded the Hizb al-Watani not as a political party but as an "emana-
tion of the people," turned it into a political party. He was followed
by Shaikh Ali Yusif, who founded a party at the Khedive's behest,
Hizb al-Islah ala al-Mabadi al-Dusturiyya.

The ideology of Hizb al-Umma was presented in the editorials
written by Lutfi from 1907 to 1914, and, though there is much that is
topical and contradictory in the manner common to editorials, they
nonetheless present a coherent gospel of liberal humanism. In the
beginning the *Jarida* became the butt of the other newspapers who
accused it of being pro-British, but in time it became recognized as
the voice of logic and of moderation, traits that seldom earn popularity, but do attract respect. *Al-Jarida* was neither pro-British, pro-
Khedive, nor pro-Ottoman, but very definitely solid, middle-class,
Egyptian-gentry oriented. It advocated moderation in nationalist demands, and would have cooperated behind the scenes with the British
authorities in return for a promise of eventual evacuation, but when
the promise was not forthcoming, they adopted an anti-British stance.[3]
They believed that the unbridled tyranny of the Khedive was much
worse than the benevolent despotism of the British, for in time the
British would have to withdraw, while the Khedive would be there
forever. They believed like Condorcet that education would lead to
democracy and that natural progression would allow them to slough
off tyranny of whatever kind. Education would allow man to develop
his faculties and a sense of judgment, and would allow him the use of
reason rather than leave him at the mercy of blind emotion.

Lutfi's articles were to produce the first coherent Egyptian expression of a sociopolitical concept of nationalism. They were derived from
Islamic principles, Greek philosophy, the ideas of the French Enlightenment and of the British liberals. (To the end of his days his
inseparable companions were the Quran and the works of Aristotle.)
Lutfi believed that religion should concern man's relations with God
and that government should be secular. Man needed religion to give
him spiritual succor and a system of ethics, but he needed a secular

3. For futher details see al-Sayyid (Marsot), *Egypt and Cromer*, Chap. 8.

form of government, built on the principles of utility, so that each generation could create that government which was best for them and not be shackled by the dictates of their forefathers, however valid they may have been in the past. To that end Lutfi preached for a political society that adopted from the East or the West or anywhere else the best elements available.

> . . . new basic principles must be introduced to our Eastern philosophy. For while it is true that knowledge has no fatherland [watan], nevertheless the marriage of the sciences of the East and those of the West is the means of our acquiring civilization, while at the same time preserving intact our own moral character.[4]

Lutfi was a sound believer in the values of reason, moderation, and compromise, and an enemy of tyranny in all its forms, intellectual and political.

> Since it is impossible for the British Occupation to last forever; and since the sovereign power of the nation is rapidly being guided through training and education toward its high and beneficent goal; and since the life of the nation is measured in generations, not in years, it is shortsighted, unduly pessimistic, and thoughtless to view the future through black glasses, or to let an unseemly haste compel us to bypass the premises to arrive at the conclusions in ignorance of the natural laws of existence. Indeed we must all haul together to extricate the nation from her sickbed, and to plant today in the belief that what we do today we will encounter tomorrow.[5]

In another editorial he wrote:

> The deplorable condition of our customs, economy or politics goes back to the same original source, namely the shocking lack of freedom in our souls, as the result of ancient despotism . . . more than anything else we Egyptians need to enlarge the freedom of action of the individual so that he may regain the qualities he had lost . . . so that we may definitely set aside our dependence on the government in all matters major

4. Charles Wendell (The Evolution of the Egyptian National Image: From Its Origins to Ahmad Lutfi al-Sayyid [Los Angeles, 1972], p. 225) has translated this passage from al-Jarida, Sept. 23, 1908.

5. Ibid., p. 293, from al-Jarida, Sept. 14, 1912.

or minor and set aside that feeling — common to the East —
that the nation is a flock and the ruler their keeper to do with
as he please.[6]

Lutfi's most violent diatribes were directed against despotism, and
specifically that of the ruler. That trait did not endear him to Abbas,
and was to cause King Fuad to detest him bitterly:

Despotism is the specific characteristic of government of whatever kind, royal or republican, and nothing can check it save
the fear of falling. The history of men and governments in
all times and places shows that despotism is a basic feature
which only ends with death or weakness. (Injustice is hidden
in the soul, strength reveals it, and weakness conceals it.)
It is therefore necessary that limits be set upon the ruler.
Clearly defined and precise limits which cannot be over-
stepped so that the people can be safe from the ruler's tyranny
and injustice. If these are not available then man is nothing
but a slave and had better leave society and live as a hermit
or as an animal.[7]

Lutfi "broke his pen" in August 1914, but he took it up again when
he helped found the Wafd with the members and sympathizers of
Hizb al-Umma. The Wafd, as we have seen, soon split into left and
right wings, the former around Zaghlul and the latter around Adli
in the Ahrar party. One can therefore regard the two parties as having
been sired by the same ideology and to have differed in techniques
and approach, a difference built on personal conflicts and vanity, more
than on ideals, although in time the Wafd built up a different set
of ideals.

When he split with the Wafd in 1922 Lutfi decided to set aside
political involvement, but he worked behind the scenes to set up the
program of the Liberal Constitutionalist party before withdrawing to
the university in 1925 where he served as the first rector until 1928
when he unhappily joined Mahmud's cabinet. When the cabinet fell
in 1929 he returned to the university as rector but resigned in 1932
over Sidqi's removal without prior agreement on Lutfi's part of Taha

6. Ismail Mazhar, brother-in-law of Lutfi, collected some of the choice editorials in
al-Jarida into one volume entitled, *al-Muntakhabat* (Cairo, 1945), p. 66. This passage
is from an editorial of Dec. 20, 1913.

7. Ibid., p. 92, from *al-Jarida*, Dec. 31, 1913.

Husain, the dean of the Faculty of the Humanities, to a position in
the Ministry of Education as belated punishment for Husain's book,
published in 1926. Lutfi, interpreting Sidqi's action as an attack on
academic freedom, resigned. He returned to the university in 1935
for another two years when he once again resigned over an issue
dealing with the need to create a campus police to cope with student
strikes. Once more he joined a cabinet headed by Muhammad Mahmud but for the fourth time he returned to the university where he
remained until his retirement. Upon retiring he was appointed senator
and became president of the Academy of the Arabic Language until
his death in 1963 at the age of 91.

Lutfi's ideology prepared the ground for the younger intelligentsia.
His office in *al-Jarida* was a salon where writers, poets, and politicians
met and discussed the issues of the day. It was a veritable school of
liberal humanism, where the concepts of democracy and constitutionalism were forged, and if Lutfi in later years was dubbed "Teacher of
the Generation" it was not solely because of his position as rector but
also because of the lessons learned in the salon of *al-Jarida*. Among
Lutfi's students and colleagues, to name but a few, were Taha Husain,
Ahmad Husain Haikal, Mayy Ziyada, and Salama Musa.

It is difficult to define the attraction that Lutfi exercised on the men
and women with whom he came in touch. It was certainly not due to
his good looks, because he was plain. He was tall and wiry with
deep-set eyes meeting above a bulbous nose, and narrow lips hidden
by the luxuriant mustachios popular at the time. His hands were his
only beautiful feature—long, tapered, and very elegant. And yet he
was a most attractive man as young and old found. When he was an
old man, his friends teased him because his table at the Cecil Hotel
in Alexandria or the Beau Rivage was always crowded with women of
all ages come to pay their respects and enjoy his gentle teasing.

Much of the attraction Lutfi exerted over the young owed to the
fact that he did not patronize. He listened and commented but never
lectured or scolded. Above all, he never dismissed the opinions of the
young as unimportant, as many older statesmen were wont to do. But,
then, he was a firm believer in the value of youth, in the idea that
every generation was born one step ahead of the preceding one, with
advantages that the past generation had not had and with new insights.

To the Englishmen among his generation Lutfi seemed to be "well
read, intelligent and generally speaking an unselfish politician but
rather conceited. As a politician he won the respect of those from

whom he differed; broad minded and modern in his views, an enemy of autocracy and the Turk."[8]

Zaghlul, who managed to insult everybody at some time or other, never quarreled with Lutfi when they were in Paris, and, although they parted ways in 1922, in a 1926 speech called him a "true patriot." Abd al-Aziz Fahmi, who quarreled with everybody, remained devoted to Lutfi to his dying day, as did Tharwat, Sidqi, and all his other friends. Oddly enough, whether opponents or friends (and the two were in no way contradictory), Lutfi managed to win and keep their respect. Perhaps it was because he never used personal invective; cold logic seemed to him more to the point, and, indeed, his irony could be devastating at times. But he preferred to demolish an argument and to leave the arguer his self respect. Perhaps it was because he was recognized as a disinterested patriot who did not join the scramble for power and office and preferred the well-stocked walls of his library to any post in a cabinet.

Lutfi's contributions to the intellectual life of his day were many. He desired to make concrete the concept of an Egyptian nationality as an independent entity, mixed in ethnic and religious configuration, but with all its elements glorying in being above all Egyptian. He then sought to point out the defects of the nation and the means by which they could be remedied. In a famous editorial he dealt with the concept of *malish*, "never mind," and showed how the virtue of forgiveness when pushed to the extreme had turned into a national vice of moral cowardice. He tried to create a civic consciousness and a sense of the rights and obligations incumbent upon a population — in his own terms, to teach *al-akhlaq al-dusturiyya*, "constitutional behavior."

Education was the key word in his philosophy, education of women as well as of men, for he did not believe that it was possible for a nation to progress when half its population was kept in ignorance. He therefore allowed and encouraged women to enter the university when most of his countrymen were scandalized at the thought of an educated woman.

He forged a new style of Arabic language, the new classical, which was capable of handling the concepts that were being introduced, and thereby started a new school of essay and prose writing. He said, "I think that the greatest service we can render our language is to make it the language of learning in Egypt and to try to unify the literary

8. Robin Furness, Notes on Egyptian Personalities, May 23, 1927, F.O. 371/12388.

and spoken languages,"[9] for he considered the spoken language to be deficient and the classical language cumbersome. It had to be reformed to become the language of learning. New words or borrowings were encouraged, and he believed that the public would determine whether these words became accepted in the language or rejected. Thus the new language he desired did indeed come to pass, and has come into use.

He set high standards in education and in journalism. He set the principle of academic freedom in the university and saw that it was respected. He made journalism a profession to which men of letters could aspire. Thus Mazini, al-Aqqad, Haikal, and other belletrists and intellectuals were influenced by his search for a more modern and flexible style of prose writing and by his ideal that a journalist was a maker of public opinion, an educator of the people, and not just someone who sold his pen to the highest bidder.

The tides of liberal humanism, Islamic reformism, or secular nationalism found an echo in the literary works of the day, and appeared in the two hundred newspapers and magazines that were then published in Egypt. For whether they were partisan papers like the Wafdist *al-Balagh* or the Liberal Constitutionalist *al-Siyasa,* independent like *al-Ahram,* or satirical like *al-Kashkul* and *Ruz al-Yusif,* it was within these papers that the new classical language was honed into a wieldy and respectable vehicle for the transmission of scientific, technical, or polemical ideas.

As all ideologies invariably do, Lutfi's liberal humanist ideology came into conflict with the political realities of the twenties. The dilemma facing Egyptian cabinets after 1922 was whether to concentrate on solving external problems, which meant wresting total independence from Britain and effecting a treaty, or to concentrate on internal problems such as social reform, constitutional rule, and the orderly transfer of power. No cabinet seemed able to cope with both at the same time and so every cabinet proved unsatisfactory. During the twenties intellectuals and politicians remained optimistic that a rapid settlement of the political issues would occur. Constitutional rule and a parliamentary regime had begun to function in Egypt. Zaghlul's dominant personality and the Wafd organization were to upset these calculations, for free elections meant a return of the Wafd to power and the other political parties had no hope of attaining

9. Wendell, *Evolution of the Egyptian National Image,* p. 277, quoting *al-Jarida,* April 23, 1913.

power, unless they earned the support of Palace or Residency. In other words, it meant that those who had set themselves up as liberals and constitutionalists had to use illiberal and unconstitutional means in order to come to power so as to rule presumably in a liberal and constitutional manner. Sidqi, neither a liberal nor a constitutionalist, justified his autocracy by saying that if a voter fell under the influence of a dominating personality like Zaghlul's he was disqualified from voting for he no longer exercised free choice.[10] Haikal, the spokesman of the Liberal Constitutionalists, said that he supported dictatorship if his party did the dictating. By the end of the decade it seemed to those who were not actors on the political scene of the day that the intellectuals were preaching an abstract ideal while the politicians were going about their own devious but concrete way.

There is always a gap between what should be and what is. There is always a chasm between man's aspirations and his achievements. The intellectuals attempted to influence both the politicians and the mass of the people by spreading as much knowledge as possible, with the accent on the importance of democratic procedures, on constitutional concepts of freedom of speech and of freedom of thought, in the hope that their teachings might fall on fertile ground. That is why the intellectual issues of the twenties centered on the works of two ulama, Ali Abd al-Raziq with his *Islam wa usul al-hukm* and Taha Husain with his *Fi-l shi*c*r al-jahili*. Both books, as we have seen, created a furore and were proscribed, yet they established two principles which in time became commonplace. Abd al-Raziq's book expressed a belief which was current among many intellectuals and which had become more palatable after Mustafa Kemal put an end to the Caliphate in Turkey, notably that the Prophet Muhammad had come not to establish a form of government but to found a religion. The break between religion and government which had been widening over the past decades was thus expressed in definite terms, and secularism in government was in time to become an established principle. Secularism meant not atheism, as the ulama immediately assumed it did, but that Islam as a religion did not need a counterpart in government, that government had nothing to do with religion. People owed loyalty to a state and to a nation, and not to a Caliph; thus any monarch was temporal and his authority was not derived from religion. It took some time for the mass of Muslims to swallow that pill, but they did do so, although to the present there are still some who find it hard to digest.

10. Ismail Sidqi, *Mudhakkirati* (Cairo, 1950), p. 47.

The second book written by Taha Husain applied Cartesian logic to literary criticism, in his case to the poetry of the pre-Islamic age. That method led Taha to question whether such poetry had indeed been written in pre-Islamic days. Taha drew blood by his methods for if applied to religious texts they could cause severe doubts as to their veracity. Under the savage onslaught that greeted his book Taha was forced to withdraw it. He wrote an open letter in which he defended himself as a Muslim and as a believer, but the following year he reedited and republished it under a different title after having excised the most offending passage.

While on one level these issues were of a religious nature, on another they were basic issues to the future political and intellectual life of the country. For if a free and rational scientific spirit was to be introduced, then logic and not emotional attachments must become the rule in methods of inquiry. In point of fact Taha claimed the right for even an atheist to declare himself without fear of reprisal. Above all he claimed the right of free inquiry according to the rules of logic. That issue magnified the conflict between the old and the new, *al-qadim wa-l jadid,* which to the present day has not been entirely resolved.

The thirties ushered in a period of despondency and a general feeling of failure. The personality of Zaghlul was no longer there to tower over political activity and to inspire confidence that all was well, that he was a worthy opponent to pit against Palace and Residency. Nahhas was a poor substitute. Second, because of inexperience within and interference from King and Britain, constitutional government never had the chance to burgeon untrammeled and had not gained any momentum, so that rule by decree reigned as long as had rule by parliament; Sidqi's repressive measures were bleaker than had been those of any of the preceding autocracies. Third, the financial crisis had focused attention on primary needs of food and clothing, reducing the struggle for power to second place for the man in the street who viewed the squabbles with a by now thoroughly jaundiced eye. Last, the crisis of democracies in the West had shaken the faith of many in the value of democracy. Admiration for Fascism grew when Mussolini made the trains run on time and forced the slackers to swallow castor oil. Some Egyptians believed that these methods might have more success in Egypt than those of the democratic institutions. Thus the Green Shirts of the Wafd and the Blue Shirts of Misr al-Fatat appeared in the streets and behaved in the same brutal and bullying fashion as their fascist counterparts.

The liberal humanist tradition obviously did not come to an end with the rise of extremist factions; both continued to exist side by side. The main exponents of liberal thought were Taha Husain and Husain Haikal. And yet both men during the thirties wrote books on religious themes, Husain his three-volume ʿAla Hamish al-Sira (1937-1943). Some authors have seen in this preoccupation with Islam a denial of his past liberal views.[11] Others have noted that in the same decade Husain also published Min Baʿid (1935), a collection of articles re-iterating his humanist beliefs in which he commented on the gap that lay between the intellectual life of the twenties and the thirties.[12]

The repressive methods that Sidqi instituted in the thirties created the need for a new approach to politics. Husain felt Sidqi's heavy hand when he was unceremoniously removed from his university position and shoved into the Ministry of Education. Thus one can interpret Husain's preoccupation with Islamic themes as a tactic designed to avoid official repression,[13] "as attempts to regild the myths of Islam in ways which will appeal to modern Egyptian consciousness,"[14] and as a restatement of his belief that the role of religion was to comfort men's souls, not to guide their political actions — and men's souls needed much comfort under Sidqi.

Husain Haikal had followed a line of reasoning similar to Taha Husain's. In the twenties he published a series of articles in al-Siyasa in which he defended Taha Husain and Ali Abd al-Raziq and attacked the ulama for being obscurantist. Although a firm believer in the values of the liberal tradition, he too published in the thirties a series of books on religious themes: Hayat Muhammad (1935), which had first appeared as a collection of articles, and Fi Manzil al-Wahy (1937), which was later followed by a series of biographies of the Rashidun. As with Husain, some historians qualified this shift in subject matter as a "crisis in orientation" whereas others described it as an attempt on Haikal's part to create an indigenous ideology centered on Islam. This shift was not a negation of the rational life of the West in favor of the spiritual life of the East but a restatement of the values of both,

11. Nadav Safran, Egypt in Search of Political Community (Cambridge, Mass., 1961), pp. 165 ff.

12. Charles Smith, "The 'Crisis of Orientation': The Shift of Egyptian Intellectuals to Islamic Subjects in the 1930's, "International Journal of Middle East Studies, 4, 4 (Oct., 1973), 382-410, a well-thought-out refutation of Safran's views.

13. Ibid.

14. Albert H. Hourani, Arabic Thought in the Liberal Age (London, 1960), p. 334.

because Haikal wanted "the greatest amount of freedom possible in the light of both western and Islamic history."[15]

Haikal saw the growing gap between the elitist philosophy of al-Ahrar, of whom he was the main exponent, and the views of the mass of the population. He was especially susceptible to the charges of atheism which the Wafd hurled at him and his party. He could not fail to note the rising interest in religion and the rapid development of the Muslim Brethren. He therefore turned to religious themes as a pedagogical necessity, a means of teaching the masses that to use reason would not undermine religion as some feared it must, but that reason would itself become the basis of religious belief, a position that ran diametrically opposite to Husain's that religion and reason operate on different spheres.

The other side of the intellectual coin revealed the use of religion in an entirely different manner. It showed the rise of an indigenous, Muslim-oriented movement, inspired by the same malaise that was sweeping the country. It did not have its roots in liberal humanist tradition but rather looked inward for its salvation within the Muslim community of the past—the far distant past. Al-Ikhwan al-Muslimun, the Muslim Brethren, blamed westernization and modernization for the sorry state of Egyptian politics and, finding them lacking, rejected them outright. Their salvation lay in a return to the precepts of Islam and to the establishment of a truly Muslim state in the manner of the Rashidun. Their message was simple and appealed to both the uneducated masses and to the educated elite who had become disabused by the political failures of the parties.

The treaty of 1936 brought the Brethren new adherents. Many felt cheated that they had struggled and fought for so many years in order to accept a treaty that could have been obtained a decade earlier. They felt betrayed by a sorry government that had promised them complete independence and then had delivered what they believed was a travesty. Nothing had changed: the King was still an autocrat, but he had won the affection of much of the population and so his power seemed to grow rather than to diminish. The British continued to be there in occupation, but now Egypt was to facilitate their continued presence by building roads and facilities for them at public expense. More important, the Wafdists, who had tasted the King's enmity and had suffered through five years of exile from political power, were

15. Smith, "Crisis of Orientation," pp. 400 ff.

growing close to the British as their one safeguard from the political
oblivion they had endured under Sidqi's rule. The Muslim Brethren
promised a change, and so successful was its propaganda and its social
and economic achievements that it won adherents to its political
program as well.

Shaikh Hasan al-Banna, the founder of al-Ikhwan al-Muslimun, was
born in 1906 in a small town of the Delta near Alexandria.[16] Hasan,
the son of a prayer leader, was attracted early in life toward a life of
religion and toward religious and Sufi groupings, some of which he
joined. After he finished his training at the Primary Teacher's Training School he attended Dar al-Ulum in Cairo in 1923. On his gradu-
ation four years later he was appointed to teach Arabic in a primary
school in Ismailiyya.

Ismailiyya was two towns in one. The European quarter bordering
the canal housed the employees of the Suez Canal Company, and it
had wide tree-lined streets with neat villas, each surrounded by a trim,
well-kept garden in which bloomed a profusion of flowers and fruit
trees. A large wood of casuarina and eucalyptus trees grew alongside
the canal and at either end were elegant sporting clubs where the
mostly French-speaking canal employees disported themselves. Life for
them was very pleasant, and summers were more frequently spent
abroad in Europe than at home. Toward the edge of the desert lay
the second half of the town, the native quarter, with its narrow streets,
its squalor, and teeming population. The contrast between the two
quarters was striking and bred in al-Banna a resentment and consequently an aversion toward all things Western.

It was in Ismailiyya that Hasan al-Banna set himself the difficult
task of reforming his society, and to that end he created the society
of the Muslim Brethren, in 1928. Within four years the organization
had set up branches in all the Canal Zone cities and in Cairo.
Contributions from the members of the organization, local merchants,
and even the Suez Canal Company had allowed them to build a
mosque and several schools, where the youngsters were given a strictly
religious training and where Western influences, which were equated
with atheism, did not penetrate.

In 1932 Hasan al-Banna requested a transfer to Cairo, which from
then on became the main target of Ikhwan activities. The following
ten years, which witnessed seven Ikhwan Conferences, developed the

16. For biographical information regarding Hasan al-Banna, see Richard Mitchell,
The Society of Muslim Brothers (London, 1969), pp. 1 ff.

theoretical and ideological foundations for al-Ikhwan and the creation of their secret apparatus.

The rapid rise of the organization did not grow unopposed, and before his transfer to Cairo al-Banna was simultaneously accused of being a communist, of being a Wafdist working against the Sidqi government, and of being a republican working against King Fuad.[17] Al-Banna was cleared of these contradictory charges, but it is interesting that the charges themselves reflected a characteristic of al-Banna — that he seemed to represent different things to different people. The ambiguity that surrounded him and his ideals allowed him to attract a wider cross-section than any definitely spelled-out political affiliations would presumably have done.

The organization was forming in the heyday of the Sidqi government, when the Wafd was agitating, when riots and strikes had become commonplace, and when the British seemed as immovable as ever. Al-Banna seemed to some people to be bringing an alternative approach to politics, one that the minority political groups recognized as a potential ally to be used against the majority party, the Wafd. Both the Wafd and the Ikhwan were popular organizations with massive followings and by 1936 they had both created paramilitary organizations. They could thus be used against each other to cancel each other out, as Ali Mahir tried to do in 1939 when he made a bid for Ikhwan support and got it. The Wafd, however, eventually acquired British support and that was stronger. But what exactly did the Ikhwan stand for?

Al-Banna said, "Our ideology is guided by the Book of God and the life of His Prophet," which sounded very grand but was not very concrete. Nevertheless it served al-Banna well in manipulating the religious affiliation of the population until religion became the quasi-exclusive domain of the Ikhwan and the legitimization of all their policies, since al-Banna also said, "In us is every goodness."[18] The concomitant was that in the others who did not join the organization resided everything else.

It seems to some historians that al-Banna stressed the religious aspects of the organization more heavily when a strong cabinet was in power and headed by a strong man, and the political aspirations when a weak cabinet resided.[19] The fact is that al-Banna changed his

17. Ibid., p. 10.
18. Anwar al-Jundi, al-Ikhwan al-Muslimun fi mizan al-haq (Damascus, n.d.), p. 11.
19. Christina Phelps Harris, Nationalism and Revolution in Egypt (The Hague, 1964), p. 182.

tactics to suit the political atmosphere of the day and to achieve his main objectives, which were to lay claim to absolute leadership over the country and to substitute his organization for all political parties, the immediate objective being to challenge and displace the Wafd. Thus Nahhas, who was called Zaim al-Umma by his followers, was insidiously discredited and his pretensions scotched when al-Ikhwan adopted the slogan *"al-rasul Zaimuna wa-l Quran dusturuna,"* "the Messenger [of God] is our leader [zaim], the Quran our constitution," a sentiment with which no Muslim could quibble and which put Nahhas in an unfavorable light for claiming the title of zaim.

There are those who bring strong evidence to bear on their belief that the Ikhwan were supported by the British authorities and owed their rise to them, as the perfect foil to use against the Wafd. In the first place the Ikhwan did not attack the British presence in Egypt until the mid-forties. And while the organization listed fifty demands, in one of their *Rasail,* "Epistles," which included an attack on colonialism couched in general terms, there was no mention of independence for Egypt, or the withdrawal of British troops from Egyptian territory,[20] a very odd omission. Second, the Ikhwan were loud in their demands for the restoration of the Caliphate just when such a demand ran sharply counter to nationalist claims. The nationalists regarded any claims made for the revival of a caliphate as a British-inspired red herring designed to entice the gullible away from the main issue, independence. It would then seem that Ikhwan activity sought to displace nationalist activity through their stress on a return to an Islamic caliphate.[21]

Third, and even more subtle, was the stand al-Ikhwan took against secular education, a stand that ostensibly was directed against the West but which served to antagonize the Christian community in Egypt and to create dissent. At that time there was some agitation over missionary activities, which by and large failed to reform Muslims but did convert some Copts to Protestantism. The Ikhwan used missionary activities to discredit all ideas stemming from the West by equating missionary preaching with Western thought, and claiming that all Western thought was an attempt to destroy Islam. In so doing al-Banna not only alienated a number of Egyptian intellectuals, but also the non-Muslim minorities. The Copts, who had lost some of their fear of Muslim domination in the nationalist fervor of 1919 and who had

20. Tariq al-Bishri, *al-Haraka al-siyasiyya fi Misr: 1945-1952* (Cairo, 1972), p. 55.
21. Ibid., p. 59.

joined the Wafd in large numbers, now once again reverted to sec-
tarian attitudes in the face of the onslaught of the Brethren against
the West and the missionaries, and by implication against all non-
Muslims.

In brief, at a time when nationalist activities were concentrated on
uniting all Egyptians against a common enemy — the British occupation
and its tools — al-Ikhwan ran counter to them and worked toward
polarizing Egyptian society and setting each group against the other, in
the name of religion. Few people realized what was at stake. The
majority of the population was simply impressed by the morality of
the Ikhwan and by the fact that they set up mosques and schools and
cottage industries. Above all, they were impressed by the fact that the
Ikhwan claimed to be a *salafiyya* movement trying to bring religion
back to the godless who had strayed from the right path. To the small
businessman and the lower middle classes who had been hit by economic depression, they promised a future full of hope, a reign of
justice where the European exploiter would disappear, and local
industry would flourish once more, as witness their efforts in business,
which were indeed successful. To the young students the Ikhwan
provided a secret society, arms, and later a crusade to liberate Palestine. In the meantime they sought to overthrow partisan government,
al-hizbiyya, and replace it with a more just, Islamic form of government. To still others they supplied a bulwark against creeping
communism.

Once a person joined the society he was entirely and completely
swept up in the movement. He was totally indoctrinated so that a
cohesive and unified organization, subject to the dictates of the Supreme Guide, Hasan al-Banna, was produced. It was an organization
which had no room for dissidents and which allowed no member to
question its motives. Those who attacked it were accused of being
anti-Islamic, of having sold out to the West, and of having betrayed
their religion and their culture. It was of little use to pit the creed of
nationalism against religious loyalty, or the constitution against the
Quran, for "nationalism" and "constitution" were newfangled terms,
and their past performance had been unsatisfactory when set against
religious fervor. It was of little use to tell the population that that was
a false dichotomy, that nationalism and the constitution were not
opposed to religion, that one could not compare dissimilars. The
Ikhwan countered by pointing out how inept secular government had
been and argued that a religious government might have more success.
These were times that tried men's souls — political chaos and economic

depression all combined to drive an aggrieved people toward religion. Al-Ikhwan acquired some of the trappings of a millenary movement, a means of salvation from the quagmire of party politics. Although the Ikhwan promised much and delivered little in socioeconomic terms, they compensated for it by the psychological comfort they supplied the entire family. The men had their daily meetings and the weekly lectures delivered by the Supreme Guide; the women joined al-Sayyidat al Muslimat, the Muslim Women, where they were given religious instruction and were inspired in the ideals of the organization; and the children had the Ikhwan schools and their own social groupings. It seemed to the Ikhwan members that this very togetherness was saving Muslim society from disruption and from falling into the corruption of Western ways.

All the frustrations of Egyptian society, and they were many, were personified and blamed by the Ikhwan on the West. The wheel had turned full circle from the time of al-Afghani and his teachings. He had blamed the decadence of the East on the fact that Muslims had turned away from their religion. He had preached that salvation lay in a return to the true principles and the spirit of Islam, but he had also advocated the adoption of Western techniques and technology to enable the East to meet the challenge of the West on equal terms. Now Hasan al-Banna was saying that Islam needed to reform by returning to the life of the Rashidun, by conforming to the letter of the religious law, and above all by eschewing anything adopted from the West. Thirteen centuries were to be set aside; religion and religious practices were not to be reinterpreted but to be returned to the originals.

Hasan al-Banna rapidly acquired the reputation of being an Imam, a reputation he did not attempt to dispel, on the contrary he encouraged it. He helped to create it by recounting stories wherein he had been miraculously saved from harm,[22] and to perpetuate it by the institution of a form of baya, or oath of allegiance, offered to him by all the members of the organization, almost as though he were the leader of the Muslim community of early Islamic days. By 1949 the Ikhwan claimed a membership of some two million adherents, a figure hotly disputed by their opponents who believed two hundred thousand to be nearer the mark. Since many of the Brethren belonged to secret cells, and others had orders to infiltrate as many political groupings as possible in order to undermine them from within, the true figures will never be known. The fact remains that the Ikhwan organization

22. Fathi al-Aal, *Hasan al-Banna kama Ariftahu* (Cairo, 1948), pp. 128-136.

very rapidly became highly influential in the land and a factor with which political parties had to contend and make deals with. And in 1942 even the Wafd had to come to terms with the Ikhwan. At that time al-Banna decided to present himself as a candidate for the elections, and Nahhas forced him to withdraw his candidacy, but only in return for a promise to allow the organization free activity and to crack down on the sale of alcoholic drinks and on prostitution, both of which had increased because of the war and the influx of Allied troops into Egypt.[23]

The history of the Muslim Brethren and their political ideals changed later in the forties when al-Banna, who had inspired the assassination of the premier Nuqrashi Pasha, and the chief of police, Salim Zaki, was in turn assassinated, but that is not within the scope of this work.

It is not unusual in the history of Muslim countries to see revolutionary movements rise under the guise of religious dissent, and the Ikhwan was no different from other reformist/revolutionary movements throughout the ages. The only difference lay in the fact that it was better organized than most, and when it was proscribed in Egypt it spread to the other Arab lands where it continues to function to the present, but more as a religious organization than as the political entity it had been in Egypt. Whether it will ever make a political comeback, and once more rise like Phoenix from the ashes, time will tell.

Whereas Taha Husain and Husain Haikal were belletrists first and journalists second, Salama Musa, who led the third intellectual current in their era was the journalist par excellence, first, last, and always.

Salama Musa, the son of an Egyptian Copt, was born in 1887 in a village close to Zagazig in the Delta.[24] His father who was a government clerk died when Salama was two years old but the family had some land and the father's pension and so were not badly off. As a child Musa attended a variety of institutions: a Coptic kuttab, followed by a Muslim one, a Coptic school followed by a government one in Zagazig, and then to Cairo to finish his schooling in the Tawfiqiyya and Khidiwiyya secondary schools.

While in Cairo Musa was introduced to the press of the day. In *al-Muqtataf* he read about Darwin and the theory of evolution, and

23. Mitchell, *Society of Muslim Brothers*, p. 27.
24. Autobiographical material derived from Salama Musa, *Tarbiyyat Salama Musa* (Cairo, 1947).

from the writings of Shibli Shumayyil he first learned of socialism —
a concept that captured his imagination. He was later to become the
major exponent of Fabian socialism in Egypt. He also read classical
Arab authors but very rapidly switched his allegiance entirely to
Western authors read mostly in translation.

In 1909 Musa went on his first trip abroad and spent a year in Paris.
A few months after his return to Egypt he left for France to spend two
more years. There he immersed himself in the writings of the French
socialists and first read Ibsen, whose plays on the condition of women
in the West opened Musa's eyes to the sorry condition of women in
the East.

Musa spent the next four years in England where he hoped to read
for a law degree. But in England he met George Bernard Shaw,
became a member of the Fabian Society, and from then on his
original plans for law were set aside very definitely as he went about
educating himself. He read Egyptology, economics, biology, geology,
literature, and anything else that struck his fancy. While he was in
England he published his first Fabian Socialist-inspired work, *Muqqad-
imat al-Suberman,* "Introduction to the Superman" (1910), which
appeared in Jurji Zaidan's *al-Hilal.* In this work Musa expressed his
ideas on capitalism, private property, and nationalization.

The seven years that Musa spent abroad in France and in England
were the formative years of his intellectual life, as he admits in his
autobiography, *Tarbiyat Salama Musa* (1947). Darwin, France, Freud,
Ibsen, Marx, Nietzsche, Rousseau, Voltaire, and Shaw all left their
imprint on him, and once back in Egypt he struggled to communicate
their ideas to the literate public or to educate a largely gullible public
in their ideas. Among the scholars in Egypt the one who left the
greatest imprint on him was Ahmad Lufti al-Sayyid, as Musa informs
us in his autobiography. Lutfi's philosophy of nationalism, he said, had
made it possible for him, a Copt, to join a nationalist movement led
by Muslims, the Wafd, and to remain within that party for the rest
of its existence.

On returning to Egypt Salama went into journalism, and to the end
of his life continued to work in the leading magazines and newspapers
of the day, having founded a few himself. He wrote articles for
al-Liwa, al-Jamia, al-Mahrusa, al-Muqtataf, and *al-Hilal.* He was
editor-in-chief of *al-Hilal* from 1925 until 1929 and changed its style
from a historical-literary journal to one that also discussed socio-
philosophical concepts. He joined the Wafdist party organ *al-Balagh*
in 1931 having founded the magazine *al-Majalla al-Jadida* which he

continued to edit until 1942. When *Akhbar al-Yom* was launched by the Amin twins, Mustafa and Ali, in 1944 he joined their staff, and in 1952 he became an editor for another Amin publication, *al-Akhbar,* where he remained until his death in 1958 at the age of seventy-one.

Musa's outspoken writings were to land him in hot water on numerous occasions, both with the government and with his literary colleagues. He carried on a literary feud with another prominent man of letters who had turned to journalism, Abbas Mahmud al-Aqqad, but when al-Aqqad was imprisoned by the Palace, Musa was one of the first to rise to his defense in his newspaper articles. He had a feud with Taha Husain but of a more gentlemanly variety since the two men were tied by bonds of friendship in spite of their intellectual opposition. On occasion Musa's language reached a level of invective best described as obscene abuse, such as that directed at Mustafa al-Rafii.

He was not content with taking on his colleagues. In 1930 he published an article in another weekly magazine he had founded that year, *al-Misri li-l Misri,* in which he attacked one of the richest men in the country, Prince Umar Tussun, and mentioned him by name, departing from prior custom of hinting at but not naming the person in question. The article was a diatribe against tyranny and the oppression of feudal landlords, and Tussun was used as an example of a man who was fabulously wealthy and yet did nothing to help those who were in need. When he followed this article some time later by another that attacked the Khedive Ismail, King Fuad's father, in very strong terms, the King considered it sufficient provocation to warrant closing down the magazine, after fourteen issues had appeared. By then Musa had provoked many others, and when that same year he helped found al-Majmaᶜ al-Misri li-l Thaqafa al-ᶜIlmiyya, Egyptian Institute for Scientific Education, and was elected to sit on its first committee, Sidqi, then the premier, saw to it that he was immediately expelled from the Institute.

In 1946 Musa was imprisoned after he had been accused by the government of being a communist, although he was later set free without ever having been brought to trial.

In addition to his contributions to the mass media of the day, Musa's publications number well over fifty. These works cover a variety of subjects ranging from translations of Western authors, such as Dostoievski's *Crime and Punishment* which he brought out in 1913, to works on socialism, psychology, history, literature (both Eastern and Western), economics, nationalist movements all over the world (in 1934 he wrote a book on Gandhi and the Indian movement), freedom of thought, freedom of speech, self-education, women's emancipation, birth control, and politics. To summarize Musa's major contributions to the intellectual life of Egypt is not an easy task; what he sought to do was to introduce the sum total of Western learning to the Egyptians, no mean feat.

Musa was a firm believer in Fabian socialist thought, and he tried to introduce it in Egypt in a practical fashion when he and three friends founded the Socialist party, al-Hizb al-Ishtiraki. He also wrote a number of books explaining socialism and its principles to the public. For a brief period of time the Socialist party acquired links with a small labor organization led by a Russian of Jewish extraction named Joseph Rosenthal. At that time labor organizations were a novelty and were mostly limited to workers of alien origin, but Rosenthal who had obvious communist tendencies thought that it would give his organization a wider gathering among the native workers if he could get a few local intellectuals to join him. When Rosenthal came out in support of Moscow and the Third Communist International, he clashed with Musa's Fabian principles. Musa chose to regard this support of Moscow as a step toward communism, which he deemed one step this side of anarchy, and therefore he split with Rosenthal after six months of cooperation.[25] While Musa never had further active links with labor organizations, none of which had much importance until the end of World War II, he continued, as a socialist and a social reformer, to be concerned with rural and urban labor problems, to write on the need for helping the working classes rise from their low condition, and to put an end to their shameful exploitation by the landed rich and the foreign capitalists. His cry against social injustice is perhaps the most consistent element in his various books.

To put an end to social injustice; Musa preached that man must shed his reliance on past traditions; he must set aside his ignorance and enlighten himself by learning and by absolute freedom of thought. In his book al-Tajdid fi-l Adab al-Injilizi al-Hadith, "New Trends in Modern English Literature" (1936), he used Shelley, Shaw, and Wells as examples to show that hidebound tradition must be replaced by a spirit of free inquiry and of scientific thought. Herein lay Salama Musa's major contribution: to help spread a new current of intellectual thought in Egypt along with other intellectuals like Ismail Mazhar and Huain Fawzi, more eminent scholars than Musa but not as widely

25. Abd al-Adhim Ramadan, Tatawwur al-haraka al-wataniyya fi Misr (Cairo, 1968), p. 532.

known as the full-time journalist. These men started a new school which accentuated the importance of secular and scientific knowledge, which set religion aside, and which looked to the men of the future as *homo scientiae,* men who were to be guided by scientific thought alone.

To enable Egyptians in particular and Easterners in general to achieve that dream of a future generation of scientific men, Musa believed that they would have to rid themselves of what he called *kabus al-sharq,* "incubus of the East," and replace it wholesale with the benefits of Western civilization. The French occupation of Egypt in 1798 was a blessing, thought Musa, for he mistakenly believed that Bonaparte had planted in Egypt the seeds of European civilization. More important, and equally as mistaken, Musa claimed that all the Arabs of Egypt, Syria, and Iraq, and all of North Africa should come to realize that they are Europeans by race, culture, and civilization.[26] Eastern societies can therefore progress only if they follow Europe's example and reform themselves by modernizing, that is, westernizing all fields of knowledge and all aspects of life. Western culture was to be adopted in toto, warts and all, by the East. People's thought must be shaped by Western intellectual developments, their industry and agriculture must follow suit. Thus he came out strongly in support of an Egyptian industry in order to compete with Europe on an equal footing. Even in the matter of clothing, Egyptians were enjoined to blindly follow the West and wear trousers and hat instead of clinging to vestiges of Turkish dress such as the *tarbush.* Musa's pleas might have fallen on less deaf ears if he had adduced some sort of rational argument for his claims, such as that the hat is better suited to sunny Egypt than the *tarbush* which heated the skull considerably and did not protect the wearer's face from the sun as did a hat.

Above all, he contended, Arabic speakers must transform Arabic script into Latin script. Just as Bernard Shaw had tried to modify and improve English, and Mustafa Kemal had tried to improve Turkish by replacing words of Arabic or Persian origin with French expressions, Salama Musa believed that similar changes should take place in Arabic. Such changes would facilitate the spread of Arabic and increase the rate of literacy. In short *al-qadim* "the old," was to be radically expunged from Egyptian society and give way to *al-jadid,* "the new," and classical Arabic was to be completely replaced by the

26. Article he wrote in *al-Hilal,* July 1927, p. 1074.

colloquial version. It is no wonder that Musa's extremist ideas, baldly stated, could incite his opposition to rage.

There was much that was contradictory in Musa's writings and in his actions. He wanted to tear out tradition by the very roots and plant Western civilization in its place, yet he was fascinated by Pharaonic Egypt and by the folk traditions of Upper Egypt. He campaigned for birth control, yet his wife bore him eight children. He played down the importance of religion, yet he founded a newspaper for the Coptic community and for twenty years gave a weekly lecture to the Young Men's Christian Association. All these contradictions his opponents were quick to point out.

Salama Musa was a gadfly to prod Egyptians into thinking, to prod them into seeing that ideas other than their own existed, and if they became infuriated in the process and refuted his ideas, at least that was a positive step, for it led them into intellectual debate and into eventual revitalization of thought, and hopefully of action.

Even though Musa advocated the wholesale adoption of Western manners and customs it did not mean that he advocated the subservience of the East to the West. Egypt, he claimed, must rid itself of the British occupation, and he threw his pen into the service of the nationalist cause. Rational man could not overthrow the domination of tradition and accept the domination of his fellowman even when that domination stemmed from a group that possessed a superior culture. For tyranny in all its forms was abhorrent, whether benevolent, as the British claimed their rule to be in Egypt, or unjust, as Egyptians agreed the Egyptian monarchy was. But if Egyptians were to be able to throw off a foreign yoke and to take their place among the family of nations, they would have to compete with the West on their own terms, and they could not hope to do that unless they adopted all the terms of the West, good or bad. To beat the West at their own game they would have to adopt it. After adopting it they could then become free: Egyptian industry could not grow when it lay in the hands of foreigners—it would have to be taken over by Egyptians; Egyptian literature could not become international unless it acquired the Latin script—some of his opponents wondered sarcastically why they should keep Arabic at all, why they should not be content to write only in a European language just to please Musa.

During his lifetime Musa believed that he had witnessed the realization of his fondest hopes. The British occupation of Egypt had come to an end in the fifties, the industry had been totally Egyptianized, the monarchy had been replaced by a republic. In 1957, after the revolution he wrote: "Today, in 1957, I find the Republic is established; it was the cry for which I was imprisoned in 1946. I find my call for industrialization is attained; a call on which I spent thirty years urging its deployment. I also find my appeal for education is being answered and that people have begun to believe in my advocacy of the theory of evolution. Lastly I can say, 'I succeeded'."[27]

Salama's school of thought did acquire a following among bureaucrats and technicians as well as among intellectuals, although it was not as popular as some other schools. Many of Musa's more outrageous ideas were discarded, but what was sensible attracted a following. His advocacy of an Egyptianized industry met with approval from many disparate sources beginning with Talaat Harb (who had come to the same conclusion on his own) and down to every worker. Musa's plea for increased education was one which Taha Husain also espoused and which, when he became minister of education in 1951, culminated in free university education as well as primary and secondary education. His call for a scientific approach to problems and for free speech and freedom of thought found its echo in the work of most intellectuals and in acceptance by the majority of educated Egyptians. His advocacy of a colloquial language manifested itself in a new generation of authors who wrote in the spoken language. His praise of Western attire, which had taken over in the urban areas among the middle and upper classes, became regulation wear in industry where the indigenous galabiyya was discovered to be a safety hazard, and trousers and shirt became mandatory. Salama was thus advocating things that were on their way to becoming established because they were useful and valuable to any society, Eastern or Western.

In the emergence to power of the technocrats after the 1952 revolution one can perhaps see Musa's dream of scientific man reach fruition. Where scientific man will lead Egypt time will tell.

27. Salama Musa, *Tarbiyyat Salama Musa* (2d ed.; Cairo, 1962), pp. 267-268.

Conclusion

T HE unprecedented unity of Egyptians dur-
ing the 1919 revolution and the feeling of euphoria roused by the
belief in imminent independence were to last for only a brief span of
time. The Wafd as a coalition of all Egyptians was to meet the
inevitable fate of coalitions, dissolution. But because the stakes were
high, the consequent ill-feeling generated between former allies became equally intense, and they were soon locked in a deadly struggle
for survival as politicians, as the future leaders of a "new" Egypt. The
shape and direction that the "new" Egypt was to take depended
entirely on who those leaders were to be: members of the old Turco-
Circassian establishment, or the new indigenous fallah elite, Yakan or
Zaghlul. To the old establishment the choice of leader depended on the
King (and the British authorities behind him), to the new leadership
the choice of leader depended on the people. Zaghlul hence accused
Adli of usurping his role as leader of the country, for he was the
Zaim of Egypt, and the only man entitled to lead the country to
independence by virtue of the "will of the nation."

The conflict between the two men and by extension between the
Wafd and Ahrar, the two parties that gathered around them, can be
summed up as the struggle by the Egyptian fallah and the urban
middle class — the outsiders — to gain recognition against the pretensions of the establishment — the elite, whether an elite of wealth or of
intellect. The Wafd, even though it had the people's votes, did not
have their interests at heart. It was a popular party with a national
cause. The Ahrar definitely represented a small elite. And yet Zaghlul
both admired and envied that elite and despised the populist aspect
of his closest lieutenants, like Nahhas, even when he recognized its
virtues to his party.

Had the conflict been limited to these two parties it may not have
reached the degree of venom that it did for the opponents, for all
their so-called differences, had a strong common goal. Socially they

remained friends outside the political arena. The presence of the King with his machinations even more than the presence of the British added an extra poisoned dimension to Egyptian political life. British motives were clear-cut, royal motives were not. The British acted when they believed British "interests" were threatened, and while that irked the Egyptians they could still see some sense to it. King Fuad interfered at all times, because every move the Egyptians took toward political independence was interpreted as an act aimed at himself and his prerogatives. His claim to rule the country untrammeled by constitution, parliament, or even advisors was the undoing of constitutional life in Egypt. He seemed to have determined that if he was not allowed to rule Egypt by himself, then he would see to it that nobody else ruled Egypt with any degree of success. Fuad was therefore the major obstacle to Egyptian liberal government in political terms. His presence cast a blight on every cabinet member who expended time and energy parrying his thrusts—even when they were his appointees—instead of governing the land. Politics has always been the art of intrigue and compromise, but Fuad gave it a twist of viciousness that was degrading to the men involved.

In all his tilts with Fuad, Zaghlul emerges as a man of honor and Fuad as an egocentric autocrat who would rather see Egypt sink than swim without him.

Zaghlul was the epitome of the fallah with all his vices and virtues. He was an Egyptian Everyman, and that was the secret of the unanimous identification with him on the part of his countrymen. His words and actions were those of a fallah, even his shabby behavior on occasion was in the fallah tradition, therefore comprehensible to the masses. The same could be said in lesser measure of Nahhas, and explains why he remained popular for so long a time in spite of the corruption that characterized his governments. The fallah, who took it for granted that all governments were corrupt, gloried in the Wafd's attainment of power as an extension of himself and accepted its corruption as benefiting one of his own. On the other hand, because it was aloof, the Ahrar could never win public sympathy. One could almost say that the Ahrar were statesmen but not true politicians, for they failed to recognize, or admit, that all actions in the political forum are struggles for power and clothed their actions in liberal principles. They may have been better men than the men of the Wafd; they were certainly more capable. But the population could not identify with them, and therefore could not sympathize with or condone their errors. Elitism may be more efficient but it is far less palatable. Without popular support, a party, whatever it chooses to call itself, will always remain "nonliberal" because it will have to rule from the top, in a paternalistic and, in the final analysis, authoritarian manner. The Ahrar ranted against the "dictatorship of the majority" and offered little more than a "dictatorship of the minority" larded with good intentions for some future utopian day.

Conflict between the two parties was therefore not only one of personality but also of basic political approach. In the abstract both groups shared a belief in liberal humanism, in the value of popular participation in government, and in freedom of speech. But where the Wafd used the myth that the masses were actively participating in the political process through elections and a pork-barrel form of reward — a claim that contained a large element of demagoguery — the Ahrar despised that approach. No doubt there was a touch of sour grapes in that attitude. They knew that they could not attract the masses away from Zaghlul, and therefore made little effort toward them, and thus hid behind a barrier of ideals and principles. Nonetheless, when the time came, the Ahrar smashed their ideals of liberalism with authoritarian zeal, all with the best of intentions.

There is nothing unusual in such behavior among political parties, either on the part of the Ahrar or of the Wafd. Their counterparts are to be found in all countries during the birth pangs of liberalism and during the most liberal periods. The role of King Fuad also had its historical counterparts in other countries and at various other times. It was the combination of King, aided and abetted — or thwarted — by the British authorities playing their own political game in Egypt, which stacked the deck against the development of liberalism. For, like the Ahrar, the British authorities in Egypt negated their own liberalism and behaved autocratically toward a people whom they refused to recognize as political equals. However much British officials admired individual Egyptians, there was frequently a snide or patronizing note in their comments on them. With very minor exceptions few Englishmen in Egypt could regard Egyptians as other than social, political, and intellectual inferiors. Zaghlul's laudable attempts to limit the King's autocracy were dubbed demagoguery, and he was classified as a dangerous rabble-rouser whose pretensions were to be crushed. That was the tragedy of the years between 1924 and 1927, the year of Zaghlul's death. They were years that should have laid the political groundwork for liberalism in Egypt and instead they became years of repression and intrigue, and set the tone for the partisan animosity that plagued parliament and characterized the successive periods.

Nahhas and his associates exacerbated that animosity by their exclusivist, power-grabbing approach to politics, but at least they had the excuse that they were supported by the majority of the population. The Ahrar, who became equally exclusive and grabbing, although on occasion they manifested a bipartisan approach, represented only a minority of vested interests.

Vis-à-vis the mass of the population all the parties failed radically in their basic duties toward their electorate. As landowners they were blind to the needs of the fallah, not because they did not see them, but because they were not willing to face the alternatives—higher taxation, land reform, agricultural unions. As capitalists or entrepreneur/industrialists of the first generation they were equally obtuse to the problems of labor. Thus there was a solid economic reason militating against the adoption of a genuinely liberal approach in parliament, and explains why a second "revolution" of a more social than political nature was necessary in order to bring about socio-economic reforms.

It was much easier for the rulers to shelve socioeconomic problems "until total independence had been effected" than to face them and attempt to undertake some measures of reform, for then they would have had to overcome two enormous obstacles. The first was the continued existence of the capitulations which allowed the Egyptian economy to be dominated by aliens and to be directed toward alien interests primarily and toward national needs peripherally. The first group of Egyptians who recognized the need to Egyptianize the economy, Talaat Harb and his associates, were as great patriots as those who fought against the physical presence of the British in the land. The second obstacle was the general economic situation of the country, where one depression followed another and culminated in the 1929-1933 cycle. Every one felt threatened and therefore became more grasping and greedy. Bankruptcy was perhaps more real to the landowner than to the fallah and rendered him more ruthless to those below him in the economic scale.

The political aspects of a society are arranged contrapuntually with its economics, but throughout both runs the intellectual theme, which highlights them both, which runs ahead of them and presages future chords, and which harks back to past passages, all the while expressing the psychological mood of that society at that point in time, whether discordant or harmonious. The thought of Lutfi al-Sayyid expressed the needs and hopes of the newly affluent and liberated man, the property owner who aspired toward the establishment of a liberal humanism that would defend his rights and above all express the basic worth of the individual, an individual who believed that if Man was shaped in God's image then he was master of his destiny and slave to no one, that he had rights and also obligations toward society, and who believed above all in the basic value of progress toward an ultimate good, an ideal or idealized goal, that of a truly egalitarian society. And while that was an externalization of theoretical assumptions, nonetheless they were more or less the guiding principles of the first nationalists.

Dueling in the political arena tarnished that pristine liberal image with cynicism and self-interest, and in its place grew an authoritarian concept of vested interests and the need for their preservation. In reaction other philosophies arose which stressed the lack of worth of the individual save within the womb of the nation or the religious community and which idealized the whole at the expense of its parts. Whether Ikhwan or Misr al-Fatat, the former talking in terms of the Muslim umma and the latter in terms of the nation, these groups were to my mind the outcome of the psychological negation of liberalism and all it stood for. Since the exponents of liberalism had failed to abide by their own principles, the others reasoned, the fault must lie not in the men but in the very principles they espoused. A return to the status quo ante, they insisted, was the answer. In the case of Hasan al-Banna a return to the early days of Islam was the outcome of a genuine religious fervor, and in the case of Ahmad Husain, a return to prior autocracy disguised under a new name was the outcome of a destructive and unscrupulous mentality. The intellectual concepts expressed by these two currents of thought more than any overt political manifestation revealed how deeply disoriented society had become.

The third and final current, that represented by Salama Musa, was a ray of hope shining out of an authoritarian night, and it brought liberal principles refurbished with new concepts once more into intellectual prominence. These currents existed simultaneously and revealed the conflicting orientations in a society that was growing and seeking to find itself as any society must.

The history of the years between 1922 and 1936 therefore holds the key to understanding much about the present. While understanding is of necessity a function of hindsight it serves a people when it exorcises frustrations and eliminates residual feelings of guilt or of inferiority. Although the establishment of liberal institutions was thwarted, liberal ideas did burgeon and Egyptian society was pushed willy-nilly along the path of progress, by which I mean toward a development of the potential in its society. What should amaze modern-day readers is not that the Egyptian leaders failed to establish democratic institutions in Egypt, but that they got as far along the path of constitutional rule as they did.

I have recounted the events of 1922-1936 and described them as the struggle for mastery in Egypt among the British occupiers, the Egyptian politicians, and the King. While that struggle was certainly not resolved by 1936, and lasted for another two decades, nevertheless it ended in a clear victory for Egypt. On that count progress is clear and definite. The early nationalists, Zaghlul, Tharwat, Yakan, and the others, were men with courage and vision, a fact that is entirely forgotten today when we talk about them patronizingly as though their achievements were negligible because they had failed to achieve complete independence and because they were the ancien regime. Without these men there would have been no "new" Egypt. They had the vision to see an independent Egypt rising from the ashes of Ottoman autocracy and British colonialism, and they fought for that vision with as much success as was possible at a time when the odds were extremely high. They had to fight an empire which was great, which had just emerged victorious from a world war, and which had an army of occupation in absolute control of the land. They had to fight a king who lived in the shadow of the nineteenth century and nurtured the myth of absolute rule, sustained by the British authorities. They had to cope with a society that was only just beginning to slough off the skin of Ottomanism and pan-Islamic traditionalism and to think in terms of national interests and patriotism. They had to contend with an international state of mind that approved of a system of colonizers and colonized as a right and proper way of life. They were not windmills that the nationalists tilted at, they were real, massive juggernauts.

The nationalists succeeded, not in forging complete and total independence, but in implanting in Egyptian youth the vision of such a future society and the desire to reach it. In so doing they implanted two important elements in their society: freedom of speech and freedom of thought. I have described how on occasion freedom of speech was hedged, but if Ali Abd al-Raziq and Taha Husain could write the books they did and simply lose a job for a short period of time instead of life or liberty, as would have happened at other times or in other countries, that is a great achievement for a country that for so many centuries had known little of free speech or free thought, an achievement that successive generations of Egyptians would do well to remember, although the lesson seems to have been forgotten for some time. For all their endemic weaknesses, Egyptian politicians could and did stand up to King and Resident. The press published as it pleased and sustained only temporary censorship. Whatever repression was carried out by the opposition inevitably ended in the reestablishment of free thought and speech. That is a heartening lesson to remember and recent events have simply confirmed it.

The most important element in national victory was not that after the 1952 revolution the last British soldier evacuated Egyptian soil— important though that was—or that a corrupt and useless system of hereditary exploitation disguised as a monarchy had ended, but that from that period onward Egyptians bore the sole responsibility for their actions, right or wrong, positive or negative. In the past the British presence and the king were used indiscriminately as a crutch or scapegoat or actual villain to explain real and imagined political diseases. No society can develop a healthy political life when it has such a crutch to lean on or such liabilities to contend with. Society can only become healthy when it faces its responsibilities squarely and places the blame where it belongs, on itself and on its people.

Not only is the political growth of a people hindered by its political dependence on outside forces but also and more surely is its economic growth. Only from 1960 onward can Egyptian economic developments be measured; once having nationalized foreign interests, Egyptian governments could no longer plead foreign plutocracy as an extenuating circumstance for economic mismanagement nor have to sit by and see it take the credit for economic achievements.

Egyptian society can only truly progress through the free exercise of the talents of her intellectuals, and I include all the educated in the land. The wholesale importation of concepts from the East or the West, for all the advantages those ideas have offered—and we must not forget that free speech and liberal humanism were Western imports—is nonetheless only a temporary expedient until indigenous ideas develop, adapt, and modify those concepts which suit their society. Today we can measure the difference in intellectual approach between the thinkers of the past and those of the present and see how they have changed. In the past educated Egyptians tried desperately to become acceptable to the West as the intellectual arbiter of the world, as did Salama Musa and his school, but today the scene has changed. Intellectuals tend more to express themselves for themselves and their society than to gain admission into a Western cultural club. Should any outsiders wish to be informed in the process, then well and good, but if they reject the local output, then the reaction of the locals is now indifference. In brief, Egyptian intellectuals do not feel the need to apologize for their ideas or to seek approval, although some still do. The majority are by and large too busy searching for and trying to express ideas, and helping to shape and mold a society that is growing.

Egypt's social problems are tremendous, and they multiply with each new birth. Overpopulation erodes the benefits of any economic investment before it even comes to fruition, so that unless population growth can be arrested the shadow of poverty looms ever darker over the land. Disease continues to take its toll: trachoma, bilharzia, and ankylostoma remain the three dreaded incubi of the Egyptian peasant, while malnutrition and tuberculosis dog the urban slum dweller. A more active social consciousness is necessary in the ruling elite and in the rest of the population to enable a system of government to become established — a system of laws, not one based on personal relations and appeals to those in power, a system that will allow for the continuity of government in spite of changes at the top.

To those who feel helpless before the magnitude of Egypt's problems one can only say, look back and see what has been achieved and how much Egypt has progressed. Surely that is encouragement enough for the most fainthearted and an incitement to work harder in the future, which can only be better than the past. It is no accident that the technocrats have come into their own in postrevolutionary Egypt. After all, modern techniques have caused many of Egypt's problems — for example, better hygiene and lower infant mortality are two causes of overpopulation — and it is to modern techniques that we must turn for a solution to poverty, disease, and ignorance. And solution there surely is as long as men of goodwill seek to find one.

Appendix

Treaty of Alliance

between His Majesty, in respect to the United Kingdom,
and His Majesty the King of Egypt[1]

London, August 26, 1936

[*Ratifications exchanged at Cairo on December* 22, 1936].

His Majesty The King of Great Britain, Ireland and the British
Dominions beyond the Seas, Emperor of India, and His Majesty the
King of Egypt;

Being anxious to consolidate the friendship and the relations of
good understanding between them and to co-operate in the execution
of their international obligations in preserving the peace of the world;

And considering that these objects will best be achieved by the
conclusion of a treaty of friendship and alliance, which in their
common interest will provide for effective co-operation in preserving
peace and ensuring the defence of their respective territories, and shall
govern their mutual relations in the future;

Have agreed to conclude a treaty for this purpose, and have appointed as their plenipotentiaries: —

His Majesty The King of Great Britain, Ireland and the British
Dominions beyond the Seas, Emperor of India (hereinafter referred to
as His Majesty The King and Emperor):

For Great Britain and Northern Ireland:

The Rt. Hon. Anthony Eden, M.C., M.P., His Principal Secretary of State
for Foreign Affairs.

The Rt. Hon. James Ramsay MacDonald, M.P., Lord President of the
Council.

The Rt. Hon. Sir John Simon, G.C.S.I., K.C.V.O., O.B.E., K.C., M.P.,
His Principal Secretary of State for the Home Department.

1. Cmd. 5360 published by H.M.S.O., 1937.

The Rt. Hon. Viscount Halifax, K.G., G.C.S.I., G.C.I.E., Lord Privy Seal.
Sir Miles Wedderburn Lampson, K.C.M.G., C.B., M.V.O., His High
  Commissioner for Egypt and the Sudan.
His Majesty the King of Egypt:
  Moustapha El Nahas Pacha, President of the Council of Ministers.
  Dr. Ahmed Maher, President of the Chamber of Deputies.
  Mohamed Mahmoud Pacha, former President of the Council of Ministers.
  Ismail Sedky Pacha, former President of the Council of Ministers.
  Abdel Fattah Yéhia Pacha, former President of the Council of Ministers.
  Wacyf Boutros Ghali Pacha, Minister of Foreign Affairs.
  Osman Moharram Pacha, Minister of Public Works.
  Makram Ebeid Pacha, Minister of Finance.
  Mahmoud Fahmy El-Nokrachi Pacha, Minister of Communications.
  Ahmed Hamdi Seif El Nasr Pacha, Minister of Agriculture.
  Aly El Chamsi Pacha, former Minister.
  Mohamed Helmi Issa Pacha, former Minister.
  Hafez Afifi Pacha, former Minister.

Who, having communicated their full powers, found in good and
due form, have agreed as follows: —

ARTICLE 1.

The military occupation of Egypt by the forces of His Majesty The
King and Emperor is terminated.

ARTICLE 2.

His Majesty The King and Emperor will henceforth be represented
at the Court of His Majesty the King of Egypt and His Majesty the
King of Egypt will be represented at the Court of St. James's by
Ambassadors duly accredited.

ARTICLE 3.

Egypt intends to apply for membership to the League of Nations.
His Majesty's Government in the United Kingdom, recognising Egypt
as a sovereign independent State, will support any request for admission which the Egyptian Government may present in the conditions
prescribed by Article 1 of the Covenant.

ARTICLE 4.

An alliance is established between the High Contracting Parties
with a view to consolidating their friendship, their cordial understanding and their good relations.

ARTICLE 5.

Each of the High Contracting Parties undertakes not to adopt in relation to foreign countries an attitude which is inconsistent with the alliance, nor to conclude political treaties inconsistent with the provisions of the present treaty.

ARTICLE 6.

Should any dispute with a third State produce a situation which involves a risk of a rupture with that State, the High Contracting Parties will consult each other with a view to the settlement of the said dispute by peaceful means, in accordance with the provisions of the Covenant of the League of Nations and of any other international obligations which may be applicable to the case.

ARTICLE 7.

Should, notwithstanding the provisions of Article 6 above, either of the High Contracting Parties become engaged in war, the other High Contracting Party will, subject always to the provisions of Article 10 below, immediately come to his aid in the capacity of an ally.

The aid of His Majesty the King of Egypt in the event of war, imminent menace of war or apprehended international emergency will consist in furnishing to His Majest The King and Emperor on Egyptian territory, in accordance with the Egyptian system of administration and legislation, all the facilities and assistance in his power, including the use of his ports, aerodromes and means of communication. It will accordingly be for the Egyptian Government to take all the administrative and legislative measures, including the establishment of martial law and an effective censorship, necessary to render these facilities and assistance effective.

ARTICLE 8.

In view of the fact that the Suez Canal, whilst being an integral part of Egypt, is a universal means of communication as also an essential means of communication between the different parts of the British Empire, His Majesty the King of Egypt, until such time as the High Contracting Parties agree that the Egyptian Army is in a position to ensure by its own resources the liberty and entire security of navigation of the Canal, authorises His Majesty The King and Emperor to station forces in Egyptian territory in the vicinity of the Canal, in the zone specified in the Annex to this Article, with a view to ensuring in co-operation with the Egyptian forces the defence of the Canal. The detailed arrangements for the carrying into effect of this Article are contained in the Annex hereto. The presence of these forces shall not constitute in any manner an occupation and will in no way prejudice the sovereign rights of Egypt.

It is understood that at the end of the period of twenty years specified in Article 16 the question whether the presence of British forces is no longer necessary owing to the fact that the Egyptian Army is in a position to ensure by its own resources the liberty and entire security of navigation of the Canal may, if the High Contracting Parties do not agree thereon, be submitted to the Council of the League of Nations for decision in accordance with the provisions of the Covenant in force at the time of signature of the present treaty or to such other person or body of persons for decision in accordance with such other procedure as the High Contracting Parties may agree.

Annex to Article 8.

1. Without prejudice to the provisions of Article 7, the numbers of the forces of His Majesty The King and Emperor to be maintained in the vicinity of the Canal shall not exceed, of the land forces, 10,000, and of the air forces, 400 pilots, together with necessary ancillary personnel for administrative and technical duties. These numbers do not include civilian personnel, e.g., clerks, artisans and labourers.

2. The British forces to be maintained in the vicinity of the Canal will be distributed (a) as regards the land forces, in Moascar and the Geneifa area on the south-west side of the Great Bitter Lake, and (b) as regards the air forces, within 5 miles of the Port Said-Suez railway from Kantara in the north, to the junction of the railway Suez-Cairo and Suez-Ismailia in the south, together with an extension along the Ismalia-Cairo railway to include the Royal Air Force Station at Abu Sueir and its satellite landing grounds; together with areas suitable for air firing and bombing ranges, which may have to be placed east of the Canal.

3. In the localities specified above there shall be provided for the British land and air forces of the numbers specified in paragraph 1 above, including 4,000 civilian personnel (but less 2,000 of land forces, 700 of the air forces and 450 civilian personnel for whom accommodation already exists), the necessary lands and durable barrack and technical accommodation, including an emergency water supply. The lands, accommodation and water supply shall be suitable according to

modern standards. In addition, amenities such as are reasonable, having regard to the character of those localities, will be provided by the planting of trees and the provision of gardens, playing fields, &c., for the troops, and a site for the erection of a convalescent camp on the Mediterranean coast.

4. The Egyptian Government will make available the lands and construct the accommodation, water supplies, amenities and convalescent camp, referred to in the preceding paragraph as being necessary over and above the accommodation already existing in these localities, at its own expense, but His Majesty's Government in the United Kingdom will contribute (1) the actual sum spent by the Egyptian Government before 1914 on the construction of new barracks as alternative accommodation to the Kasr-el-Nil Barracks in Cairo, and (2) the cost of one-fourth of the barrack and technical accommodation for the land forces. The first of these sums shall be paid at the time specified in paragraph 8 below for the withdrawal of the British forces from Cairo and the second at the time for the withdrawal of the British forces from Alexandria under paragraph 18 below. The Egyptian Government may charge a fair rental for the residential accommodations provided for the civilian personnel. The amount of the rent will be agreed between His Majesty's Government in the United Kingdom and the Egyptian Government.

5. The two Governments will each appoint, immediately the present treaty comes into force, two or more persons who shall together form a committee to whom all questions relating to the execution of these works from the time of their commencement to the time of their completion shall be entrusted. Proposals for, or outlines of, plans and specifications put forward by the representatives of His Majesty's Government in the United Kingdom will be accepted, provided they are reasonable and do not fall outside the scope of the obligations of the Egyptian Government under paragraph 4. The plans and specifications of each of the works to be undertaken by the Egyptian Government shall be approved by the representatives of both Governments on this committee before the work is begun. Any member of this committee, as well as the Commanders of the British forces or their representatives, shall have the right to examine the works at all stages of their construction, and the United Kingdom members of the committee may make suggestions as regards the manner in which the work is carried out. The United Kingdom members shall also have the right to make at any time, while the work is in progress, proposals for modifications or alterations in the plans and specifications. Effect

shall be given to suggestions and proposals by the United Kingdom members, subject to the condition that they are reasonable and do not fall outside the scope of the obligations of the Egyptian Government under paragraph 4. In the case of machinery and other stores, where standardization of type is important, it is agreed that stores, of the standard type in general use by the British forces will be obtained and installed. It is, of course, understood that His Majesty's Government in the United Kingdom may, when the barracks and accommodation are being used by the British forces, make at their own expense improvements or alterations thereto and construct new buildings in the areas specified in paragraph 2 above.

6. In pursuance of their programme for the development of road and railway communications in Egypt, and in order to bring the means of communications in Egypt up to modern strategic requirements, the Egyptian Government will construct and maintain the following roads, bridges and railways: —

(A)—Roads.

(i) Ismailia-Alexandria, via Tel-el-Kebir, Zagazig, Zifta, Tanta, Kafr-el-Zayat, Damanhour.

(ii) Ismailia-Cairo, via Tel-el-Kebir and thence continuing along the Sweet Water Canal to Heliopolis.

(iii) Port Said-Ismailia-Suez.

(iv) A link between the south end of the Great Bitter Lake and the Cairo-Suez road about 15 miles west of Suez.

In order to bring them up to the general standard of good-class roads for general traffic, these roads will be 20 feet wide, have byepasses round villages, &c., and be made of such material as to be permanently utilisable for military purposes, and will be constructed in the above order of importance. They will comply with the technical specifications set out below which are the ordinary specifications for a good-class road for general traffic.

Bridges and roads shall be capable of carrying a double line of continuous columns of either heavy four-wheeled mechanical transport, six-wheeled mechanical transport or medium tanks. With regard to four-wheeled vehicles, the distance between the front axle of one vehicle and the rear axle of the vehicle next ahead shall be calculated at 20 feet, the load on each rear axle to be 14 tons, on each front axle to be 6 tons and the distance between axles 18 feet. With regard to six-wheeled vehicles, the distance between the front axle of one vehicle and the rear axle of the next ahead shall be calculated to be 20 feet, between rear axle and middle axle to be 4 feet and between middle axle and front axle 13 feet; the load on each rear and middle axle to be 8.1 tons and on each front axle to be 4 tons. Tanks shall be calculated for as weighing 19.25 tons, to be 25 feet over all in length and to have a distance of 3 feet between the front of one tank and the rear of the next ahead; the load of 19.25 tons to be carried by tracks which have a bearing of 13 feet upon the road or bridge.

(B)—Railways.

(i) (1) Railway facilities in the Canal Zone will be increased and improved to meet the needs of the increased garrison in the zone and to provide facilities for rapid entrainment of personnel, guns' vehicles and stores according to the requirements of a modern army. His Majesty's Government in the United Kingdom are hereby authorised to make at their own expense such subsequent additions and modifications to these railway facilities as the future requirements of the British forces may demand. Where such additions or modifications affect railway lines used for general traffic, the permission of the Egyptian Government must be obtained.

(ii) The line between Zagazig and Tanta will be doubled.

(iii) The Alexandria-Mersa Matruh line will be improved and made permanent.

7. In addition to the roads specified in paragraph 6 (A) above, and for the same purposes, the Egyptian Governemnt will construct and maintain the following roads: —

(i) Cairo south along the Nile to Kena and Kus;

(ii) Kus to Kosseir;

(iii) Kena to Hurghada.

These roads and the bridges thereon will be constructed to satisfy the same standards as those specified in paragraph 6 above.

It may not be possible for the construction of the roads referred to in this paragraph to be undertaken at the same time as the roads referred to in paragraph 6, but they will be constructed as soon as possible.

8. When, to the satisfaction of both the High Contracting Parties, the accommodation referred to in paragraph 4 is ready (accommodation for the forces retained temporarily at Alexandria in accordance with paragraph 18 below not being included) and the works referred to in paragraph 6 above (other than the railways referred to in (ii)

and (iii) of part (B) of that paragraph) have been completed, then the British forces in parts of Egypt other than the areas in the Canal Zone specified in paragraph 2 above and except for those maintained temporarily at Alexandria, will withdraw and the lands, barracks, aircraft landing grounds, seaplane anchorages and accommodation occupied by them will be vacated and, save in so far as they may belong to private persons, be handed over to the Egyptian Government.

9. Any difference of opinion between the Governments relating to the execution of paragraphs 3, 4, 5, 6, 7, and 8 above wil be submitted to the decision of an Arbitral Board, composed of three members, the two Governments nominating each a member and the third being nominated by the two Governments in common agreement. The decision of the Board shall be final.

10. In order to ensure proper training of British troops, it is agreed that the area defined below will be available for the training of British forces: (a) and (b) at all times of the year, and (c) during February and March for annual maneuvers: —

(a) West of the Canal: From Kantara in the north to the Suez-Cairo railway (inclusive) in the south and as far as longitude 31 degrees 30 minutes east, exclusive of all cultivation;

(b) East of the Canal as required;

(c) A continuation of (a) as far south as latitude 29 degrees 52 minutes north, thence south-east to the junction of latitude 29 degrees 30 minutes north and longitude 31 degrees 44 minutes east and from that point eastwards along latitude 29 degrees 30 minutes north.

The areas of the localities referred to above are included in the map (scale 1:500,000) which is annexed to the present Treaty.(1)

11. Unless the two Goverments agree to the contrary, the Egyptian Government will prohibit the passage of aircraft over the territories situated on either side of the Suez Canal and within 20 kilometres of it, except for the purpose of passage from east to west or *vice versa* by means of a corridor 10 kilometres wide at Kantara. This prohibition will not, however, apply to the forces of the High Contracting Parties or to genuinely Egyptian air organisations or to air organisations genuinely belonging to any part of the British Commonwealth of Nations operating under the authority of the Egyptian Government.

12. The Egyptian Government will provide when necessary reasonable means of communication and access to and from the localities where the British forces are situated and will also accord facilities at Port Said and Suez for the landing and storage of material and supplies

for the British forces, including the maintenance of a small detachment of the British forces in these ports to handle and guard this material and these supplies in transit.

13. In view of the fact that the speed and range of modern aircraft necessitate the use of wide areas for the efficient training of air forces, the Egyptian Government will accord permission to the British air forces to fly wherever they consider it necessary for the purpose of training. Reciprocal treatment will be accorded to Egyptian air forces in British territories.

14. In view of the fact that the safety of flying is dependent upon provision of a large number of places where aircraft can alight, the Egyptian Government will secure the maintenance and constant availability of adequate landing grounds and seaplane anchorages in Egyptian territory and waters. The Egyptian Government will accede to any request from the British air forces for such additional landing grounds and seaplane anchorages as experience may show to be necessary to make the number adequate for allied requirements.

15. The Egyptian Government will accord permission for the British air forces to use the said landings and seaplane anchorages, and in the case of certain of them to send stocks of fuel and stores thereto, to be kept in sheds to be erected thereon for this purpose, and in case of urgency to undertake such work as may be necessary for the safety of aircraft.

16. The Egyptian Government will give all necessary facilities for the passage of the personnel of the British forces, aircraft and stores to and from the said landing grounds and seaplane anchorages. Similar facilities will be afforded to the personnel, aircraft and stores of the Egyptian forces at the air bases of the British forces.

17. The British military authorities shall be at liberty to request permission from the Egyptian Government to send parties of officers in civilian clothes to the Western Desert to study the ground and draw up tactical schemes. This permission shall not be unreasonably withheld.

18. His Majesty the King of Egypt authorises His Majesty The King and Emperor to maintain units of his forces at or near Alexandria for a period not exceeding eight years from the date of the coming into force of the present treaty, this being the approximate period considered necessary by the two High Contracting Parties —

   (a) For the final completion of the barrack accommodation in the Canal zone;
   (b) (1) For the improvement of the roads —

(i)   Cairo-Suez;

(ii) Cairo-Alexandria via Giza and the desert;

(iii) Alexandria-Mersa Matruh;

so as to bring them up to the standard specified in part (A) of paragraph 6;

(c) The improvement of the railway facilities between Ismailia and Alexandria, and Alexandria and Mersa Matruh referred to in (ii) and (iii) of part (B) of paragraph 6.

The Egyptian Government will complete the work specified in (a), (b) and (c) above before the expiry of the period of eight years aforesaid. The roads and railway facilities mentioned above will, of course, be maintained by the Egyptian Goverment.

19. The British forces in or near Cairo shall, until the time for withdrawal under paragraph 8 above, and the British forces in or near Alexandria until the expiry of the time specified in paragraph 18 above, continue to enjoy the same facilities as at present.

ARTICLE 9.

The immunities and privileges in jurisdictional and fiscal matters to be enjoyed by the forces of His Majesty The King and Emperor who are in Egypt in accordance with the provisions of the present treaty will be determined in a separate convention to be concluded between the Egyptian Government and His Majesty's Government in the United Kingdom.

ARTICLE 10.

Nothing in the present treaty is intended to or shall in any way prejudice the rights and obligations which devolve, or may devolve, upon either of the High Contracting Parties under the Covenant of the League of Nations or the Treaty for the Renunciation of War signed at Paris on 27th August, 1928.[2]

ARTICLE 11.

1. While reserving liberty to conclude new conventions in future, modifying the agreements of the 19th January and the 10th July, 1899, the High Contracting Parties agree that the administration of the Sudan shall continue to be that resulting from the said agreements. The Governor-General shall continue to exercise on the joint behalf of the High Contracting Parties the powers conferred upon him by the said agreements.

2. Treaty Series No. 29 (1929) (Cmd. 3410).

The High Contracting Parties agree that the primary aim of their administration in the Sudan must be the welfare of the Sudanese.

Nothing in this article prejudices the question of sovereignty over the Sudan.

2. 1 Appointments and promotions of officials in the Sudan will in consequence remain vested in the Governor-General, who, in making new appointments to posts for which qualified Sudanese are not available, will select suitable candidates of British and Egyptian nationality.

3. In addition to Sudanese troops, both British and Egyptian troops shall be placed at the disposal of the Governor-General for the defence of the Sudan.

4. Egyptian immigration into the Sudan shall be unrestricted except for reasons of public order and health.

5. There shall be no discrimination in the Sudan between British subjects and Egyptian nationals in matters of commerce, immigration or the possession of property.

6. The High Contracting Parties are agreed on the provisions set out in the Annex to this Article as regards the method by which international conventions are to be made applicable to the Sudan.

Annex to Article 11.

1. Unless and until the High Contracting Parties agree to the contrary in application of paragraph 1 of this Article, the general principle for the future shall be that international conventions shall only become applicable to the Sudan by the joint action of the Governments of the United Kingdom and of Egypt, and that such joint action shall similarly also be required if it is desired to terminate the participation of the Sudan in an international convention which already applies to this territory.

2. Conventions to which it will be desired that the Sudan should be a party will generally be conventions of a technical or humanitarian character. Such conventions almost invariably contain a provision for subsequent accession, and in such cases this method of making the convention applicable to the Sudan will be adopted. Accession will be effected by a joint instrument, signed on behalf of Egypt and the United Kingdom respectively by two persons duly authorised for the purpose. The method of depositing the instruments of accession will be the subject of agreement in each case between the two Governments. In the event of its being desired to apply to the Sudan a convention which does not contain an accession clause, the method

by which this should be effected will be the subject of consultation
and agreement between the two Governments.

3. If the Sudan is already a party to a convention, and it is desired
to terminate the participation of the Sudan therein, the necessary
notice of termination will be given jointly by the United Kingdom and
by Egypt.

4. It is understood that the participation of the Sudan in a convention and the termination of such participation can only be effected
by joint action specifically taken in respect of the Sudan, and does not
follow merely from the fact that the United Kingdom and Egypt are
both parties to a convention or have both denounced a convention.

5. At international conferences where such conventions are negotiated, the Egyptian and the United Kingdom delegates would naturally keep in touch with a view to any action which they may agree to
be desirable in the interests of the Sudan.

ARTICLE 12.

His Majesty The King and Emperor recognises that the responsibility
for the lives and property of foreigners in Egypt devolves exclusively
upon the Egyptian Government, who will ensure the fulfilment of
their obligations in this respect.

ARTICLE 13.

His Majesty The King and Emperor recognises that the capitulatory
régime now existing in Egypt is no longer in accordance with the
spirit of the times and with the present state of Egypt.

His Majesty the King of Egypt desires the abolition of this régime
without delay.

Both High Contracting Parties are agreed upon the arrangements
with regard to this matter as set forth in the Annex to this Article.

Annex to Article 13.

1. It is the object of the arrangements set out in this Annex: —
(i) To bring about speedily the abolition of the Capitulations in
Egypt with the disappearance of the existing restrictions on
Egyptian sovereignty in the matter of the application of Egyptian
legislation (including financial legislation) to foreigners as its
necessary consequence;
(ii) To institute a transitional régime for a reasonable and not
unduly prolonged period to be fixed, during which the Mixed
Tribunals will remain and will, in addition to their present

judicial jurisdiction, exercise the jurisdiction at present vested in the Consular Courts.

At the end of this transitional period the Egyptian Government will be free to dispense with the Mixed Tribunals.

2. As a first step, the Egyptian Government will approach the Capitulatory Powers as soon as possible with a view to (a) the removal of all restrictions on the application of Egyptian legislation to foreigners and (b) the institution of a transitional régime for the Mixed Tribunals as provided in paragraph 1 (ii) above.

3. His Majesty's Government in the United Kingdom, as the Government of a Capitulatory Power and as an ally of Egypt, are in no way opposed to the arrangements referred to in the preceding paragraph and will collaborate actively with the Egyptian Government in giving effect to them by using all their influence with the Powers exercising capitulatory rights in Egypt.

4. It is understood that in the event of its being found impossible to bring into effect the arrangements referred to in paragraph 2, the Egyptian Government retains its full rights unimpaired with regard to the capitulatory régime, including the Mixed Tribunals.

5. It is understood that paragraph 2 (a) involves not merely that the assent of the Capitulatory Powers will be no longer necessary for the application of any Egyptian legislation to their nationals but also that the present legislative functions of the Mixed Tribunals as regards the application of Egyptian legislation to foreigners will terminate. It would follow from this that the Mixed Tribunals in their judicial capacity would no longer have to pronounce upon the validity of the application to foreigners of an Egyptian law or decree which has been applied to foreigners by the Egyptian Parliament or Government, as the case may be.

6. His Majesty the King of Egypt hereby declares that no Egyptian legislation made applicable to foreigners will be inconsistent with the principles generally adopted in modern legislation or, with particular relation to legislation of a fiscal nature, discriminate against foreigners, including foreign corporate bodies.

7. In view of the fact that it is the practice in most countries to apply to foreigners the law of their nationality in matters of "statut personnel," consideration will be given to the desirability of excepting from the transfer of jurisdiction, at any rate in the first place, matters relating to "statut personnel" affecting nationals of those Capitulatory Powers who wish that their Consular authorities should continue to exercise such jurisdiction.

8. The transitional régime for the Mixed Tribunals and the transfer to them of the jurisdiction at present exercised by the Consular Courts (which régime and transfer will, of course, be subject to the provisions of the special convention referred to in Article 9) will necessitate the revision of existing laws relating to the organisation and jurisdiction of the Mixed Tribunals, including the preparation and promulgation of a new Code of Criminal Procedure. It is understood that this revision will include amongst other matters: —

(i) The definition of the word "foreigner" for the purpose of the future jurisdiction of the Mixed Tribunals;

(ii) The increase of the personnel of the Mixed Tribunals and the Mixed Parquet, which will be necessitated by the proposed extension of their jurisdiction;

(iii) The procedure in the case of pardons or remissions of sentences imposed on foreigners and also in connection with the execution of capital sentences passed on foreigners.

ARTICLE 14.

The present treaty abrogates any existing agreements or other instruments whose continued existence is inconsistent with its provisions. Should either High Contracting Party so request, a list of the agreements and instruments thus abrogated shall be drawn up in agreement between them within six months of the coming into force of the present treaty.

ARTICLE 15.

The High Contracting Parties agree that any difference on the subject of the application or interpretation of the provisions of the present treaty which they are unable to settle by direct negotiation shall be dealt with in accordance with the provisions of the Convenant of the League of Nations.

ARTICLE 16.

At any time after the expiration of a period of twenty years from the coming into force of the treaty, the High Contracting Parties will, at the request of either of them, enter into negotiations with a view to such revisoin of its terms by agreement between them as may be appropriate in the circumstances as they then exist. In case of the High Contracting Parties being unable to agree upon the terms of the revised treaty, the difference will be submitted to the Council of the League of Nations for decision in accordance with the provisions of the Covenant in force at the time of signature of the present treaty or to such other person or body of persons for decision in accordance with such procedure as the High Contracting Parties may agree. It is agreed that any revision of this treaty will provide for the continuation of the Alliance between the High Contracting Parties in accordance with the principles contained in Articles 4, 5, 6 and 7. Nevertheless, with the consent of both High Contracting Parties, negotiations may be entered into at any time after the expiration of a period of ten years after the coming into force of the treaty, with a view to such revision as aforesaid.

ARTICLE 17.

The present treaty is subject to ratification. Ratifications shall be exchanged in Cairo as soon as possible. The treaty shall come into force on the date of the exchange of ratifications, and shall thereupon be registered with the Secretary-General of the League of Nations.

In witness whereof the above-named plenipotentiaries have signed the present treaty and affixed thereto their seals.

Done at London in duplicate this 26th day of August, 1936.

(L.S.) ANTHONY EDEN.

(L.S.) J. RAMSAY MACDONALD.

(L.S.) JOHN SIMON.

(L.S.) HALIFAX.

(L.S.) MILES W. LAMPSON.

(L.S.) MOUSTAPHA EL-NAHAS.

(L.S.) AHMAD MAHER.

(L.S.) M. MAHMOUD.

(L.S.) I. SEDKI.

(L.S.) A. YEHIA.

(L.S.) WACYF BOUTROS GHALI.

(L.S.) O. MOHARRAM.

(L.S.) MAKRAM EBEID.

(L.S.) MAHMOUD FAHMY EL-NOKRACHY.

(L.S.) A. HAMDY SEIF EL NASR.

(L.S.) ALY EL CHAMSI.

(L.S.) M. H. ISSA.

(L.S.) HAFEZ AFIFI.

Sources and
Select Bibliography

UNPUBLISHED SOURCES

Ali M. M. Barakat. "Tatawwur al-milkiyya al-ziraᶜiyya fi-Misr wa atharuh ᶜala-l haraka al-siyasiyya." Unpub. Ph.D. dis. Cairo University, 1972.

Fathallah Barakat Memoirs. Egypt.

Egypt. State Archives. Saad Zaghlul Memoirs.

Great Britain. Foreign Office. Drafts and Despatches. Public Records Office. F.O. 371 series.

St. Antony's Papers. St. Antony's College, Oxford. Gerald Delaney Memorandum. Sept. 1970.

———. Stanley Parker Memorandum.

GOVERNMENT PUBLICATIONS

Egypt. *Annuaire Statistique: 1932-33.* Cairo, 1934.

———. *Annuaire Statistique: 1949-51.* Cairo, 1953.

Great Britain. *Accounts and Papers.* 1919-1936.

———. Commons. *Parliamentary Debates.*

WORKS IN ARABIC

al-Aal, Fathi. *Hasan al-Banna kama ariftahu.* Cairo, 1948.

Abd al-Rahim, Abd al-Rahim. *al-Rif al-Misri fi al-qarn al-thamin ashr.* Cairo, 1974.

Anis, Muhammad. *Dirasat fi thawrat sanat 1919.* Cairo, 1963.

al-Aqqad, Abbas Mahmud. *Zaᶜim al-thawra: Saad Zaghlul.* Cairo, 1952.

al-Bishri, Tariq. *al-Haraka al-siyasiyya fi Misr: 1945-1952.* Cairo, 1972.

Fahmi, Abd al-Aziz. *Hadhihi hayati.* Cairo, 1952.

Ghorbal, Shafiq. *Tarikh al-mufawadat al-Misriyya al-Biritaniyya.* Vol. I. Cairo, 1952.

Haikal, Ahmad Husain. *Mudhakkirat fi-l siyasa al-Misriyya.* 2 vols. Cairo, 1951.

al-Jundi, Anwar. *al-Ikhwan al-Muslimun fi mizan al-haq.* Damascus, n.d.

Lajin, Abd al-Khaliq. *Saad Zaghlul: Dawruh fi-l siyasa al-Misriyya hatta 1914.* Cairo, 1971.

_____. *Saad Zaghlul: Wa dawruh fi-l siyasa al-Misriyya.* Beirut, 1975.

Muhammad, Rauf Abbas Hamid. *al-Haraka al-ummaliyya fi Misr: 1899-1952.* Cairo, 1968.

Musa, Salama. *Tarbiyyat Salama Musa.* Cairo, 1947. 2d ed., 1962.

Mustafa, Abd al-Rahim. *Misr wa-l mas'ala al-Misriyya.* Cairo, 1958.

al-Rafii, Abd al-Rahman. *Mustafa Kamil.* Cairo, 1945.

_____. *Thawrat sanat 1919.* Cairo, 1955.

_____. *Fi aᶜqab al-thawra al-Misriyya.* 2 vols. Cairo, 1958-1966.

_____. *Muhammad Farid.* Cairo, 1962.

Ramadan, Abd al-Adhim. *Tatawur al-haraka al-wataniyya fi Misr.* Cairo, 1968.

al-Sayyid, Ahmad Lutfi. *al-Muntakhabat.* Ed. Ismail Mazhar. Cairo, 1945.

_____. *Safahat matwiya.* Ed. Ismail Mazhar. Cairo, 1946.

_____. *Qissat Hayati.* Cairo, 1962.

al-Shirbini, Yusif. *Hazz al-quhuf fi sharh qasidat Abi Shaduf.* Bulaq, 1857.

Sidqi, Ismail. *Mudhakkirati.* Cairo, 1950.

WORKS IN OTHER LANGUAGES

Abdel Malek, Anouar. *Idéologie et Renaissance Nationale.* Paris, 1969.

Abu-Lughod, Janet. *Cairo.* Princeton, 1971.

Ahmad, Jamal. *Intellectual Origins of Egyptian Nationalism.* London, 1960.

Ammar, Hamed. *Growing Up in an Egyptian Village.* London, 1954.

Ayrout, Henri Habib. *The Egyptian Peasant.* Trans. J. A. Williams. Boston, 1968.

Baer, Gabriel. *A History of Landownership in Modern Egypt.* London, 1963.

Berque, Jacques. *L'Egypte: Impérialisme et Révolution.* Paris, 1967.

Cleland, Wendell. *The Population Problem in Egypt.* New York, 1936.

Earl of Cromer. *Modern Egypt.* 2 vols. New York: Macmillan, 1916.

Crouchley, A. E. *The Economic Development of Modern Egypt.* London, 1938.

Ericson, Eric. *Young Man Luther.* New York, 1958.

Grafftey-Smith, Laurence. *Bright Levant.* London, 1970.

Harbison, F., and I. A. Ibrahim. *Human Resources for Egyptian Enterprise.* London, 1958.

Harris, Christina Phelps. *Nationalism and Revolution in Egypt.* The Hague, 1964.

Harik, Iliya. *The Political Mobilization of Peasants: A Study of an Egyptian Community.* Bloomington, 1974.

Holt, P. M. ed. *Political and Social Change in Modern Egypt.* London, 1968.

Hourani, Albert H. *Arabic Thought in the Liberal Age.* London, 1960.

Issawi, Charles. *Egypt at Mid-Century.* London, 1954.

_____. "Economic and Social Foundations of Democracy in the Middle East." *International Affairs,* 32, 1 (Jan. 1956), 27-42.

_____. *Egypt in Revolution.* London, 1963.

Kedourie, Elie. *Saad Zaghlul and the British.* St. Antony's Papers, no. 11. London, 1961.

Killearn, Lord. *The Killearn Diaries: 1934-1946.* Ed. Trefor Evans. London, 1972.

Lloyd, Lord. *Egypt Since Cromer.* 2 vols. London, 1934.

Mitchell, Richard. *The Society of Muslim Brothers.* London, 1969.

Monroe, Elizabeth. *Britain's Moment in the Middle East.* London, 1963.

Owen, E. R. J. *Cotton and the Egyptian Economy.* London, 1969.

Rivlin, Helen. *The Agricultural Policy of Muhammad Ali in Egypt.* Cambridge, Mass., 1961.

Safran, Nadav. *Egypt in Search of Political Community.* Cambridge, Mass., 1961.

al-Sayyid (Marsot), Afaf Lutfi. *Egypt and Cromer.* London, 1968.

———. "The Cartoon in Egypt." *Comparative Studies in Society and History,* 13, 1 (January 1971), pp. 2-15.

Smith, Charles. "The 'Crisis of Orientation': The Shift of Egyptian Intellectuals to Islamic Subjects in the 1930's," *International Journal of Middle East Studies.* 4, 4 (Oct. 1973), 382-410.

Tignor, Robert. *Modernization and British Colonial Rule in Egypt: 1882-1914.* Princeton, 1966.

Van den Bosch, Baron F. *Vingt Années en Egypte.* Paris, 1932.

Vatikiotis, P. J. *A Modern History of Egypt.* New York, 1969.

Waterfield, Gordon. *Professional Diplomat: Sir Percy Loraine.* London, 1973.

Wendell, Charles. *The Evolution of the Egyptian National Image: From Its Origins to Ahmad Lutfi al-Sayyid.* Berkeley and Los Angeles, 1972.

Zayid, Mahmud. *Egypt's Struggle for Independence.* Beirut, 1965.

NEWSPAPERS AND JOURNALS

Times   *al-Ahram*   *al-Musawwar*

Index

Abbud, Ahmad, 205
Abd al-Hadi, Ibrahim, 151
Abd al-Munim, Prince, 195
Abd al-Nasir, Jamal, 5, 193
Abd al-Nur, Fakhri, 164, 161
Abd al-Raziq, Ali, 86, 87, 228, 249
Abd al-Raziq, Hasan, 61
Abd al-Raziq, Mahmud, 122, 151, 182
Abduh, Shaikh Muhammad, 8, 219, 221
Abu Ali, al-Sayyid, 220
Abu Lughod, Janet, 33
Abu al-Nasr, Mahmud, 62
Abu Shaduf, 20
Abu-l Suud, Zaki, 94
al-Afghani, Jamal al-Din, 46, 236
Afifi, Atta, 150, 151, 154, 159, 161
Afifi, Hafiz, 113, 157, 175, 178
Agricultural Credit Bank. *See* Crédit
    Agricole Bank
al-Ahram, 160, 227
al-Ahrar al-Dusturiyyun, 65, 67, 84, 106,
    109-124, 149, 150, 152, 153, 157, 159,
    176, 180, 211
al-Akhbar, 55, 239
Akhbar al-Yom, 239
Allenby, E. H. H., Lord, 51, 60, 61, 63,
    83
Alluba, Muhammad Ali, 49, 87
Amin, Ali, 239
Amin, Mustafa, 239
Amin, Qasim, 197, 221
Anglo-Egyptian Treaty, 181, 182-184, 187-
    189. See *the appendix*
al-Aqqad, Abbas Mahmud, 134, 227
Ayrout, Henri Habib, 21, 25
al-Azhar, 30, 38-39, 41, 46, 51, 81, 86,
    151, 153, 190-191, 219, 220
Azzam, Abd al-Rahman, 131

Badrawi family, 205
al-Balagh, 124, 142
al-Banna, Hasan, 164, 232-237
Barakat, Atif, 61

Barakat, Bahi Eddine, 195
Barakat, Fathallah, 61, 73, 76, 98, 105,
    106, 113, 131-136, 141, 142, 150, 151,
    152-153, 154, 161
Barakat, Hidiya Hanim, 200
al-Basil, Hamad, 50, 56, 154, 161
Berque, Jacques, 114
Blue Shirts. *See* al-Qumsan al-Zarqa
Bonaparte, 1, 38, 241
Boyle, Harry, 46
Budairi, 162
Bulfin, E. S., General, 51
Butler, H. B., 167

Campbell, Cecil, 115, 127, 131, 137, 153,
    176
Capitulations, 43, 69, 70, 125, 169, 182,
    183, 188
Chamberlain, Austen, 103
Cheetham, Milne, 50
Churchill, Winston, 101
Cleland, Wendell, 213
Constitution, 64, 67-68, 153-144, 145
Crédit Agricole Bank, 164, 166.
Crédit Hypothéquaire, 164, 166
Cromer, Evelyn Baring, Lord, 7, 8, 13, 43,
    218
Curzon, George Nathaniel, Lord, 57

Dalton, Hugh, 128
Declaration of Independence (1922), 63,
    80, 100, 117
Delaney, Gerald, 91, 93, 101-102, 127
Doss, Tawfiq, 87, 157

Eden, Anthony, 174, 195
Education, 197, 199-200, 201, 203
Emancipation of women, 197-200
Entomological Society, 179

Fahmi, Abd al-Aziz, 45, 47-49, 66, 87, 94,
    162, 182
Fahmi, Abd al-Rahman, 207

Fakhri, Jaafar, 110
Fallah, 10-31, 32, 33, 120, 121, 122, 166-
    169, 193, 206
Farid, Muhammad, 33
Faruq, King, 172, 180, 183, 189, 190-191,
    193-195
Fatima, Princess, 179
Fawzi, Husain, 219, 240
Free Officers, 192
Fuad, King, 59-60, 64, 74, 86, 95-100,
    107, 109-110, 133-138, 147-148, 157-
    162, 172-173, 177-178
Furness, Robert (Robin), 104, 112

General Association of Egyptian Labor
    Unions. See al-Ittihad al-ʿAm li Niqabat
    ʿUmmal al-Qutr al-Misri
General Association of Labor Unions. See
    Ittihad ʿAm al-Niqabat
George V, King of England, 58
Ghali, Wasif, 74, 75, 133, 149, 161, 178
Gharabli, Najib, 133, 151, 154, 161
Grafftey-Smith, Laurence, 92, 102, 156
Grand Cordon of the Nile, 81
Greg, Robert, 156
Green Shirts. See al-Qumsan al-Khadra

Haikal, Ahmad Husain, 21, 65, 118, 123,
    127, 154, 160, 182, 186-187, 230-231
al-Hakim, Tawfiq, 130
Halim, al-Nabil Abbas, 119, 166-167
Hanna, Morcos, 73, 94, 95
Hanna, Sinut, 140, 155
Harb, Talaat, 33, 70, 204, 243
Harik Iliya, 15
Hasanain, Ahmad, 160, 190
Hasib, Hasan, 154
Hayter, William, 61
Henderson, Arthur, 127-128, 129, 132,
    152
Henderson, Nevile, 82, 95, 105
al-Hilal, 238
Hoare, Samuel, 175
Husain, Ahmad, 163, 191. See also Misr
    al-Fatat
Husain, Taha, 94, 202, 228-229, 230
al-Husri, Sati, 191

Ibrahim, Yahia, 67, 87
al-Ibrashi, Zaki, 147, 171, 172
al-Ikhwan al-Muslimun, 31, 164, 219, 231,
    235-237. See also al-Banna, Hasan
International Federation of Trade Unions,
    167

Iskandar, Najib, 161
Ismail, Khedive, 13, 25, 37, 44, 59, 147,
    217, 239
Issa, Hilmi, 178
Issawi, Charles, 13-14
al-Ittihad al-ʿAm li Niqabat ʿUmmal al-
    Qutr al-Misri, 118, 166
Ittihad ʿAm al-Niqabat, 166

Al-Jabarti, Abd al-Rahman, 3, 198
Jaghbub, 88
al-Jarida, 48, 222, 225
al-Jazzar, Ilwi, 151, 154, 161

Kamil, Mustafa, 44, 221
al-Kashkul, 227
al-Kawakibi, Abd al-Rahman, 191
Kellogg Pact, 181
Kemal, Mustafa, 131, 228, 241
Kershaw, J. F., Judge, 91
Khairi, Badi, 40
Khashaba, Ahmad, 97
Khayyat, George, 154
Killearn, Lord. See Lampson, Miles
al-Kutla al-Wafdiyya, 189

Labor, 33, 36, 76-77, 118-119, 135, 141,
    166-168, 176, 204-210, 212-213. See also
    Trade Unions
Lacouture, Jean, 207
Lacouture, Simone, 207
Lamlum, Salih, 64
Lampson, Miles, 171, 173-174, 176-177,
    183, 190, 194-195
Landowners, 11, 15-17, 27-28, 121, 166-
    167, 204-205, 210-211, 214. See also
    Fallah
League of Nations, 125, 182, 183, 188
League of Wafdist Youth. See Rabitat al-
    Shubban al-Wafdiyya
Liberal Constitutionalist Party. See al-
    Ahrar al-Dusturiyyun
Lloyd, George, Lord, 88-89, 91-93, 96-97,
    100-103, 108-109, 117, 126
Loraine, Percy, 129, 136-137, 146-147,
    152-153, 155-158, 160, 162, 171

McDonald, Ramsay, 76, 126-127, 140, 172
Mahfuz, Najib, 37
Mahir, Ahmad, 83, 91, 134, 155, 173, 178,
    189
Mahir, Ali, 113, 162, 174, 178, 191-192,
    194

Mahmud, Muhammad, 13, 45, 48, 56, 106, 111, 115-118, 123, 125-129, 132-133, 145, 149-150, 152, 159-160, 174-176, 178, 182, 186, 194
al-Majalla al-Jadida, 238
al-Majmaᶜ al-Misri li-l Thaqafa al-ᶜIlmiyya, 239
Makram, Umar, 3
Mansur, Shafiq, 83
al-Marᵓa al-Jadida, 200
al-Maraghi, Shaikh Mustafa, 151, 152-153, 190
Mazhar, Ismail, 219, 240
al-Mazini, Abd al-Qadir, 160
Mazlum, Ahmad, 73
Misr Bank, 33, 118. *See also* Harb Talaat
Misr Company, 118
Misr al-Fatat, 191-193. *See also* Husain, Ahmad
al-Misri, Aziz Ali, 192
al-Misri li-l Misri, 239
Montreux Convention, 169
Mortgage Credit Bank. *See* Crédit Hypothéquaire Bank
al-Muayyad, 220-221
Mubarat Muhammad Ali, 200
Muhammad Ali, Pasha of Egypt, 3, 11, 13, 24, 25, 41, 43
Muhanna, Rashad, 195
Muharram, Uthman, 178
Mukabatti, Abd al-Latif, 49, 56
al-Muqattam, 221
al-Muqtataf, 237-238
Musa, Salama, 219, 237-243
Muslim Brethren. *See* al-Ikhwan al-Muslimun

al-Nadim, Abdallah, 220
al-Nahhas, Mustafa, 13, 26, 61, 73-74, 98, 105, 108, 110-120, 124, 129, 131-136, 141, 144-155, 159, 161, 173, 175-176, 178, 180, 183, 189-191, 194, 200
al-Naqshabandi, Shaikh, 20
Nashat, Hasan, 86, 89
Nasim, Tawfiq, 172-174, 177
Nationalist movement, 44, 197
Nile Waters Agreement, 125
Nuqrashi, Mahmud Fahmi, 83, 91, 131, 141, 151, 154, 173, 178, 189

Palestine, 183, 207
Parmoor, C. A. Cripps, Lord, 80
Peterson, Maurice, 172

Political parties, 44, 46, 49, 144, 145-146, 176, 189, 191, 211-212, 222
Protectorate, 45

al-Qumsan al-Khadra, 163, 191
al-Qumsan al-Zarqa, 163, 191

Rabitat al-Shubban al-Wafdiyya, 177
al-Rafii, Abd al-Rahman, 160, 172-173
Red Crescent, 156
Rifaat, Shaikh Muhammad, 20
al-Rihani, Najib, 40
Rosenthal, Joseph, 207
Rushdi, Husain, 48, 54, 64, 67
Ruz al-Yusif, 227

Saadist Party, 194
Sabri, Abd al-Rahim, 59
Sabri, Hasan, 162
Sabri, Zuhair, 191
Said, Abd al-Hamid, 109
Said, Muhammad, 49
Saif al-Din, Prince, 110, 124
Saif al-Nasr, Ahmad Hamdi, 178
Salih, Ahmad Rushdi, 20
al-Sayyid, Ahmad Lutfi, 14, 45, 48, 56, 65, 113, 115, 199, 219-227
al-Sayyidat al-Muslimat, 236
Scavenlis, W., 167
Sennar Dam, 125
Sève, Colonel, Sulaiman al-Faransawi, 59
Shaarawi family, 205
Shaarawi, Ali, 45, 48, 200
al-Shamsi, Ali, 154, 178
al-Sharqawi, Abd al-Rahman, 21
al-Shawarbi family, 205
al-Shirai, Murad, 154, 161
al-Shishai, Shaikh Mahmud, 20
Shumayyil, Shibli, 238
Sidqi, Ismail, 5, 49, 50, 61-63, 137-147, 156, 160-162, 164, 169, 178
Sièyes, E. J., Abbé, 2
Simon, John, 161
Siraj al-Din family, 205
al-Siyasa, 65, 76, 134, 142. *See also* Haikal, Ahmad Husain
Smart, Walter, 152
Societé Royale de Géographie, 179
Spinx, Charlton, 100
Stack, Lee, 81, 91
Students, 38-39, 51, 107, 123-124, 141, 163, 175-178, 193, 201-203
Sudan, 80, 183-184

Sulaiman, Abd al-Hamid, 113
Sulaiman, Mahmud, 111
Sultan family, 204
Syndicate of Lawyers, 156

Taba, 221
Taftish Bashbish, 87
Tahsin al-Siha, 200
al-Tashriʿ, 220
Thabit, Mahjub, 208
Tharwat, Abd al-Khaliq, 6, 62, 63, 64-67,
    99-103, 105-107, 108, 117
Trade Unions, 167; 307-308. See also
    Labor
Tussun, Umar, 239

Ubaid, Makram, 109, 128, 131, 141, 154-
    155, 161, 173, 177, 178, 189
Umda, 20, 26-28, 76, 85, 97, 130, 144.
    See also Fallah; Landowners
United Front, 177, 181
Urban society, 34-40, 196-198. See also
    Labor
al-Ustadh, 220

Van den Bosch, Firmin, 75
Vera, 135

Wafd, 26, 45, 49, 50, 52, 56, 63-64, 69,
    76, 83, 89, 98, 105-109, 114, 119, 124-
    163, 173-180, 189, 193-194, 211
Wahba, Yusif, 67
al-Wakil, Zainab, 125
Wasif, Wisa, 19, 133, 139, 151
Wingate, Reginald, 48-49

Yahia, Abd al-Fattah, 162, 171, 178
Yahia, Ali Amin, 205
Yakan, Adli, 44, 52-58, 64, 66, 94-97, 99,
    102, 129, 136, 142, 154, 155
Yakan, Ahmad Midhat, 204
Young Egypt. See Misr al-Fatat
Young Men's Christian Association, 242
Yusif, Ali, 221
Yusri, Prince Saif Allah, 106

Zaghlul, Saad, 13, 26, 44-61, 67-68, 70-
    105, 122, 148
Zaghlul, Safia, 105
Zaidan, Jurji, 238
Zaki, Salim, 237
Ziwar, Ahmad, 83-84, 89, 153
Ziyada, Mayy, 225
Zuhdi, Ismail, 67